White Mythologies

Writing History and the West

Robert Young

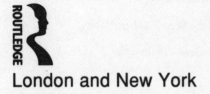

London and New York

First published 1990
by Routledge
11 New Fetter Lane, London EC4P 4EE

Simultaneously published in the USA and Canada
by Routledge
29 West 35th Street, New York, NY 10001

Reprinted 1992, 1993

© 1990 Robert Young

Typeset in 10/12pt Garamond, Linotron by
Ponting–Green Publishing Services, London

Printed in England by Clays Ltd., St. Ives plc

British Library Cataloguing in Publication Data
Young, Robert,
    White Mythologies: Writing History and the West.
    1. Historiography. Literary aspects
    I. Title
    907.2

Library of Congress Cataloging in Publication Data
Young, Robert,
    White Mythologies: Writing History and the West / Robert Young.
        p.   cm.
    1. History – Philosophy. 2. Literature, Modern – Philosophy.
I. Title.
D16.8.Y67 1990
901–dc20   90–32948

ISBN 0 415 05371 4
ISBN 0 415 05372 2 pbk

for Badar

Contents

Preface

In recent years the field of literary and cultural theory has, broadly speaking, been determined by a preoccupation with 'the political'. Within this arena one of the most vigorous debates has concerned the relation of 'theory' to 'history'. Very often these categories are presented as somehow opposed, even as mutually exclusive, or as if they operated within different hierarchical realms so that the one was in a position to vanquish and subsume the other. One popular and persuasive view suggests that theory neglects history and that, insofar as you attach a primacy to the political, you should reject theory's 'textuality' for history and 'the real'.

Here I attempt to counter this argument, though not by simply reversing it, that is, by suggesting that theory really does pay attention to history on occasion, nor even by disputing the values implicit in the category of the political. The question rather concerns history itself: we must, we are often told, get back to history. But where is this history that is so confidently invoked? If we look at some examples of the history to which theory is generally opposed, it quickly becomes clear that history itself has been, and continues to be, a deeply problematical concept, particularly for Marxism. It has never succeeded in achieving a 'concrete' existence outside theory, where it can lie in wait, ready to be invoked against it.

In this book I investigate the difficulties of a number of post-war theories of history. The following chapters do not, however, themselves represent a history, a succession of analyses that move towards the present, demonstrating the gradual production of an adequate theory. For what we discover is that the conditions of history's possibility are also its conditions of impossibility. At this point, it becomes increasingly difficult to distinguish theoretical 'failure' from 'success'. Here the difference becomes the more political one of what response can be made to such conditions, and for what purposes it can be deployed.

One such condition that all those discussed encounter is the difficult relation between history and totalization, any account of which by definition can hardly claim to be comprehensive. Instead I here focus on certain writers in a non-linear series which is determined, and constituted, by my initial starting point. The argument between theory and history in the realm of literary and cultural theory in Britain has been conducted, broadly speaking, in terms of a debate between Marxism and poststructuralism, and it is this that provides my point of departure, as well as regulating the questions to which I return. If poststructuralism is an Anglo-American response to recent French Marxist and post-Marxist theory, this has provided the frame of reference in which I have constructed my analysis. It is important to add, for it is no doubt necessary to spell it out, that all of these terms, such as 'Marxism', 'poststructuralism', and the like, are here used in a strictly improper sense, and should not be taken to imply absolute or homogeneous identities. As terms, they are merely flags of convenience, and on this basis will, therefore, henceforth be used without scare-quotes.

The interesting relation of recent French theory to that of the Frankfurt School (Adorno in particular) is discussed in part two of the first chapter. A more extended comparison between the two could be related to my general argument that a historical analysis of the terms of the theory/history debate shows that far from being radically opposed positions, both sides have in fact been working from a common problematic. It is for this reason that I have not proposed a poststructuralist history as an alternative to a Marxist one. It is rather colonialism, I argue, that constitutes the dislocating term in the theory/history debate; from this perspective, theoretical and political questions are inflected towards the way in which theory and history, together with Marxism itself, have themselves been implicated in the long history of European colonialism – and, above all, the extent to which that history continues to determine both the institutional conditions of knowledge as well as the terms of contemporary institutional practices – practices which extend beyond the limits of the academic institution. My concern is therefore in no sense simply to present an alternative form of history but rather to elaborate a different framework for thinking about it.

If this book is frequently preoccupied with the theoretical perplexities of writing history then, given that it presents certain historical arguments itself, the obvious question that follows is how can it claim to do so? My answer is that its conditions of impossibility are also those of its possibility. If all history, in Plato's terms, is a bad copy, then his stricture applies no less to this one: any history it offers is only a simulacrum of one, an historical pastiche. Certainly in the course of writing I have become familiar with that process of a continuous, unfinalizable supplementation preventing closure which I describe in the work of Sartre and others. In this context, I thank Janice Price for her patience. For constructive help along the way I would also like to thank Derek Attridge, Maud Ellmann, Ken Hirschkop, Matthew Meadows, Jacqueline Rose, Jonathan Sawday, Diana Stone, and Clair Wills. Geoffrey Bennington and Homi Bhabha were kind enough to read the complete manuscript and to give me the benefit of their rigorous thinking and questioning, and their sceptical tolerance where our views differed. I owe a special debt of gratitude to Badar Nissar Kaler, and to my mother and my father.

Wadham College, Oxford
October 1989

Chapter 1

White mythologies

If so-called 'so-called poststructuralism' is the product of a single historical moment, then that moment is probably not May 1968 but rather the Algerian War of Independence – no doubt itself both a symptom and a product. In this respect it is significant that Sartre, Althusser, Derrida and Lyotard, among others, were all either born in Algeria or personally involved with the events of the war. But let us begin instead with Hélène Cixous's remarkable account of what it was like to grow up as an Algerian French Jewish girl at that time:

> I learned everything from this first spectacle: I saw how the white (French), superior, plutocratic, civilized world founded its power on the repression of populations who had suddenly become 'invisible', like proletarians, immigrant workers, minorities who are not the right 'colour'. Women. Invisible as humans. But, of course, perceived as tools – dirty, stupid, lazy, underhanded, etc. Thanks to some annihilating dialectical magic. I saw that the great, noble, 'advanced' countries established themselves by expelling what was 'strange'; excluding it but not dismissing it; enslaving it. A commonplace gesture of History: there have to be *two* races – the masters and the slaves. [1]

Cixous has been criticized for lacking a politics and a theory of the social. [2] According to some criteria perhaps, but if so they would have to exclude from 'the political' considerations such as those described here. Which is precisely the point: if there is a politics to what has become known as poststructuralism, then it is articulated in this passage which unnervingly weaves capitalist economic exploitation, racism, colonialism, sexism, together with, perhaps unexpectedly, 'History' and the structure of the Hegelian dialectic.

A lot has been said already in the English-speaking world about poststructuralism and politics, much of it in the accusatory mode voiced from the opposing class-based verities of 'tradition' or 'History'. Such apparently secure grounds of objection amount to two narratives: their intriguing similarity brings out the extent to which poststructuralism challenges not just the politics and institutions of the right but also the politics and theoretical systems of the left. Disturbing conventional assumptions about what constitutes 'the political', poststructuralism is correspondingly difficult to place itself.

In the passage just cited for example it is striking that Cixous includes the Hegelian dialectic in the forms of political oppression which she describes. It is not a question of showing that such an allegation misinterprets or simplifies Hegel's texts. [3] Of course it does. The problem involves rather the ways in which Hegel has been read, absorbed and adapted. Nor is it just the Hegelian dialectic as such: Cixous includes 'History', and by implication therefore Marxism as well. This cannot simply be dismissed as another New Right invocation of the Gulag, for Cixous is arguing something much more specific: that Marxism, insofar as it inherits the system of the Hegelian dialectic, is also implicated in the link between the structures of knowledge and the forms of oppression of the last two hundred years: a phenomenon that has become known as Eurocentrism.

To this extent, Marxism's universalizing narrative of the unfolding of a rational system of world history is simply a negative form of the history of European imperialism: it was Hegel, after all, who declared that 'Africa has no history', and it was Marx who, though critical of British imperialism, concluded that the British colonization of India was ultimately for the best because it brought India into the evolutionary narrative of Western history, thus creating the conditions for future class struggle there. [4] Such an arrogant and arrogating narrative means that the story of 'world history' not only involves what Fredric Jameson describes as the wresting of freedom from the realm of necessity but always also the creation, subjection and final appropriation of Europe's 'others'. This is why 'History', which for Marxism promises liberation, for Cixous also entails another forgotten story of oppression:

Already I know all about the 'reality' that supports History's progress: everything throughout the centuries depends on the distinction between the Selfsame, the ownself ... and that which limits it: so now what menaces my-own-good ... is the 'other'. What is the 'Other'? If it is truly the 'other', there is nothing to say; it cannot be theorized. The 'other' escapes me. It is elsewhere, outside: absolutely other. It doesn't settle down. But in History, of course, what is called 'other' is an alterity that does settle down, that falls into the dialectical circle. It is the other in a hierarchically organized relationship in which the same is what rules, names, defines, and assigns 'its' other. With the dreadful simplicity that orders the movement Hegel erected as a system, society trots along before my eyes reproducing to perfection the mechanism of the death struggle: the reduction of a 'person' to a 'nobody' to the position of 'other' – the inexorable plot of racism. There has to be some 'other' – no master without a slave, no economico-political power without exploitation, no dominant class without cattle under the yoke, no 'Frenchmen' without wogs, no Nazis without Jews, no property without exclusion – an exclusion that has its limits and is part of the dialectic. (70–1)

Not that Hegel himself is responsible. Rather the problem, Cixous argues, is that unfortunately Hegel wasn't inventing things. The entire Hegelian machinery simply lays down the operation of a system already in place, already operating in everyday life. Politics and knowledge have worked according to the same Hegelian dialectic, with its 'phallo-logocentric *Aufhebung*' – whether it be Marxism's History, Europe's colonial annexations and accompanying racism or orientalist scholarship, or, in a typical conflation of patriarchy and colonialism, Freud's characterization of femininity as the dark unexplored continent ('within his economy, she is the strangeness he likes to appropriate' [68]). For even Freud, according to Cixous, has not helped in any project to separate history from the history of appropriation or that of phallocentrism. The patriarchal structures of psychoanalytic theory have often been defended on the grounds that they only describe the current customs of a patriarchal society. But this does not alter the fact that psychoanalysis therefore repeats the same masculine 'Empire of the Selfsame', and that as soon as such descriptions become institutionalized – as a structure of knowledge, or as psychoanalytic practice – then they become agents of the system they describe. [5] The point is to change it.

But why this emphasis on Hegel? The problem of the Hegelian model, particularly of a historicism which presupposes a governing structure of self-realization in all historical process, is by no means confined to post-war French Marxism, but the dominance of Hegelian Marxism from the thirties to the fifties does explain the particular context for the French post-structuralist assault. [6] Here it is not a question of suggesting that Hegel is somehow answerable for the excesses of capitalism or even socialism in the past two hundred years: rather what is at stake is the argument that the dominant force of opposition to capitalism, Marxism, as a body of knowledge itself remains complicit with, and even extends, the system to which it is opposed. Hegel articulates a philosophical structure of the appropriation of the other as a form of knowledge which uncannily simulates the project of nineteenth-century imperialism; the construction of knowledges which all operate through forms of expropriation and incorporation of the other mimics at a conceptual level the geographical and economic absorption of the non-European world by the West. Marxism's standing Hegel on his head may have reversed his idealism, but it did not change the mode of operation of a conceptual system which remains collusively Eurocentric. It is thus entirely appropriate that Hegelian Marxism has become generally known as 'Western Marxism'.

As Cixous suggests, the mode of knowledge as a politics of arrogation pivots at a theoretical level on the dialectic of the same and the other. Such knowledge is always centred in a self even though it is outward looking, searching for power and control of what is other to it. Anthropology has always provided the clearest symptomatic instance, as was foreseen by Rousseau from the outset. History, with a capital H, similarly cannot tolerate otherness or leave it outside its economy of inclusion. The appropriation of the other as a form of knowledge within a totalizing system can thus be set alongside the history (if not the project) of European imperialism, and the constitution of the other as 'other' alongside racism and sexism. The reaction against this structure has produced forms of politics that do not fit into traditional political categories. Here the problem rests on the fact that for orthodox Marxism there can be only one 'other', that of the working class, into which all other oppressed groups, so-called 'minorities', must in the last instance be subsumed.

Such a position is by no means confined to a Marxism of a Stalinist past. In *Making History*, published in 1987, for example, Alex Callinicos argues that the so-called poststructuralist critique of the category of the subject can be avoided by shifting the subject out of the problematic realm of consciousness into a theory of human agency. This provides something closer to historical Marxism, although it does mean that he quickly becomes involved in assumptions about rationality and intentionality, and has to propose a 'Principle of Humanity', that is a common human nature, to hold them all together. Perhaps not unexpectedly, the 'Principle of Humanity' also turns out to involve the assumption that class is the primary form of collective agency, because, we are told, it is more fundamental than any other interests or forms of social power. Callinicos writes:

> Feminists and black nationalists [sic] often complain that the concepts of Marxist class theory are 'gender-blind' and 'race-blind'. This is indeed true. Agents' class position derives from their place in production relations, not their gender or supposed race. But of itself this does not provide grounds for rejecting Marxism, since its chief theoretical claim is precisely to explain power-relations and forms of conflict such as those denoted by the terms 'nation', 'gender' and 'race' in terms of the forces and relations of production. The mere existence of national, sexual and racial oppression does not refute historical materialism, but rather constitutes its *explanandum*. The only interesting question is whether or not Marxism can actually explain these phenomena. [7]

The only interesting question? So as long as gender and race can be satisfactorily subordinated to class then Marxism does not need refuting, and history can be reasserted as the single narrative of the Third International. [8]

Conversely, as Callinicos implicitly recognizes, the problem with contemporary politics for the left is that the dialectic of class depends on a historicist History and vice versa; any failure of the former necessarily also involves a waning of the latter. Marxism's inability to deal with the political interventions of other oppositional groups has meant that its History can no longer claim to subsume all processes of change. The straightforward oppositional structure of capital and class does not necessarily work any more: if we think in terms of Hegel's master/slave dialectic, then rather than the working class being the obvious universal subject-victim, many others are also oppressed: particularly women, black people, and all other so-called ethnic and minority groups. Any single individual may belong to several of these, but the forms of oppression, as of resistance or change, may not only overlap but may also differ or even conflict. As soon as there is no longer a single master and no single slave, then the classic Hegelian reversal model on which Marxism depends and on which it bases its theory of revolution (literally, an overturning) is no longer adequate. In fact it is arguable whether such dualistic conditions ever existed anyway: marginal groups which could not be assimilated into the category of the working class were merely relegated by Marx to the *Lumpenproletariat*. Even the formulation of a dualistic class division, Laclau and Mouffe have argued persuasively, is itself nothing less than a nostalgic attempt to recreate for the nineteenth century the imagined simplicity of the conditions of the aristocracy/ bourgeoisie conflict of the French Revolution which had originally inspired Hegel. [9] A similarly straightforward opposition also provides much of the attraction which has fuelled the recent growth of interest in the historical analysis of colonialism – in which you apparently have the simple binary of master and slave, colonizer and colonized. With colonialism it's easy to tell the good guys from the bad guys, which makes it tempting to substitute the colonized for the lost working class. Already in 1957 Roland Barthes was claiming that 'today it is the colonized peoples who assume the full ethical and political condition described by Marx as being that of the proletariat'. [10] But politics today are much more complex, much more difficult to disentangle. The dialectical structure of oppositional politics no longer works for the micro-politics of the post-war period in the West. This is the context of Foucault's critique of what he calls the sovereign model of power, of the idea that power has a single source in a master, king, or class – and can thus easily be reversed.

This shift from a conflictual dyadic political structure is not simply a question of historical change, of the recent appearance of 'minorities': after all the slave was already constituted simultaneously according to different groups (for example male or female), the *Lumpenproletariat* always had to be excluded. The problem begins at a conceptual level with the initial division between master and slave as such, as if relations of power work according to the binary opposition of Hegel's fight to the death between two individuals. [11] This structure is not, as might at first be imagined, derived from a fantasy of power relations modelled on a medieval joust but from the phenomenological account of the constitution of knowledge that works according to the structure of a subject perceiving an object, a same/ other dialectic in which the other is first constituted by the same through its negation as other before being incorporated within it. No possibility of dialogue or exchange here. As Cixous argues, nor can there be any place in this schema for the other as other, unless it becomes, like God, an absolute other, literally unknowable. The difficulties which arise from this structure are familiar from the debates in feminism, where 'woman' seems to be offered an alternative of either being the 'other' as constituted by man, that is, conforming to the stereotypes of patriarchy, or, if she is to avoid this, of being an absolute 'other' outside knowledge, necessarily confined to inarticulate expressions of mysticism or *jouissance*. The only way to side-step these alternatives seems to be to reject the other altogether and become the same, that is, equal to men – but then with no difference from them. Exactly the same double bind is encountered in any theorization of racial difference.

In his influential *Le Même et l'autre* Vincent Descombes has described the entire history of twentieth-century philosophy in France as a succession of moves which attempt to get out of this Hegelian dialectic: the recent phenomenon of poststructuralism is part of a long philosophical story and distinguished only by what appears to be a certain success, or at least an avoidance of failure to the extent that it has at least managed to keep the game with Hegel in play. [12] The real difficulty has always been to find an alternative to the Hegelian dialectic – difficult because strictly speaking it is impossible, insofar as the operation of the dialectic already includes its negation. You cannot get out of Hegel by simply contradicting him, any more than you can get out of those other Hegelian systems, Marxism and psychoanalysis, by simply opposing them: for in both your opposition is likewise always recuperable, as the workings of ideology or psychic resistance.

Nor can you get away from Hegel by simply removing him, like the excision of Trotsky from the side of Lenin in certain official Soviet photographs. This is the lesson of Althusser. Althusser's historical interest derives from the fact that he represents the only orthodox Marxist theorist who has tried to get out of Hegel while remaining a Marxist – though for many Marxists he did sacrifice Marxism in the process, which only suggests how closely Marxism and Hegelianism are intertwined. Althusser's theoretical interest, on the other hand, is that he demonstrates the impossibility of any attempt simply to exclude, excise or extirpate Hegel. Other strategies are required.

II HISTORICISM AND IMPERIALISM

Metaphysics – the white mythology which reassembles and reflects the culture of the West: the white man takes his own mythology, Indo-European mythology, his own *logos*, that is, the *mythos* of his idiom, for the universal form of that he must still wish to call Reason.

Jacques Derrida [13]

If poststructuralism has involved an attempted disruption or reworking of Hegelianism through the detection of its own fissures, it is not by any means unique in such an enterprise. For, as Foucault argued in 1978, the work of the Frankfurt School could also be regarded as a reassessment of Hegelianism and the metaphysics of dialectical thought. [14] However, it is too simplistic a reaction to suggest that French poststructuralism can therefore be invalidated by judging it against the claims of a comparable endeavour in Germany, a procedure which can only operate by turning the former into a failed version of the latter, which obviously leaves open the possibility of exactly the reverse argument being made. [15] Though the two may have isolated similar problems, the political and intellectual context of their work was by no means the same. The key Frankfurt School text in this regard is obviously Horkheimer and Adorno's *Dialectic of Enlightenment* of 1944. [16] The date, and the exiled place of composition of its authors, suggests tellingly that the situation with which it attempts to deal is the phenomenon of fascism which seemed to have stopped in its tracks the long march of the progress of reason, and its liberating enlightenment ideals, of which Marxism was the fullest political development. Horkheimer and Adorno therefore pose the question: how has the dialectic deviated into fascism? Why has History gone wrong? Their answer, briefly, was that reason had always contained a measure of irrationality, which, despite its best intentions, had led to its involvement with tyranny and domination: 'Enlightenment is totalitarian'. [17] The very powers of rationality which enabled modern man to free himself from nature and control it had also become an instrumental device to dominate him. If nature had been modelled by man into productive commodities, man's own subjectivity had also become reified into a self-identical instrument; man had become an empty and passive consumer. The project, therefore, was to return to the enlightenment in the wake of fascism, to excise the forms of instrumental rationality that had produced this self-defeating and, ironically, irrational dialectical structure of domination, and to redefine reason and the forms of identity thinking that had defined the individual simply as an indistinguishable element in the collective. In this way the autonomy and spontaneity of the individual subject that had been the original goal of enlightenment might be retrieved.

If for the Frankfurt School the problem to be dealt with was the relation of the phenomena of fascism, and particularly Auschwitz, to the ideals of the enlightenment and the progress of reason, for the French poststructuralists the historical perspective was similarly long. But it comprised, rather, a history of the West in which fascism was itself merely a symptom, and included not only the history of European imperialism but also the defeats of the European colonial powers by Japan in World War II, the subsequent French (and American) defeat in South-East Asia, the war in Algeria, as well as the many other colonial wars of national liberation. From this point of view the French have never regarded fascism as an aberration, concurring rather with Césaire and Fanon that it can be explained quite simply as European colonialism brought home to Europe by a country that had been deprived of its overseas empire after World War I. French poststructuralism, therefore, involves a critique of reason as a system of domination comparable to that of the Frankfurt School, but rather than setting up the possibility of a purged reason operating in an unblocked, ideal speech situation as a defence against tyranny and coercion in the manner of a Habermas, it reanalyses the operations of reason as such. Here the focus is placed not so much upon the continued presence of irrationality, for irrationality after all is simply reason's own excluded but necessary negative other, but rather on the possibility of other logics being imbricated within reason which might serve to undo its own tendency to domination. Here we have a major difference from the historical pessimism of Adorno's negative dialectics which in certain respects poststructuralism might appear to resemble.

Another such project was initiated by Adorno's contemporary Jean-Paul Sartre, whose attempt to define a new form of Hegelian Marxism via a reworked philosophy of consciousness in many ways more closely resembled that of the Frankfurt School. In both cases revisionary work of this kind was embodied in a historical and political analysis of the relation of individual consciousness to society, from within the aegis of an Hegelian Marxism in some respects still impossibly bound to its own enlightenment heritage. This meant that Adorno in particular tended to project science as something exterior and exclusively instrumental; he reacted against it, as well as 'objective' reason generally, by trying to retrieve the individual subject as the means to salvation. In France, however, there also existed a very different tradition, that of the history of the sciences, a tradition in which Foucault has placed himself. Having been overshadowed since the war by Sartrean Marxism, in the crises of the 1960s it emerged as the more influential of the two. Foucault traces its history back to Husserl's *Cartesian Meditations* (1929) and the *Crisis of the European Sciences* (1936) – in which Husserl 'posed the question of the relations between the "Western" project of a universal deployment of reason, [and] the positivity of the sciences and the radicality of philosophy'. [18] This enabled the establishment of a critical position in relation to science which for Adorno remained so elusive.

In larger terms, however, the questions posed in the French tradition were comparable to those of the Frankfurt School, particularly the interrogation of rationality in its claims to universality. As Foucault puts it:

> In the history of the sciences in France, as in German critical theory, it is a matter at bottom of examining a reason, the autonomy of whose structures carries with it a history of dogmatism and despotism – a reason, consequently, which can only have an effect of emancipation on condition that it manages to liberate itself from itself. (54)

The final emancipatory gesture of enlightenment thought would thus be its own liberation from itself, so that it is no longer recognizable as reason. But what was it that brought about the return of the question of the enlightenment to contemporary philosophical enquiry? Foucault identifies three reasons: first of all the ever-increasing importance of technology, secondly the place of rationalism in the optimism attached to the notion of 'revolution' – as well as in the despotism that so often followed its realization – and thirdly:

> the movement which, at the close of the colonial era, led it to be asked of the West what entitles its culture, its science, its social organization, and finally its rationality itself, to be able to claim universal validity: was this not a mirage associated with economic domination and political hegemony? Two centuries later, the Enlightenment returns: but not at all as a way for the West to take cognizance of its present possibilities and of the liberties to which it can have access, but as a way of interrogating it on its limits and on the powers which it has abused. Reason as despotic enlightenment. (54)

Foucault's account is particularly useful insofar as it gives a good indication of the characteristic French, as opposed to German, emphasis on the relation of Marxism to enlightenment rationality and the questioning of enlightenment claims to the universality of its values. The first element, the role of science, is common to both, though they approach the question from opposite perspectives. The second, the role of enlightenment thinking in the subsequent history of European despotism, is the particular focus of interest for the German critical theorists, most memorably and most forcibly articulated in Benjamin's 'Theses on the Philosophy of History'. It is the third element, however, which represents the special interest of the French, whether of the Sartrean or Foucauldian tradition: the relation of the enlightenment, its grand projects and universal truth-claims, to the history of European colonialism. This need not necessarily involve a direct analysis of the effects of colonialism as such, but can also consist of a relentless anatomization of the collusive forms of European knowledge. For Foucault this has comprised a vigorous critique of historicism, including Marxist historicism, and its relation to the operations of knowledge and power. It is from this perspective that it becomes possible to understand the basis of the distrust of totalizing systems of knowledge which depend upon theory and concepts, so characteristic of Foucault or Lyotard, both of whom have been predominantly concerned with the attempt to isolate and foreground singularity as opposed to universality. [19] This quest for the singular, the contingent event which by definition refuses all conceptualization, can clearly be related to the project of constructing a form of knowledge that respects the other without absorbing it into the same.

It is in the work of Edward Said that we can find the problematic of historicist forms of knowledge linked most forcibly to the question of European imperialism. He writes:

> So far as Orientalism in particular and European knowledge of other societies in general have been concerned, historicism meant that one human history uniting humanity either culminated in or was observed from the vantage point of Europe, or the West.... What ... has never taken place is an epistemological critique at the most fundamental level of the connection between the development of a historicism which has expanded and developed enough to include antithetical attitudes such as ideologies of Western imperialism and critiques of imperialism on the one hand, and on the other, the actual practice of imperialism by which the accumulation of territories and population, the control of economies, and the incorporation and homogenisation of histories are maintained. [20]

This was the difficult project of his own book, *Orientalism* (1978), which we shall later be examining in detail. For the moment let us focus on Said's subsequent point that if Orientalism and anthropology derive from historicism, this is by no means a thing of the past: of more recent sciences, Said singles out in particular that of world history as practised by Braudel, Wallerstein, Anderson and Wolf, which he contends is still derived from the enterprise of Orientalism and its colluding companion anthropology, and which has refused to encounter and to interrogate its own relationship as a discipline to European imperialism. For Said, the problem amounts simply to historicism and 'the universalising and self-validating that has been endemic to it':

> the theories of accumulation on a world scale, or the capitalist world state, or lineages of absolutism depend (a) on the same displaced percipient and historicist observer who had been an Orientalist or colonial traveller three generations ago; (b) they depend also on a homogenising and incorporating world historical scheme that assimilated non-synchronous developments, histories, cultures, and peoples to it; and (c) they block and keep down latent epistemological critiques of the institutional, cultural and disciplinary instruments linking the incorporative practice of world history with partial knowledges like Orientalism on the one hand, and on the other, with continued 'Western' hegemony of the non-European, peripheral world. (22)

A new type of knowledge, Said contends, must be produced that can analyse plural objects as such rather than offering forms of integrated understanding that simply comprehend them within totalizing schemas. Already across a wide range of different activities he points to advances in the process of 'breaking up, dissolving and methodologically as well as critically reconceiving the unitary field ruled hitherto by Orientalism, historicism, and what could be called essentialist universalism'. In this last phrase, Said thus links his critique of Orientalism to other critiques, such as those of racism or of patriarchy. The more difficult question remains of what form this new kind of knowledge can take. Here we return to the theoretical problem of how the other can be articulated as such. How can we represent other cultures? asks Said, as Lévi-Strauss had done before him. His own dismissal of deconstruction as a merely textual practice means that he is himself at a loss when faced with the complex conceptual dialectics of the same and the other. As will be demonstrated with respect to *Orientalism* itself, Said cannot get out of the Hegelian problematic that he articulates, and indeed tends himself to repeat the very processes that he criticizes. His advocacy of an analytic pluralism in itself does not solve, or even address, the conceptual problems.

Nevertheless, Said's comments suggest the wider significance of his project. The demise of an orthodox Marxism may have left theory with a sense that everything is now in flux, that the old verities have gone, but it has also involved the important realization, articulated so forcibly by writers such as Foucault or Said, of the deep articulation of knowledge with power. The politics of poststructuralism forces the recognition that all knowledge may be variously contaminated, implicated in its very formal or 'objective' structures. This means that in particular colonial discourse analysis is not merely a marginal adjunct to more mainstream studies, a specialized activity only for minorities or for historians of imperialism and colonialism, but itself forms the point of questioning of Western knowledge's categories and assumptions.

In the same way, Fanon suggests that at the political level the so-called 'Third World' constitutes the disruptive term for the European political dialectic of capitalism and socialism. Everyone feels the need nowadays to qualify the term 'Third World', stating quite correctly that it should not be taken to imply a homogeneous entity. The inadequateness of the term, however, insofar as it offers a univocal description of an extremely heterogeneous section of the world, also means that a suitable alternative general category cannot by definition be produced. In this situation, abject apologies in some respects remain complicit with the patronizing attitudes from which they attempt to disassociate themselves. For the 'Third World' was invented in the context of the 1955 Bandung Conference, on the model of the French Revolution's 'Third Estate', and incorporating equally revolutionary ideals of providing a radical alternative to the hegemonic capitalist-socialist power blocks of the post-war period. [21] The Third World as a term needs to retrieve this lost positive sense – even if today the political order has changed so that to some extent the various forms of Islamic fundamentalism have taken over the role of providing a direct alternative to First and Second World ideologies. [22] 'Third World' will, therefore, be used in this book without (further) apology, or scare quotes, as a positive term of radical critique even if it also necessarily signals its negative sense of economic dependency and exploitation.

III THE PHILOSOPHICAL ALLERGY

Although Said rejects them, and Foucault characteristically does not mention them, the most effective ploys that have recently been played in this project of articulating another form of knowledge, of redefining the basis of knowledge as such, derive from a different although related body of work to that which Foucault describes – namely the phenomenological tradition of Heidegger, Levinas, and Derrida, which, seemingly like all twentieth-century European philosophy, also traces its apparent origins back to Husserl. As we have seen, the fundamental problem concerns the way in which knowledge – and therefore theory, or history – is constituted through the comprehension and incorporation of the other. This has led to a series of attempts to reinscribe a place for, and a relation with, the other as other, outside the sphere of mastery and therefore, logically speaking, both infinite and beyond the scope of knowledge. Emmanuel Levinas, for example, whose career has been long enough to have introduced Husserl to Sartre in the thirties and to have been able to reply to Derrida in the seventies, proposes a rather different critique of such models of knowledge to those which we have encountered so far. [23] According to Levinas,

> Western philosophy coincides with the disclosure of the other where the other, in manifesting itself as a being, loses its alterity. From its infancy philosophy has been struck with a horror of the other that remains other – with an insurmountable allergy.... Hegel's philosophy represents the logical outcome of this underlying allergy of philosophy. [24]

Levinas objects to the implicit violence in the process of knowledge which appropriates and sublates the essence of the other into itself. But as we can see, he does not just blame Hegel here, for according to Levinas ontology itself is the problem. Concerned to find a way to allow the other to remain as other, Levinas therefore rejects not only Hegel but Husserl, Heidegger and Sartre also, and abjures ontology altogether. Because ontology involves an ethico-political violence towards the other, always to some degree seen as a threat, Levinas proposes ethics in its place, substituting a respect for the other for a grasping of it, and a theory of desire not as negation and assimilation but as infinite separation.

In *Totality and Infinity* (1961), a book self-consciously written under the shadow of two 'world' wars in which Europe, at the limit of its attempt to devour the world, turned in on itself in two violent acts of self-consummation, Levinas questions the accepted relation between morality and politics. [25] It must always, he suggests, be possible to criticize politics from the point of view of the ethical. As Althusser was keen to emphasize, according to Marx morality works simply as a form of ideological control, and Levinas concurs that 'everyone will readily agree that it is the highest importance to know whether we are not duped by morality' (21). But, he argues, the placing of politics – 'the art of foreseeing war and of winning it by every means' – before morality overlooks the extent to which war constitutes the philosophical concept of being itself. For being is always defined as the appropriation of either difference into identity, or of identities into a greater order, be it absolute knowledge, History, or the state. For its part, violence involves not just physical force, injuring or annihilating persons, but also

> interrupting their continuity, making them play roles in which they no longer recognize themselves, making them betray not only commitments but their own substance.... Not only modern war but every war employs arms that turn against those who wield them. It establishes an order from which no one can keep his distance; nothing henceforth is exterior. (21)

War, then, is another form of the appropriation of the other, and underpins all ontological thinking with its violence. [26] Its corollary, or 'visage', is the concept of totality, which, as Levinas observes, has dominated Western philosophy in its long history of desire for Unity and the One. Through the totality, itself a kind of rational self writ large, the individual takes on meaning; the present is sacrificed to a future which will bring forth an ultimate, objective meaning when the totality of history is realized. The objection therefore to totalization is not founded on any simple analogy with totalitarianism – though neither can this be excluded – but rather on the implicit violence of ontology itself, in which the same constitutes itself through a form of negativity in relation to the other, producing all knowledge by appropriating and sublating the other within itself. As Levinas puts it, 'the idea of truth as a grasp on things must necessarily have a non-metaphorical sense somewhere'. [27]

In Western philosophy, when knowledge or theory comprehends the other, then the alterity of the latter vanishes as it becomes part of the same. This 'ontological imperialism', Levinas argues, goes back at least to Socrates but can be found as recently as Heidegger. In all cases the other is neutralized as a means of encompassing it: ontology amounts to a philosophy of power, an egotism in which the relation with the other is accomplished through its assimilation into the self. Its political implications are clear enough:

Heidegger, with the whole of Western history, takes the relation with the Other as enacted in the destiny of sedentary peoples, the possessors and builders of the earth. Possession is preeminently the form in which the other becomes the same, by becoming mine. (46)

Ontology, therefore, though outwardly directed, remains always centred in an incorporating self: 'this imperialism of the same', Levinas suggests, 'is the whole essence of freedom' (87). For freedom is maintained by a self-possession which extends itself to anything that threatens its identity. In this structure European philosophy reduplicates Western foreign policy, where democracy at home is maintained through colonial or neocolonial oppression abroad. Levinas opposes freedom, based on self-interest, to justice, which respects the alterity of the other and can only be proposed through the asymmetry of dialogue. [28]

This also implies an interrogation of the imperialism of theory itself. For theory, as a form of knowledge and understanding of the spectator, is constitutively unable to let the other remain outside itself, outside its representation of the panorama which it surveys, in a state of singularity or separation. [29] This will also be true of any concept, because by definition the concept 'cannot capture the absolutely-other'; and, to the extent that it must invoke a form of generality, of language itself. Any conventional form of understanding must appropriate the other, in an act of violence and reduction. This leads Levinas to denounce the inability of theory, in its drive to comprehension and representation, to do justice to any radical exteriority. [30]

But how can we know *and* respect the other? Is there a means of bridging the gap between knowledge and morality that avoids the problems of Kant's recourse to the aesthetic but also resists Lyotard's argument that the two are simply incommensurable? [31] How can Levinas' ethics work differently from ontology? Against the egotism of the preoccupation of being with itself, he posits a relation of sociality, whereby the self instead of assimilating the other opens itself to it through a relation with it. In the place of the correlation of knowledge with vision and light, the visual metaphor by which the adequation of the idea with the thing has been thought from Plato to Heidegger, Levinas proposes language, which in the form of speech enables a kind of invisible contact between subjects that leaves them both intact. Language, however, should take the form of dialogue: whereas the universality of reason means that it must necessarily renounce all singularity, and whereas language's function in conceptualizing thought is to suppress the other and bring it within the aegis of the same, in dialogue language maintains the distance between the two; 'their commerce', as Levinas puts it, 'is ethical'. Dialogism allows for 'radical separation, the strangeness of the interlocutors, the revelation of the other to me' (73). The structure of dialogue, moreover, disallows the taking up of any position beyond the interlocutors from which they can be integrated into a larger totality. The relation between them, therefore, is not oppositional, nor limitrophe, but one of alterity.

Dialogue, face to face conversation, maintains a non-symmetrical relation, a separation through speech. In so doing it breaches any totality, including History:

> To say that the other can remain absolutely other, that he enters only into the relationship of conversation, is to say that history itself, an identification of the same, cannot claim to totalise the same and the other. The absolutely other, whose alterity is overcome in the philosophy of immanence on the allegedly common plane of history, maintains his transcendence in the midst of history. The same is essentially identification within the diverse, or history, or system. It is not I who resist the system, as Kierkegaard thought; it is the other. (40)

The thesis of the primacy of History, Levinas argues, forms part of the imperialism of the same. For 'totalization is accomplished only in history' when the historiographer assimilates all particular existences and punctual moments into the time of universal history, whose chronological order, it is assumed, 'outlines the plot of being in itself, analogous to nature' (55). If History claims to incorporate the other within a larger impersonal spirit or idea, albeit the ruse of reason, Levinas contends that 'this alleged integration is cruelty and injustice, that is, [it] ignores the Other' (52). History is the realm of violence and war; it constitutes another form by which the other is appropriated into the same. For the other to remain other it must not derive its meaning from History but must instead have a separate time which differs from historical time. [32] Whereas for Heidegger time and history are the horizon of Being, for Levinas 'when man truly approaches the Other he is uprooted from history' (52). Time itself involves the 'relationship to unattainable alterity', an absolute past. [33] It is in temporality, in anteriority, that we find an otherness beyond being.

Levinas calls the relation in which an infinite distance is maintained from the other 'metaphysics'. Metaphysics, he writes, 'transcendence, the welcoming of the other by the same, of the Other by me, is concretely produced as the calling into question of the same by the other, that is, as the ethics that accomplishes the critical essence of knowledge' (43). Metaphysics therefore precedes ontology. Though a troubling term, metaphysics for Levinas names a counter-tradition in philosophy in which the idea of infinity breaches all totality because 'it is a relationship *with a surplus always exterior to the totality*' (22). This surplus is the effect of the radical alterity of the other, whether as 'face' or as 'death', which prevents the totality from being constituted as such. As might be expected, it is the possibility of this absolute otherness, and the ability to excise all violence in the relation with it, which Derrida questions in the first of his discussions of Levinas. [34]

Whereas Levinas, like Habermas, posits an authentic language of expression which abhors the distortions of 'rhetoric', Derrida argues that such alterity is constituted not through dialogue but rather through the operation of language itself: Levinas' transcendence-as-surplus is therefore redefined as a Derridean supplement. This would mean that there can never be an authentic speech of the other as such, a position which certainly troubles Levinas' fundamental argument. [35]

Despite their differences, Derrida's keen interest in Levinas, as Christopher Norris has argued in scrupulously non-Derridean terms, points to 'the ultimately ethical nature of his enterprise'. [36] The early essay on Levinas, dating from 1964, shows the extent to which Derrida has been implicated in such questions from the first – though, *contra* Norris, he has always shown that the conditions of 'writing' that make ethics possible also makes them impossible. Certain orientations of his work can be affiliated to Levinas' attempt to shift the relation to alterity from an appropriation by the same into its totality to a respect for the other's heterogeneity. Derrida has even described the critique of logocentrism as 'above all else the search for the "other"'. [37] This can be related to the concern in Derrida's work with the politics of feminism and other positions which contest institutional and political appropriation and exclusion.

In recent years Levinas has himself articulated more explicitly his account of the relation of the ethical to the political. If there were just two, as in the face-to-face dialogue, then the ethical would preside as the injunction of responsibility for the other. But as soon as there are three, he suggests, then the ethical moves into politics. 'We can never', Levinas concedes to Derrida, 'completely escape from the language of ontology and politics'. [38] But this does not mean that the ethical has to renounce the moral order in the political world of the third person – of justice, of government, institutions, or the law. The political can retain an ethical foundation: Levinas finds his example for this, unexpectedly, in Marx's famous comment on idealist philosophers – that the point is not to describe the world but to change it:

> In Marx's critique we find an ethical conscience cutting through the ontological identification of truth with an ideal intelligibility and demanding that theory be converted into a concrete praxis of concern for the other. [39]

From this perspective Levinas proposes the possibility that the much lamented 'subject' be brought back not as the ontological subject which seeks to reduce everything to itself but as an ethical subject defined in relation to the other: 'Ethics redefines subjectivity as this heteronomous responsibility in contrast to autonomous freedom'. [40]

We might compare this ethical relation to Cixous' remarks about the need to love the other or Kristeva's recent preoccupation with love which, from this perspective, hardly involves the sudden apostasy of which she has been accused, but rather as for Levinas consists of a way of formulating a 'responsibility for the Other, being-for-the-other'. [41] In each case these writers can be shown to be trying to place the other outside the sphere of mastery rather than in a relation of negation or of reduplication of the self. Unlike a conventional ethics of altruism, such a relation remains one of alterity. There will always be some return for the self in any gift – unless it can be articulated in an economy of ingratitude, a movement without return. Unless, that is, philosophy can become dissemination: *'a work conceived radically is a movement of the same unto the other which never returns to the same'*. [42] To the story of Ulysses, Levinas opposes that of Abraham who leaves his fatherland for ever, never to return.

This figure of the diaspora returns us to one of the most important aspects of Levinas' formulation of the relation of the ethical to the political, that is the connections which he makes between the structure of ontology and Eurocentrism, the latter 'disqualified', as he puts it, 'by so many horrors'. [43] He connects the form of knowledge that is self-centred but directed outwards, philosophy as 'egology', quite explicitly with the appropriating narcissism of the West. So in the past few hundred years Europe has been, as Gayatri Chakravorty Spivak has suggested, constituted and consolidated as 'sovereign subject, indeed sovereign and subject'. Just as the colonized has been constructed according to the terms of the colonizer's own self-image, as the 'self-consolidating other', so Europe

consolidated itself as sovereign subject by defining its colonies as 'Others', even as it constituted them, for purposes of administration and the expansion of markets, into programmed near-images of that very sovereign self. [44]

It is this sovereign self of Europe which is today being deconstructed, showing the extent to which Europe's other has been a narcissistic self-image through which it has constituted itself while never allowing it to achieve a perfect fit. This can be allied to Derrida's critique of 'a certain fundamental Europeanization of world culture'. [45] Derrida has sometimes been criticized for the generality of phrases such as 'the history of the West', or the claim that his work involves a critique of 'Western metaphysics'. Although one of the earliest questions put to him in England concerned this category of 'the West', in the subsequent fervour that accompanied the transformation of Derrida's work into the method of deconstruction, this problem tended to slip out of view. [46] In its largest and perhaps most significant perspective, deconstruction involves not just a critique of the grounds of knowledge in general, but specifically of the grounds of Occidental knowledge. The equation of knowledge with 'what is called Western thought, the thought whose destiny is to extend its domains while the boundaries of the West are drawn back' involves the very kind of assumption that Derrida is interrogating – and this is the reason for his constant emphasis on its being the knowledge of the West; in the same way Foucault also emphasizes that he is specifically discussing the 'Western *episteme*'. [47] The assertion that Derrida's work incurs a form of relativism is thus exactly to the point, though its implications are rather different from those generally assumed in such a complaint.

For we can say that deconstruction involves the decentralization and decolonization of European thought – insofar as it is 'incapable of respecting the Being and meaning of the other', and to the extent that its philosophical tradition makes 'common cause with oppression and with the totalitarianism of the same'. [48] This has been the significance of Levinas' thought for Derrida. As he puts it in *Writing and Difference*, at the very moment when the fundamental conceptual systems of Europe are in the process of taking over all of humanity, Levinas leads us instead to 'an inconceivable process of dismantling and dispossession'. For Levinas' thought

> seeks to liberate itself from the Greek domination of the Same and the One ... as if from oppression itself – an oppression certainly comparable to none other in the world, an ontological or transcendental oppression, but also the origin or alibi of all oppression in the world. [49]

This is the context in which to set Derrida's own intervention in *Of Grammatology*. Everyone knows that that book is a critique of 'logocentrism'; what is less often recalled is that the terms of the critique with which it opens announce the design of focusing attention on logocentrism's '*ethnocentrism*' which, Derrida suggests, is 'nothing but the most original and powerful ethnocentrism, in the process of imposing itself upon the world'. [50] It is this preoccupation which accounts for Derrida's choice, and forceful interrogation, of the privileged examples of Saussure – where he focuses on the 'profound ethnocentrism' of his exclusion of writing – Rousseau and Lévi-Strauss. [51] In the case of the latter, Derrida's interest also focuses particularly on the way in which Lévi-Strauss produces his knowledge of a non-European civilization according to a doubled but non-contradictory logic which evades identity-thinking. The well-known deconstruction carried out in 'Structure, Sign, and Play' shows how the constitution of anthropological knowledge, though often paraded as scientific and objective, is nevertheless governed by a problematic of which it remains unaware: the philosophical category of the centre – which Derrida then proceeds to articulate with the problem of Eurocentrism. [52] The analysis of the dialectics of the centre and the margin can thus operate geographically as well as conceptually, articulating the power relationships between the metropolitan and the colonial cultures at their geographical peripheries. This is not to suggest, however, that deconstruction in any sense brings another knowledge to bear: rather it involves a critique of Western knowledge that works by exploiting the ambivalent resources of Western writing, as if Marxism were to produce a critique of ideology without the advantage of its science (which, given the current ambiguous status of Marxist science is not a possibility to be dismissed lightly). If one had to answer, therefore, the general question of what is deconstruction a deconstruction of, the answer would be, of the concept, the authority, and assumed primacy of, the category of 'the West'.

If deconstruction forms part of a more widespread attempt to decolonize the forms of European thought, from this perspective Derrida's work can be understood as characteristically postmodern. Postmodernism can best be defined as European culture's awareness that it is no longer the unquestioned and dominant centre of the world. Significantly enough one of the very earliest uses of the term 'postmodern', dating from the time of the Second World War, was that of Arnold Toynbee in his *A Study of History*. He used it to describe the new age of Western history which, according to Toynbee, began in the 1870s with the simultaneous globalization of Western culture and the re-empowerment of non-Western states. [53] If this new period brought with it a phase of Spenglerian pessimism after the long years of Victorian optimism, Toynbee did not himself assume that the West was in decline as such, but rather that paradoxically the globalization of Western civilization was being accompanied by a self-consciousness of its own cultural relativization, a process to which Toynbee's own equally totalizing and relativizing history was designed to contribute. Reviewing the genesis of his whole project, he recounts that his history was written

> against a current Late Modern Western convention of identifying a parvenue and provincial Western Society's history with 'History', writ large, *sans phrase*. In the writer's view this convention was the preposterous off-spring of a distorting egocentric illusion to which the children of a Western Civilisation had succumbed like the children of all other known civilisations and known primitive societies. [54]

Postmodernism, therefore, becomes a certain self-consciousness about a culture's own historical relativity – which begins to explain why, as its critics complain, it also involves the loss of the sense of an absoluteness of any Western account of History. Today, if we pose the difficult question of the relation of poststructuralism to postmodernism, one distinction between them that might be drawn would be that whereas postmodernism seems to include the problematic of the place of Western culture in relation to non-Western cultures, poststructuralism as a category seems not to imply such a perspective. This, however, is hardly the case, for it rather involves if anything a more active critique of the Eurocentric premises of Western knowledge. The difference would be that it does not offer a *critique* by positioning itself outside 'the West', but rather uses its own alterity and duplicity in order to effect its deconstruction. In this context, we may note, attempts to account for poststructuralism in terms of the aftermath of the events of May 68 seem positively myopic, lacking the very historical perspective to which they lay claim. Contrary, then, to some of its more overreaching definitions, postmodernism itself could be said to mark not just the cultural effects of a new stage of 'late' capitalism, but the sense of the loss of European history and culture as History and Culture, the loss of their unquestioned place at the centre of the world. [55] We could say that if, according to Foucault, the centrality of 'Man' dissolved at the end of the eighteenth century as the 'Classical Order' gave way to 'History', today at the end of the twentieth century, as 'History' gives way to the 'Postmodern', we are witnessing the dissolution of 'the West'.

Chapter 2

Marxism and the question of history

Marxist literary criticism has not produced a new theory in over twenty years. Not since Macherey's *A Theory of Literary Production* of 1966 has there been any fundamental theoretical innovation. [1] This date and this gap are by no means fortuitous.

For much of this century Marxist literary criticism monopolized the realm of literary theory, for the simple reason that only Marxists consistently believed in its value and strategic necessity. [2] But since the rise of structuralism in the sixties Marxist criticism has been more and more on the defensive. Marxist humanists still often consider structuralism simply as an attack on Marxism; this theory would be more persuasive if so many structuralists had not also been Marxists. By contrast, it is certainly the case that, with certain notable exceptions, there are few Marxist poststructuralists. If by the late seventies the intellectual arguments of poststructuralism began to seem virtually unanswerable, resistance eventually crystallized around the question of history. In its preoccupation with textuality, poststructuralism had apparently forgotten all about it.

The earliest such critique in the field of literary theory was that of Frank Lentricchia, who organized his entire account of modern criticism around the premise of a 'repeated and extremely subtle denial of history by a variety of contemporary theorists'. [3] Lentricchia's argument was quickly endorsed by Terry Eagleton who claimed first that poststructuralism represented a 'hedonist withdrawal from history' (aestheticism) and, a year later, that it amounted to a more menacing holocaust-like 'liquidation of history'. [4] Moving beyond the confines of the literary, Perry Anderson has similarly dismissed all poststructuralism on the grounds that it represents '*the randomisation of history*'. [5] But what, we might pause to ask, is this remark supposed to suggest? Is Anderson using the word 'random' in its mathematical sense, as one out of a series, or in its statistical sense in which each item has an individual chance? It seems not. More likely he is using it in the more everyday usage of 'not sent or guided in any special direction; having no definite aim or purpose' (OED), which suggests that any such view of history must have no end, and therefore no teleology. In other words, what we are really dealing with here is a defence of a belief in the rationality of the historical process. Anderson's history must work according to a rational principle, the dialectic, and be moving towards an end which will reveal and enact its meaning. Without such a purpose, it is assumed, history must be meaningless.

The terms of this argument repeat exactly those of the critical debate about univocal meaning, according to which the only alternative to the idea that history has a single meaning must be that it has none at all. But of course no one has really been suggesting that history has no meaning, for the obvious reason that any interpretation of history as such must *ipso facto* assert meaning. What is in dispute is whether history has a meaning as 'History'. One alternative would be that history may be made up of the multiple meanings of specific, particular histories – without their necessarily being in turn part of a larger meaning of an underlying Idea or force. Anderson's accusation, which conflates the concept of the differential with the notion of the random, is therefore really directed against the possibility that different histories may have different meanings. But why deny that history can have multiple meanings? *De facto*, it already has – for even for a Marxist who believes in the possibility of 'science' there exists the multiplicity of meanings of truth and of error. We are therefore not so much talking about a single meaning as a true one versus all the others which are false. In a similar way, even 'History' as a metahistorical category achieves its single meaning by subsuming a range of ethico-political concepts, such as 'progress', 'human freedom', 'necessity' and the like, which then form the basis of the regulation and authorization of historical interpretation. This shifts the discussion away from any simple antithesis. The question about history then becomes the more interesting one of the relation between different significa- tions, and the ways in which such differences can, or cannot, be articulated and unified under the same horizon of totalization to produce a single meaning. Until the lonely hour arrives in which the philosophical proof of the truth of history is produced, then history will inevitably continue as a representation and interpretation of the past – rather than Marxist truth and the false or limited interpretation of all other historians. As a form of understanding history will necessarily also be subject to the whole range of questions that surround interpretation, representation and narrative in any form. This is the reason why in recent years theorists have turned their attention back to the question of the historicity of historical understanding, to its status as interpretation, representation or narrative, and, more radically, to the problem of temporality as such. [6]

Lentricchia and Eagleton, by contrast, invoke history rather like 'the political': an outside, a concrete, that somehow remains exterior to 'theory', unaffected by it, capable of enclosing it and even swallowing it up – as if history were in a position to consume theory. History here is self-evident and needs no elaboration. We all know what it is (apparently). But the

problem with the idea that it is possible to dismiss structuralism and
poststructuralism with the charge that they neglect history is that this
argument itself neglects history. For history, as Althusser noted, has always
been a problematical concept. [7] Any examination of the history of 'history'
will demonstrate that it has never had the immediate certainty that is implied
in the all too frequent invocation of 'concrete history'. Far from being the
concrete, it has always rather been the theoretical problem. To acknowledge
that amounts to something very different from simply excising history as
such. [8]

Nevertheless the suggestion that structuralism and poststructuralism have
denied history is a persuasive one which now has wide currency. Such an
argument, in implying that the problem is simply a question of the lack of
history or of its presence, as if history were some undifferentiated entity
that could just be added or taken away, stepped into or got out of, skates
over the fact that the real question has always focused on the much more
difficult issue of what *kind* of history, and of what status can be accorded to
historical thought. The reproach that poststructuralism has neglected history
really consists of the complaint that it has questioned History. This becomes
clearer if it is considered from the more general perspective of postmodernism which has been widely characterized as involving a return of
history, albeit as a category of representation. In fact it was rather modernism,
as its name implies (from latin *modo*, just now, or *hodie*, today), that tried to
awake from the nightmare of history, self-consciously setting itself against
the past, and rejecting forms of historical understanding. The argument
against poststructuralism really just repeats Lukács' reproach, set out in his
1957 essay 'The Ideology of Modernism', that modernism involves a
'negation of history'. [9] If Lukács' objections to modernism laid the basis for
all contemporary objections to poststructuralism, his continuing influence
can help us to understand why history in particular is privileged here.

II 'IN HISTORY'

For why, after all, 'history' at all? Why, from the point of view of Marxism
proper, not the class-struggle, or economics, the state, or social relations?
The stress on history as paramount provides a straightforward indication as
to where such arguments are coming from: not Marxism in general as a
political practice, but the Hegelian Marxism of the philosophical tradition
initiated by Lukács' *History and Class Consciousness* (1923). Criticizing the
orthodox Marxism which regarded dialectics as an external law validated by
natural science, Lukács argued for the primacy of history over economics as
the most significant element in the methodology of Marxism. His stress on
Marxism as a historical method that presupposed and required the idea of
totality initiated a course that determined the history of Western Marxism
to our own day. [10] That history, from one perspective, could be seen as a

consistent struggle to retain Lukács' legacy in which history, the dialectic and the totality are interdependent to the extent that each is essential to the operation of the other in the production of a Marxist science. Post-structuralism, which in its own way also takes part in that history of Western Marxism, differs only insofar as it foregrounds the implications of the theoretical difficulties involved rather than repressing them in pursuit of the unrealized ideal.

For Lukács' legacy could also be seen to have bequeathed a curse. The insistence on history as a totality, necessary if historical materialism is to justify itself as true, left Marxism with a fragile category that from the very first was always on the point of breaking apart. To characterize only recent French thought as 'the logic of disintegration', as Peter Dews has recently done, masks over the fact that such a logic is fundamental to Marxism itself, the unassimilable dark other to its 'primacy of the category of totality'. [11] Yet if Lukács laid this theoretical burden upon Western Marxism, he had, ironically, already written the narrative of its subsequent history in his earlier, pre-Marxist, *Theory of the Novel* (1920). In that work it is possible to see clearly the relation between his insistence on totality and the Romantic aesthetic of totality as the inner necessity that moulds all works of art. More significantly, totality is defined in terms of its absence for modern man who exists in a relation of alienation from the world. The novel, according to Lukács, consists of a striving for unity, a lost state of being represented for him as for many German Romantics by an idealized picture of classical Greece, punctuated by the continual intrusion of a heterogeneous discontinuity. Lukács argues that the novel can transcend this threat of dispersal through an assertion of a continuous temporality, but at the same time he formulates the process in the structure of a fall: 'Once this unity disintegrated, there could be no more spontaneous totality of being'. [12] This account, whose origins in German Romanticism are obviously comparable to Marx's, points to the subsequent difficulty for Marxism itself: the lost 'spontaneous' totality of being can never be retrieved. The objections to poststructuralism at one level therefore represent merely the latest version of the Romantic nostalgia for this unfallen totality of being.

The history of Western Marxism amounts to a history of attempts to provide a means for transcending the condition of alienation and achieving that lost totality, not through irony or a reified homogeneous temporality, as in Lukács' novel, but, according to his formulation of Marxism, through history and class consciousness. The problem, however, is that that reconstituted totality is never certain, its status always remains ambivalent. The appearance of *History and Class Consciousness* at the height of the Modernist movement suggests the degree to which history was being totalized by Lukács at the very moment when the process of detotalization had already begun – even in the aporetic possibilities of his own writings. So in *The*

Historical Novel (1937) Lukács himself would reject as delusion what he calls 'a specially strong temptation to try and produce an extensively complete totality', advocating instead a dramatic concentration and intensification of 'outwardly insignificant events'. [13] Their relation to the totality emerges not through the form of synecdoche – the typical detail which can then be generalized as metaphor – but should, according to Lukács, be drawn out through the narrative which inscribes and extends a connection between such moments of empirical reality and the general laws of history as a totality. Lukács' historicism depends upon the resolution of this tension between the idea of history and the singular detail. But the fundamental incommensurability of idea and event re-emerges in a precariousness in this narrativization of history where each disturbance in the writing punctuates it with the unassimilable, discontinuous and disjunctive temporality of the event.

Lukács' early assault on Marxist economism, subsequently retracted under criticism from the Leninist orthodoxy of the Comintern, became particularly influential in the post-war period among Marxist intellectuals who sought to redefine a new Marxist humanism against the economism of Stalinism with which Lukács' name had by that time itself become associated. Most prominent among those was Sartre, who, in the spirit of Lukács, declared that 'both sociology and economism must be dissolved in *History*'. [14] Today when the primacy of history above all else – the economic, even class conflict – is asserted within a Marxist discourse, together with an accompanying defence of humanism, it can usually be traced back to a Marxism of a Sartrean existentialist form. It comes as no surprise, for example, to discover that the argument about poststructuralism neglecting history was initiated by those whose own intellectual formation can be identified with the existential Marxist humanism of the New Left of the 1950s and early 1960s. [15]

But the case of Sartre poignantly demonstrates that the return-to-history argument can really only succeed through a form of historical amnesia which conveniently forgets that history was almost impossible to find. Any historical investigation will show that history has always been a problematic concept for Marxism, not something that has the status of a 'concrete' existence outside and beyond theory. This could be demonstrated for Lukács or indeed for Marx himself. [16] But in the context of the alleged neglect of history by poststructuralism, it will be more appropriate to confine our discussion to the Marxism of the post-war period. Here too history has always been the problem not the solution – which is why both structuralism and poststructuralism can be positioned within the broad trajectory of a post-war Marxism that has taken the form of a sustained enquiry into concepts of history and even the very possibility of its conceptualization.

III THE CRISIS OF STALINISM

Sartre's existential Marxism, as Ronald Aronson has recently emphasized, was itself formulated in response to criticisms of the function of history in his work by the untimely post-war 'post-Marxist', Maurice Merleau-Ponty. In *Adventures of the Dialectic* (1955), Merleau-Ponty accused the Sartre of *The Communists and Peace* (1952) of using an existentialist ontology to justify communism 'as a completely voluntary effort to go beyond, to destroy and to recreate history':

> Sartre founds communist action precisely by refusing any productivity to history and by making history, insofar as it is intelligible, the immediate result of our volitions. As for the rest, it is an impenetrable opacity. [17]

Through his 'extreme subjectivism', Merleau-Ponty argued, Sartre avoided the traditional claims of Marxism to be the realization of history – and thus also the problem of the relation of Marxism to Stalinism. With the growing recognition of the real nature of the Stalinist regime, the ideological divisions of pre-war Europe became too simplistic to sustain, and even the *attentiste* (wait-and-see) attitude taken after the war by many Marxists, including Merleau-Ponty himself in *Humanism and Terror* (1947), became no longer tenable. [18] Stalinism posed a crisis for Marxism from which it could, in a sense, be said never to have recovered, the conundrum being that if Marxism is true, as it claims that it is, how did the first Marxist state end up as Stalinist? There are basically two positions that can be taken with respect to this irrevocable split between theory and practice: either Marxism has been shown to be not true, or the Marxism of Stalinist Russia was not proper Marxism. The second alternative poses a serious problem, however, insofar as it leads to the further question, how could such Marxism not be true – in the sense of how could History, in the objective processes on which a scientific Marxism places so much faith, be undialectical enough to produce Stalinism from the October Revolution? How could History have failed to bring about an end to history? Merleau-Ponty's response was to argue that history itself had shown Marxist philosophy to have been flawed; such philosophy must therefore give up its claim to truth. [19] Ironically, then, the trajectory which today produces the Marxist argument that poststructuralism neglects history was itself initiated by the claim that Marxism itself had been invalidated by history.

In this context, the major challenge for Marxism became how to explain Marxism's 'detour' from itself, a question on which Sartre's project was to founder in the second volume of the *Critique of Dialectical Reason*. It was Stalin's unfortunate deviation which led to the whole series of attempts by Western European Marxists to return-to-Marx – the major examples in France being Sartre and Althusser, and in Germany the Frankfurt School. Merleau-Ponty, on the other hand, arguing that only one Marxism,

Stalinism, could be said to be the product of actual history, rejected any possibility of trying to define a new, more genuine Marxism as the return-to-Marxists tried to do. According to Merleau-Ponty, Western academic Marxism, starting with Lukács, amounted only to the production of 'ideas without historical equivalents' (204). He therefore repudiated any attempt to begin the painful separation of an 'authentic' from a 'false', orthodox or official Marxism, choosing rather to stress the ambivalence of Marxism itself. For Merleau-Ponty no sublation could resolve Marxism's own division between its theory and the history of its practice, itself, he argued, an acting out of its theoretical equivocation between history as a process of natural necessity and history as the product of human praxis. These conflicts, he contended, although highlighted in the differences between the Western Marxism of Lukács and the orthodoxy of Marxist-Leninism, could be traced back to the work of Marx himself. Merleau-Ponty's argument thus meant acknowledging a certain equivocalness in Marxist claims to truth, which could no longer claim exemption from critical examination, and led inevitably, therefore, to an early form of what, even then, was characterized as 'post-Marxism'.

Merleau-Ponty, whose anticipations of later post-Marxists such as Foucault and Lyotard are readily apparent, therefore rejected not the dialectic as such, nor history, but the closed dialectic as an autonomous principle that was supposed to produce the grand narrative of History:

> The illusion was only to precipitate into a historical fact – the proletariat's birth and growth – history's total meaning, to believe that history itself organized its own recovery, that the proletariat's power would be its own suppression, the negation of the negation. (205)

In a provocative comparison of the failures of the French and Russian revolutions, he argued that the problem stemmed from the fact that no class, whether proletarian or bourgeoisie, can become the ruling class without taking upon itself something of the historical role of a ruling class – especially if at the same time it also considers that 'history carries within itself its own cure':

> To assume that the proletariat will be able to defend its dictatorship against entanglement is to assume in history itself a substantial and given principle which would drive ambiguity from it, sum it up, totalise it, and close it. (221)

Instead, Merleau-Ponty proposed an open dialectic which would concede Marxism's equivocalness, and give up the claim to the dialectical logic of History as a process of objective truth. [20] Or to put it another way, he maintained that Marxism can only constitute its totality through its perpetual detours from itself.

Chapter 3

Sartre's extravagances

Thus, the world and man reveal themselves by *undertakings*. And all the undertakings we might speak of reduce themselves to a single one, that of *making history*.
                                                                    Jean-Paul Sartre [1]

Sartre took the opposite course to Merleau-Ponty and sought instead to define a new authentic Marxism. His project in the *Critique of Dialectical Reason* (1960) amounted to a philosophical defence of Marxism and its dialectic through a reassertion of its claim to be the only valid interpretation of history, 'the untranscendable philosophy for our time'. [2] However, Sartre was no more prepared than Merleau-Ponty to return to what he characterized as Marxist organicism, in which the laws of history unfold according to their own autonomous momentum. Not wishing to propose History as a transcendent law outside the human, Sartre was careful to distinguish his claims from Engels' validation of the dialectic as the law of nature. [3] He sought instead to prove that history achieves its course and its meaning from the actions of men, even if men are also simultaneously the products of history. Merleau-Ponty had accused the existentialist Sartre of denying history and trying to hold everything together instead 'only by the hopeless heroism of the I'. Sartre therefore tried to show that the two were not opposed: arguing that the dialectic is produced by human subjectivity rather than inscribed within history itself, at the same time he also asserted the truth of the Marxist account of there being one history with a single meaning – a history, that is, in which all differences return as the same. Everything, therefore, hinged on Sartre's ability to substantiate the interdependence of these two claims.

'There is a crisis in Marxism', Sartre announced at the beginning of the *Critique*; this crisis, not the first and not to be the last, Sartre characterized as the result of a paradox in which historical materialism had become 'at one and the same time, the only truth of History and a total *indetermination* of the Truth' (I, 19). Today we might say that it had been shown to be different from itself. This was the aporia detected by Merleau-Ponty: but rather than question Marxism's truth, Sartre sought to remove its indetermination. He argued that though historical materialism had satisfactorily explained the forms and conditions of human reality it had never established theoretically the validity of its own existence, never shown how it constituted not just the substance of reality but its logical form as well. In order to prove the truth of History's prospective totalization into one meaning, therefore, Sartre's initial philosophical task was to ground his argument epistemologically by proving the legitimacy of the dialectic itself, thus demonstrating not only that history was dialectically intelligible but also why it necessarily should be so. 'The dialectic', according to Sartre, 'is both a method *and* a movement in the object' (I, 20): Marxism asserts simultaneously that both the process of knowledge and the structure of the real are dialectical, but it has never proved the former – basing its claim to truth instead on the 'dogmatic dialectic' of natural science. Accordingly, much of Volume I of the *Critique* is taken up with the attempt to prove the dialectic *a priori* as the universal method and the law of anthropology, superseding that which Kant had provided for analytical reason. [4] Volume Two, Sartre announces, will then prove 'the *Truth of History*' (I, 52):

> it will attempt to establish that there is *one* human history, with *one* truth and *one* intelligibility – not by considering the material content of this history, but by demonstrating that a practical multiplicity, whatever it may be, must unceasingly totalise itself through interiorizing its multiplicity at all levels. (I, 69)

The point, therefore, is to validate Marxism, to show that it is not simply a method of interpretation, nor even that it is the best method of interpretation that can most successfully account for the facts and the course of history, but to prove *a priori* that history works according to dialectical structures, and to demonstrate 'the moments of their inter-relations, the ever vaster and more complex movement which totalises them and, finally, the very direction of the totalization, that is to say, the "meaning of History" and its Truth' (I, 69). Had he succeeded, Sartre would have established dialectical reason as successfully for the human sciences as Kant had established analytical reason for natural science. But he was unable to do it. The indetermination that he sought to banish increasingly returned to haunt him; he could never demonstrate how the unceasing totalization of multiplicity would ever reach its promised moment of finality.

Sartre's claim for the continued validity of Marxism as a method of understanding necessarily meant that he had to respond to the problem of Stalinism. His was the first attempt to explain Stalinism as an aberration through the forms of Marxist analysis itself. [5] Rather than reject Marxism on the grounds that it had been disproved by history, as Merleau-Ponty had done, he sought to account for Stalinism through a dialectical analysis of the specific history of the Soviet Union since the Revolution: theory and practice, he argued, had become separated with the result that the former had become 'sclerosed' while the latter had become 'blind' and 'unprincipled' (I, 50). According to Sartre, if the dialectic had become blocked, an understanding of its detour could nevertheless only be achieved through the use of a dialectical logic. He therefore sought to prove both that the structures of history were necessarily dialectical and that the course of actual history could be shown to be so. But in attempting to discover why the Russian Revolution followed the path it did, he found himself arriving at the conclusion that, far from being a 'false' deviation, in the circumstances of history Stalinism had been necessary. Having set out to demonstrate how, through its understanding of the structure of history, Marxism was in a position to forecast the future, he came to the conclusion that there was no guarantee that history could promise anything better that what had just passed.

II THE FIRST *CRITIQUE*

Unity had been easy during the Resistance, because relationships were almost always man-to-man. Over against the German army or the Vichy government, where social generality ruled, as it does in all machines of state, the Resistance offered the rare phenomenon of historical action which remained personal. The psychological and moral elements of political action were almost the only ones to appear here, which is why intellectuals least inclined to politics were to be seen in the Resistance. The Resistance was a unique experience for them, and they wanted to preserve its experience in the new French politics because this experience broke away from the famous dilemma of being and doing, which confronts all intellectuals in the face of action.... It is only too obvious that this balance between action and personal life was intimately bound up with the conditions of clandestine action and could not survive it. And in this sense it must be said that the Resistance experience, by making us believe that politics is a relationship between man and man or between conscious-nesses, fostered our illusions of 1939 and masked the truth of the incredible power of history which the Occupation taught us in another connection. [6]

If by 1945 Merleau-Ponty had here already indicated the historical basis for what was to become Sartre's project in the *Critique*, the theoretical problem that followed was how to unite orthodox Marxist concepts of economic determinism and historical necessity with the individualism of Sartre's earlier work, that is the existentialist notion of the authentic self and the possibility of choosing one's own freedom: how to relocate human practice within historical determinism, to reconcile the individual with the social, the idea of agency with that of necessity, or freedom with history? [7] For Marxist or Hegelian thought, such an age-old contradiction ought to be resolvable through the operations of dialectical logic. [8] Citing Marx's famous remark in

The Eighteenth Brumaire, 'Men make their own History ... but under circumstances ... given and transmitted from the past', Sartre suggested that this implied 'the permanent and dialectical unity of freedom and necessity' (I, 35). Accordingly, he attempted to shift Marxism away from orthodox theories of an absolute determinism towards the primacy of a concept of 'History' which, while still a totality as it had been for Lukács, a process with a determinate meaning and end, could also include a concept of human agency and thus articulate the individual with the social, freedom with determinism.

Today, Sartre's voluntarism is to some extent returning to favour as the result of a desire to retrieve the categories of agency and the subject, which goes together with the wish to get out of the apparently totalizing systems of Adorno, Althusser or Foucault. Sartre's stress on the role of the subject also finds approval because many of those no longer prepared to argue for a general theory of history as the progress of a single narrative of class-struggle, have begun to argue instead for a return of its correlative, the subject, almost as if it was the next best thing in the absence of history itself. [9] But it still leaves us with the crucial problem that Sartre had to solve, namely how to link human consciousness with the processes of history so that the former can be said to be the agent of the latter.

How could this take place? As Sartre had put it in *What is Literature?*: 'Never has *homo faber* better understood that he has *made* history and never has he felt so powerless before history'. [10] How can man make history if at the same time it is history which makes him? Sartre considered that orthodox dialectical materialism takes the easy way out by merely eliminating the first in favour of the second, making man a passive product entirely determined by economic circumstances. Unwilling to follow Merleau-Ponty by dropping the second in favour of the first, Sartre argued that it was possible for man to be both at once through the movement of *praxis*, that is intentional actions which produce material effects. [11] Its corollary, whereby praxis becomes determining history, he called the 'practico-inert', by which he meant the material circumstances that have themselves been created by previous praxes and which form the conditions for new praxis. The individual is thus both totalizer and totalized, deftly uniting freedom with necessity. Though this neatly solves the problem of how man can make history while at the same time history makes him, it does not answer the larger question of how a multiplicity of the products of individual acts, 'totalizations', can themselves be totalized into the overall totalization required by the logic of dialectical rationality – rather than being the arbitrary, blind and self-cancelling movements of, say, Hardy's immanent will. Sartre's fundamental thesis, that 'History continually effects totalisations of totalisations' (I, 15), does not in itself answer what Ronald Aronson has rightly characterized as *the* question for Sartre: 'how do separate, antagonistic actions yield *a* history; how do individual totalizations lead to Totalization (and also progress, the direction of history, its truth and its meaning)?' [12]

For the whole basis of Sartre's argument is that the dialectic of history is not a metaphysical law, 'some powerful unitary force revealing itself behind History like the will of God', but the continuously produced effect of individual conflicts; each action is in its turn subsumed as a part of the whole in an ever broader, developing totalization (I, 37). What Sartre needs to demonstrate, therefore, is that if the law of the dialectic works from the individual level, overall it produces nothing less than the intelligibility or the meaning of History as such:

> The dialectic is the law of totalization which creates *several* collectivities, *several* societies, and *one* history – realities, that is, which impose themselves on individuals; but at the same time it must be woven out of millions of individual actions. We must show that it is possible for it to be both a *resultant* ... and a *totalizing force* ... how it can continually bring about the unity of dispersive profusion and integration. (I, 36)

But what produces the overall direction of History? How does it 'continually bring about the unity of dispersive profusion and integration'? Sartre does not attempt to answer this question, shifting rather to the notion of a lack of self-consciousness. The dialectic is the law that remains hidden. At the moment, 'history is made without being known (*l'histoire se fait sans se connaître*)' – history constitutes, we might say today, a political unconscious. [13] 'Marxism', on the other hand, Sartre claims, 'is History itself becoming conscious of itself' (I, 40): as for Lukács, it is by becoming conscious of itself as the subject of history that the working class will understand history's meaning – and so recognize itself as the meaning of history. While he suggests in apocalyptic tones in *The Problem of Method* that this process of self-consciousness is at last beginning to take place, and that civil, foreign and colonial wars are becoming apparent as different forms of a single class struggle, Sartre also admits that the divorce between theory and praxis which ensued under Stalinism has generally prevented any clear self-consciousness among the masses. [14] The 'detour' of Stalinism is thus formalized as Marxism's own descent into its unconscious, resulting in a dream-work of heterogeneous histories that have eluded systematization and subsumption into the single meaning of Marxism's own reading of history. It is therefore, Sartre argues, our historical task to make it known, promoting not just the historical process as such, but also the general recognition whereby the plurality of the meanings of individual histories can be seen to combine to make one history, with one meaning – the 'Truth of humanity' (I, 822). Sartre's account thus sets up the articulation of history, univocal meaning, and totality as the indissoluble set of elements required for the validation of Marxism, necessary in order to save it from its detour from itself. The problem, however, remains how such universals are produced from the multiplicity of initiating individual praxes.

If History is a history of conflict, how could it be both one and internally diversified without the inner moving principle of the dialectic? How can History be a unity if it is also conflictual, if each action is aimed at destroying the other and results in a double negation in which the original aims of each action have been destroyed by the other? If each action negates the aim of the other, where is the 'unity' totalized in the conflict? How does History constantly totalize itself? (I, 817–18) Sartre arrives at what he calls 'the real problem of History', that is how there can be totalization without a totalizer, only at the very end of Volume I. [15] It is not until the next volume, however, that he intends to show how individual actions, separate multiplicities, make up 'one human history, with one truth and one intelligibility' (I, 69). Throughout, Sartre has nevertheless taken it 'for granted that such a totalisation is constantly developing both as History and as historical Truth' (I, 822). His History, therefore, is always in process: but its teleology of a final totalization always has to be assumed. He thus asserts the Truth of History while constantly projecting forwards and deferring its proof. But when the proof comes it also turns out to rest on the assumption that it is already true.

III THE SECOND CRITIQUE:
'We are trying to establish the Truth of History'

Sartre produces a persuasive formulation of the relation of the individual to the determining historical circumstance through his concepts of praxis and the practico-inert; it is also obvious to him how the larger question of History ought to be solved. He asserts it often enough: 'History continually effects totalisations of totalisations' (I, 15). But in Volume I of the Critique, as we have seen, he continually defers the demonstration of his proof. For the 'dogmatic dialectic', as he describes dialectical materialism, the whole question naturally poses no problem, for each person or group simply constitutes a partial moment of an already operative movement of totalization that produces them and then goes beyond them. But Sartre's dispensing with all historicist schemas creates the problem of how, between two autonomous and contradictory totalizations, there could be 'one dialectical intelligibility of the ongoing process' (II, 13). He attempts to solve this through matching his account of contradiction with a new concept derived from the conjunction of work and labour: 'anti-labour' (anti-travail), a category of negation. The products of a conflict, as well as its residues, may seem incomprehensible insofar as they differ from the original intentions of any of the combatants. [16] Nevertheless they constitute the basis and conditions for further actions and history. Dialectical reason encounters such products as undecidables:

aporias – because they seem to be at once the results of a communal enterprise while at the same time bearing witness to the fact that this enterprise never existed except as the inhuman reverse side of two opposed actions in which each aims to destroy the other. In the dialectical perspective, we encounter these objects as productions which are human and provided with a future.... thus they seem by themselves to be totalizations in process. (II, 20)

This means that first, they lead to unforseeable results, and second, that the internal structure of social objects contains 'the double negation of themselves and of each constituent part by the other' (II, 22). There is, therefore, before any understanding of historic agents and movements, a certain *aporia* in all social ensembles: from afar they may appear whole, but close to, they can be seen as riddled with holes. This increasingly comes to resemble nothing so much as Sartre's own account of History.

In the context of the negativity of this formulation, Sartre is obliged to pose once again the problem of whether there can be a totalization, without any independent totalizer or totalizing force such as the dialectic, or whether the structure of negation that he has described means that, as for Adorno or Bakhtin, history does not develop positively but, rather, negatively, and is therefore instead detotalizing:

Marxism is rigorously true if History is totalization; it is not so any more if human history decomposes into a plurality of particular histories, or if, in any case, within the relationship of immanence that characterizes struggle, the negation of each adversary by the other is on principle *detotalizing*. Certainly, we have neither the design nor the actual possibility of showing here the full truth of dialectical materialism.... Our goal is solely to establish whether, in a practical ensemble torn apart by antagonism (whether there are multiple conflicts or whether they are reduced to one) the breaks themselves are totalizing and carried along by the totalizing movement of the ensemble. (II, 25)

At this point Sartre confronts the possibility that the whole project of the *Critique*, stated so confidently on its very first page – 'it must be proved that a negation of a negation can be an affirmation' (I, 15) – may break down. Perhaps the Truth of History cannot be proved; its direction cannot be discerned.

Sartre's reaction to the threat that the negation of a negation may produce a detotalizing effect is to introduce a new category, a unifying force of a 'singularization' which incarnates the universal: 'If totalization really is an ongoing process', he writes, 'then it operates everywhere. That means both that there is a dialectical meaning of the practical ensemble ... and that each singular event totalizes in itself the practical ensemble in the infinite richness of its singularity' (II, 26). Unlike Lukács' insignificant event from which the universal is precariously drawn out through the narrative, Sartre's singularity works synecdochally in a conventional antinomy with the universal, the relation between the two structured according to the familiar nineteenth-century model of organic growth or process in which each singular event makes up the whole while, as he puts it, 'the whole is entirely present in the part as its present meaning and as its destiny'. [17]

Sartre's 'singular universal', therefore, begs the question, for it is predicated on the assumption that, if there is not a totality as such, then there already is an overall totalization: 'If totalization really is an ongoing process...'. That developing process is itself totalized through Sartre's assertion that each totalization is the totalization of all struggles, as it must be if the singular is to incarnate the universal. The concept of the singular universal thus facilitates a circularity in the argument whereby Sartre can avoid the question which he began by posing. So the singular universal presumes the totalization he can't (yet) prove. This strategy marks a structure of repetition in Sartre's text: each time he poses the question of how there can be totalization of History without a totalizer, he retreats to a more limited example whose unity is already evident, but which in the end only brings him back to the original question again.

In this case Sartre demonstrates how the singular universal works, by appealing to the concrete example of a boxing match – a random exemplification that just happens to reproduce the single adversaries of the master/slave dialectic. Its totalization takes place through its incarnation, as part of the totality of boxing, in the overall framework within which each individual fight occurs. Each boxing match, Sartre claims, must be both a unique event and also in some sense the incarnation of all boxing, whose rules and conventions it follows, and whose past and future history it sets itself against. But it is also apparent that that totality is not completely known, nor is its future shape even presumed. By totalization, therefore, Sartre does not here mean anything like a predetermined end or final closure of a totality but rather a process of mediation among the parts, where each is determined by the other. No one can predict the future of boxing, either at the level of particular victories or defeats, in effect a structure of repetition, nor at the more general level of possible modifications or developments of the sport. Yet each individual bout articulates itself within the framework of the history of boxing, known and unknown. This allows Sartre to include chance and contingency in his scheme. Since it cannot be known as a concept that will realize itself in the future, Sartre argues instead that the totality only produces itself in the moment: 'The incarnation as such is at once unrealizable except as totalization of everything and irreducible to a pure abstract unity of that which it totalizes' (II, 58). The universal, the totality, can only be known through the singular. But its future direction remains unknown and indeterminate.

At the same time Sartre makes a larger, though less persuasive claim that the boxing-match also works synecdochally and re-exteriorizes a more fundamental violence, namely the interiorized condition of scarcity that he considers to be the basis of conflict in general. The boxing match 'is the public incarnation of *all* conflict' (II, 32), totalizing in its own struggle the whole of 'contemporary irreducibilities and fissures' (II, 26):

> thus one can and must say ... that each fight is the singularisation of all *the circumstances* of the social whole in movement and that by this singularisation, it incarnates the enveloping totalization which the historical process is. (II, 58)

But then he adds, 'I have said and I repeat that we have not yet proved that this enveloping totalization exists'. So, although it is possible to conceive of any event as an incarnation of the totality, insofar as it must itself make up a part of that totality in its determination, unlike the case of the boxing match, where we can define the overall entity 'boxing', it still remains unproven that an overall entity, 'History', can be said to exist at all. For all his use of the model of the boxing match, Sartre has really got no further with the fundamental question of how there can be totalization without a totalizer. It is simple enough for him to show that a boxing match takes place within a general totality of 'boxing', which is itself only ever present in any individual incarnation, for as a game each match is both an individual bout and something conducted according to general rules and a specific social tradition. But what about those conflicts that do not take place within such a constituted social system, such as conflictual bourgeois societies which cannot be said to be unified, except, as Sartre suggests dismissively, by appeal to a lost paradise before the class struggle? Such societies make the conflicts of history irreducible to Sartre's logic unless, like the boxing match, they can be shown to take part in a larger totalizable category. However, when he poses the question of whether his method could work as well for the class struggle as for the boxing match, Sartre admits that he finds it impossible to answer and returns instead to the much easier case of sub-groups. [18] Once again he backtracks and assumes a larger unity in which conflict takes place.

The major question thus always remains unanswered in the *Critique*: every time that Sartre announces that he is about to proceed with the fundamental problem of how History can be a totalization without a totalizer, he turns back to a previous, more easily intelligible stage on the way. His difficulty is accompanied by a no doubt symptomatic increasing distrust of universals so that, in championing specificities against them, he seems to give up the attempt to validate the universals – History as Totalization – that originally formed the object of his project. At this point a further contradiction in Sartre's whole enterprise begins to open up: for someone so deeply distrustful of universals it seems curious that he has involved himself so emphatically with the notions of totality, History, and the dialectic. [19] As Sartre insists more and more upon the virtues of specificity (II, 200–05), such is his distaste for Marxist or any other universalizing categories that he refuses even to countenance them, attempting to replace concepts with specificities, universals with singulars. His scepticism goes to the extent of even denying the existence of 'society' or 'the nation' as such (II, 24, 61) – the very totalities which his own general argument for totalization requires. Here certain similarities with later 'post-Marxist' theorists such as Foucault or Lyotard, begin to become apparent. [20] But if Sartre anticipates such later thinkers we should not assume too quickly that they have simply taken his insights further. For Sartre's singular universal could never be expected to solve the formal theoretical problem of how individual existential existence can be related to History insofar as it simply renames, in one oxymoronic category, the original antithetical terms. Without an adequate theory of their articulation, they simply begin to separate again. [21]

IV THE AMBIVALENCE OF HISTORY

The 'singular universal', with its organicist and essentialist overtones whereby the part incarnates the whole, is thus the product of Sartre's hesitation between the singular, which remains privileged as the existential basis of history, and the universal which as a Marxist he feels is required for its intelligibility and validation. [22] The effect of Sartre's oscillation between these two poles is that his argument is increasingly drawn towards the very positions that ostensibly he wishes to refute. So, for example, he compulsively returns to the idea that history might consist of several totalizations rather than one:

> Might not History, at the level of the grand ensembles, be an ambiguous interpenetration of unity and plurality, of dialectic and anti-dialectic, of sense and nonsense? Might there not be, according to the circumstances and the particular ensemble, *several* totalizations without any links between them except coexistence or no matter what other exterior link? (II, 131)

Up to this point, Sartre's notion of conflict has operated in direct antithesis to that of Bakhtin: whereas for Sartre, struggles are totalizing, always creating a larger, meaningful and developing whole out of multiplicities, for Bakhtin they are detotalizing, dissolving 'previous totalisations'. [23] But Sartre's own text here develops a dialogism in the tension between these two possibilities which becomes an increasingly dominant characteristic of his regressive-progressive method and ends up by detotalizing the very totalization which he sought to prove. Here we find the theoretical corollary of what Althusser was to characterize as the tragic 'double thesis' of Sartre's 'historicist humanism', and which produced, in Michael Sprinker's words, a 'ceaseless rebounding between the poles of revolutionary optimism and historical pessimism'. [24]

Sartre himself theorizes this growing ambivalence as the difference between his own method and that of orthodox Marxism, elaborating the distinction between concept and incarnation as two possible paths of a dialectical understanding of the same social reality. The concept, as employed by orthodox Marxism, goes from the singular to the universal and therefore, Sartre claims, detotalizes in a movement of 'decompressive expansion', whereas incarnation involves 'a way of totalizing compression which, on the contrary, seizes the centripetal movement of all the significations drawn in and condensed in the event or in the object' (II, 59). But it is rather Sartre's own text that seems to be caught between these two dialectical possibilities of expansion and compression in a double logic. Thus the very concept of totalization, distinguished from totality, must always be refused its prospective closure, for if 'History continually effects totalisation of totalisations' (I, 15) it must necessarily also mean that by definition it can never be absolutely totalized. As he puts it in *The Problem of Method*: 'For us the reality of the collective object rests on *recurrence*. It demonstrates that the totalization is never achieved and that the totality exists at best only in the form of a *detotalized totality*.' [25] How then can history totalize totalization if totalization is never accomplished? This is the point at which the dialectic, as a unity of method and movement, of subject and object, knower and known, requires the writing subject who must effectively hold them together. Thus the critical investigation

> takes place *inside* the totalisation and can be neither a contemplative recognition of the totalising movement, nor a particular, autonomous totalisation of the known totalisation. Rather it is a real moment of the developing totalisation.... (I, 48)

This means that the process of totalization must be kept moving by the critical investigation itself on which it comes to depend but which by the same token it can never subsume. Every time that Sartre asserts the enveloping movement of the historical process, while adding emphatically that he has yet not proved that such a totalization exists, he must always simultaneously introduce a counterstructure of repetition, so that his argument seems to fluctuate, like the groups that he describes, 'in a state of perpetual *detotalisation*' (I, 579). This is why although he dares to pose his overwhelming question, he can never be in a position to answer it with more than an assertion and the promise of more totalizations. The indetermination he sought to excise returns to govern him. The *Critiques* can do nothing but proliferate extravagantly into the writing of a perpetual process of deferral.

If the singular universal increasingly punctuates the forward movement of Sartre's text instead of providing it with a dialectical meaning and direction, the problem that it was invoked to solve meanwhile takes its own aberrant course. Denying that conflict is an *a priori* structure actualized in historical struggle, we have seen that Sartre does explain, through the category of the 'practico-inert' (determining material conditions which have themselves been created by previous praxis), how individuals or classes in conflict produce a historical movement to which they are then subject. Actions, in turn, create the conditions for their own contradiction when the successful fulfilment of praxis is prevented by the action of another praxis whose aims conflict with it. The fact that conflict produces anti-labour, or a contingent situation that was not the original aim of either conflictual group, must mean that in this schema History has a negative unity, notwithstanding the troubled formulation of the singular-universal. If Sartre denies all possibility both of an underlying historical structure and of a larger unity, a 'hyper-organism' as he puts it, within which conflict takes place, then history as he conceptualizes it here has no specific or necessary direction. More seriously, it suggests that history will always deviate from any intended route and take an unforeseen one instead. If political struggle takes place for specific purposes and anticipated results, here Sartre seems to condemn it to an unending series of detours that will never arrive at their destination. Insofar as 'History' names the horizon of totalization of those ethico-political meanings that point in the direction of social change, it here not only loses its single meaning, but threatens to lose even the bases on which its meaning is constituted. Sartre, therefore, cannot after all be said to substitute a simple voluntarism for an underlying historical structure.

In the second *Critique* Sartre seems remarkably equivocal with regard to his central question of how struggles which have no controlling totalizer or underlying structure of totalization can be intelligible. He begins by allowing the possibility of schism, such as that which took place in the Roman Empire (II, 84), which implies that humans can choose not to allow totalization. He then admits that the result of any conflict, though it may be intelligible, may not necessarily imply any progress. Progress or improvement is no more likely than decline: he now repeatedly disowns any necessary historical logic of progress; its incarnations will always, strictly speaking, be accidental ones in relation to the objectives which were at the origin of praxis:

> [History] is not rigorous because it always proceeds by faults and corrections, because it is not *in any way* a universal schema but a unique adventure that unfolds on the basis of prehistoric circumstances which constitute in themselves, and in relation to all the objectives and all the practices, a heavy and badly understood legacy of fundamental deviations. (II, 238)

History therefore does have a structure of sorts – a legacy of continual aberration.

By abandoning any logic of progress for the negative synthesis of anti-labour which produces deviation, Sartre is, on the other hand, able to account for the major detour that provides the context for his whole debate with Merleau-Ponty, and indeed for all post-war Marxism: the spectre of Stalinism. The problem, however, is that though Sartre produces a provocative analysis of why Stalin was successful, this imperceptibly slides into an account of why Stalin had to do what he did, to the extent that Sartre appears to justify his actions according to the particular necessities of his historical circumstances. Thus Sartre argues that it was necessary to choose between the break-up of the Revolution and its deviation. [26] Stalinism, in fact, accords all too perfectly with the perverse structures of Sartre's own theoretical argument. It also serves, appropriately enough, as a way of closing down the aporias which have opened up in Sartre's text.

Sartre takes the slogan 'socialism in one country' as an example of the unintended but necessary product of the anti-labour of the Stalin-Trotsky conflict. He translates the 'socialism in one country' of the one versus the 'internationalism' of the other into a conflict between his own, now reified and separated, terms of concrete incarnation and abstract universalism: 'the revolutionary incarnation chose the singular against the universal and the national against the international' (II, 223). Stalin therefore becomes the authentic Marxist, able to deal with specific historical circumstances, as against Trotsky who is regarded as having been hopelessly caught up with the *a priori* universalism of an abstract Marxism. According to Sartre, the Revolution's 'incarnation directly contradicts its universalization' (II, 116). If he therefore demonstrates why socialism in one country was historically necessary, he ends up by apparently justifying Stalinism: in showing how anti-labour produces deviation, he seems to endorse its course while rejecting any overall schema which can provide the basis of a claim that it will be ultimately corrected. The analysis stops at the point where even Stalin's anti-semitism begins to appear necessary (II, 281). Sartre never broaches the question of the other crimes committed by Stalin (which is just as well in view of the way the argument is going) nor does he address the obvious problem that his own identification of Stalin as the practical Marxist of specificities against Trotsky's abstract universalism runs directly counter to the fact that Stalinism produced the most clear-cut example of a Marxism which internalized an abstract schema within itself. Instead, at this point Sartre at last abandons all hope of proving History as a totalization without a totalizer. He moves into a long attempt, which takes up the rest of the book, to revise the earlier ontology of *Being and Nothingness* into a new ontology of action and even of History, as if, after all, he is investigating the prospect of accrediting the latter with ontological status – a possibility which has always haunted his text in its insistent negation. This analysis, though lengthy, remains incomplete. [27] In studying the deviation, Sartre himself deviated from his original project. But this was not just the effect of Stalin *per se*, despite his perverse attraction as a sort of singular-universal who did in effect unite 'man' with 'history': it was also the result of the theoretical collapse of the singular-universal as a totalizing concept that could save history from the aberrant consequences of anti-labour.

Sartre's philosophical grounding of 'History', therefore, foundered in the second volume when the logic of history inexorably brought him, not to totalization without a totalizer, but to the very reverse: the figure of Stalin and the conclusion that Stalinism had been indispensable for the development of socialism in the Soviet Union. Although the *Critique* had been intended to rescue Marxism from the sclerosis of Stalinism, Sartre found that his theory of history, far from explaining what had gone wrong when the most radical political theory turned out in practice to be one of the most oppressive, had rather shown why it had necessarily happened that way. Volume II was never completed, and only published, unfinished, in 1985.

Thus Sartre's attempt to prove the truth of Marxism and of History at a philosophical level was abandoned. The basic theoretical problem had been to show how two or more autonomous and contradictory totalizations make up one dialectical intelligibility: to do this he needed to totalize the classes in struggle, and to discover the synthetic unity of a conflictual society. The articulation of individual *praxis* with History stood or fell with the concept of history as totalization without a totalizer. The stakes had been painfully clear to Sartre himself: 'Marxism is rigorously true if History is totalization; it is not so any more if human history decomposes into a plurality of particular histories' (II, 25). The problem was that the premises of his own theory required the answer to this question to remain always in abeyance, while his text enacts rather than resolves the equivocality of the choice which it sets up. If Sartre began by attempting to unite man with history, in the notes at the very end of the manuscript he poses once more the fundamental ontological question, and immediately follows it with a decidedly unequivocal answer:

IS HISTORY ESSENTIAL TO MAN?
No. (II, 454)

Sartre's argument for History as totalization, then, was already caught up in interminable difficulties by the time he was drafting Volume II of the *Critique* in 1958. No sooner had he published Volume I in 1960 than the whole status that he claimed for History, for man, and for their articulation, came under attack.

V HISTORY AND ETHNOCENTRICITY

The case of Sartre demonstrates why the assertion of 'history' against structuralism and poststructuralism must always remain problematical. In this context it is ironic that it was a structuralist critique of Sartre's claims for history that, in historical terms, brought about the abrupt intellectual demise of existential Marxism itself. Lévi-Strauss' famous objections to

Sartre, which appeared in the last chapter of *The Savage Mind* (1962), are sometimes represented as if they were merely a structuralist attack on Marxism. [28] But their immediate occasion was as a response to the use that Sartre himself had made of Lévi-Strauss' *The Elementary Structures of Kinship* (1949) in the first *Critique*. Sartre had stated that

> If there is to be any such thing as the Truth of History (rather than *several* truths, even if they are organized into a system), our investigation must show that the kind of dialectical intelligibility which we have described ... applies to the process of human history as a whole (I, 64).

For Sartre 'human history' was identified with the history of the West, and it was for this reason that Lévi-Strauss contested Sartre's claim to have established the human foundation of 'a structural, historical anthropology' for Marxism. [29] In retrospect, it was highly significant that resistance to Sartre's 'History' began by drawing attention to its ethnocentrism and Eurocentrism.

Lévi-Strauss' critique of Sartre effectively takes the form of a deconstructive analysis: he begins by arguing that the *Critique* works by a double movement – just as, only four years later, Derrida was to suggest that the anthropologist's own work functions in exactly the same way. [30] Lévi-Strauss focuses on the ambivalence which we have already seen to be such a distinctive feature of the *Critique*, pointing in particular to Sartre's vacillation between two concepts of dialectical reason. In the first he regards it as antithetical to analytical reason, as truth to error, while in the second he sees it as complementary to it. [31] If this is the case, then Lévi-Strauss argues that Sartre disqualifies his own *Critique*, which establishes the truth of dialectical reason partly through the exercise of analytical reason, as any critique, which separates subject from object, knower from known, inevitably must. But then 'it is difficult to see how analytical reason could be applied to dialectical reason and claim to establish it, if the two are defined by mutually exclusive characteristics'. [32] Moreover, if the two eventually arrive at the same truth anyway then there seems to be little need for dialectical reason at all. 'Sartre's endeavour seems contradictory in the one case and superfluous in the other' (246).

While stressing that they both take their point of departure from Marx, Lévi-Strauss suggests that for him Marxism implies that

> the opposition between the two sorts of reason is relative, not absolute. It corresponds to a tension within human thought which may persist indefinitely *de facto*, but which has no basis *de jure*. (246)

The two forms of reason do not exist independently of each other, as different forms of reality, but exist in relation to each other in an economy comparable to Derrida's differential 'stricture'. [33] Unknown to Lévi-Strauss, Sartre himself had already proposed that dialectical understanding itself works along two paths, one of 'expansion' and one of 'compression', which suggests that having separated dialectical from analytical reason, he had then to reintroduce the latter under a new guise. The argument about the relation of the different kinds of reason to each other will doubtless (and necessarily) continue without resolution; what is important in the present context is that, in rearticulating the possibility that there is no absolute difference between the two, Lévi-Strauss puts into question Sartre's definitions of man, human history, and finally his concept of history *in toto* – all of which are predicated on the dialectic.

If conflict is the motive force of history, and history a series of progressive dialectical totalizations, then Sartre claims that what he calls 'backward societies' have existed in a state of equilibrium and are therefore without history. He writes:

> There is no logical (dialectical) absurdity in the idea of a country with no History, where human groups would vegetate and never break out of a cycle of repetition, producing their lives with primitive techniques and instruments and knowing absolutely nothing of one another (I, 126).

In the background here is Hegel. According to Sartre, history is only born from a sudden imbalance of scarcity which disrupts all levels of society and initiates conflict and therefore progression. Many have objected that this analysis is hardly Marxist – insofar as Marxism takes the form of an analysis of the misappropriation of surplus value. [34] But Lévi-Strauss rather objects to the ethnocentrism of Sartre's argument, for it means that 'man', the constituents of whom should have been the result and product of Sartre's anthropology, is defined in advance in terms of the dialectic as historical humanity, with history effectively restricted to societies of the West. [35] The rest are excluded. It is exactly this assumption, however, that shows the extent to which Western society is indistinguishable from all other cultures, for each, according to Lévi-Strauss, has always assumed that it represents the full meaning and significance of human society:

> a good deal of egocentricity and naïvety is necessary to believe that man has taken refuge in a single one of the historical or geographical modes of his existence, when the truth about man resides in the system of their differences and common properties. (249)

Sartre's ethnocentricity derives from the whole project of his existentialism and his phenomenological definition of man in terms of the experiencing self defined against an other. Lévi-Strauss suggests that as a science anthropology should be attempting not to provide a definition of man as he is known experientially in our own society – an unscientific subjectivism – but should rather begin by 'dissolving' him. Here we encounter the first attempt to undo the category of 'man', an enterprise which has caused more distress than most in the recent history of the social sciences. Lévi-Strauss' point here, however, is simply the objection that Sartre defines 'man' in advance, predetermined by the particular experience of what it is to be a man in twentieth-century post-war French society. The assumption that one's own experience, one's own gender, one's own society, constitutes the sole reality is in fact the very antithesis of the whole concept of any anthropology. Sartre, as Simon Clarke argues, 'takes the conscious rationalization of his own culture for the ultimate meaning of humanity'. [36] But how can Sartre claim to found a general anthropology when he defines it solely in terms of his own society? As soon as Lévi-Strauss shows that the experience on which Sartre bases his philosophy is not a universal one, then the general inferences for all humanity that he draws from it can no longer be justified. [37] Sartre's existential consciousness cannot be dehistoricized into a general foundation for a concept of History.

Having questioned the basis of Sartre's definition of man and the human according to the categories of civilization and primitivism, Lévi-Strauss focuses on this relation to history. It cannot, he argues, be tied to the notion of 'man' as if they were images of each other:

> We need only recognize that history is a method with no distinct object corresponding to it to reject the equivalence between the notion of history and the notion of humanity which some have tried to foist on us with the unavowed aim of making historicity the last refuge of a transcendental humanism: as if men could regain the illusion of liberty on the plane of the 'we' merely by giving up the 'I's that are too obviously wanting in consistency. (262)

In other words, Sartre's attempt to combine Marxism with existentialist subjectivity cannot resolve its difficulties through a shift from economism to history, for history implicitly continues to fulfil the same function anyway. Here Lévi-Strauss argues that behind the original question from which Sartre began – how can man make history if history makes him? – lurks another: if it is man who makes history, how does 'History' gain its exorbitant status as the desired, unachievable object of Sartre's text? His emphasis on the primacy of history means that he forms 'an almost mystical conception of it'.

> Sartre seems to have remembered only half of Marx's and Freud's combined lesson. They have taught us that man has meaning only on the condition that he view himself as meaningful. So far I agree with Sartre. But it must be added that *this meaning is never the right one*: superstructures are *faulty acts* which have 'made it' socially. Hence it is vain to go to historical consciousness for the truest meaning. (253)

Historical consciousness is necessarily ideological, even if dialectical, and can never in itself provide the one true meaning of history. Despite Sartre's reiteration that it is man who makes it, history increasingly assumes its own ontological status in the *Critiques*.

Above all, Lévi-Strauss questions its status as totalization. The idea of history as the totalization of totalizations does not work. How total, he asks in a critique of totalization which Derrida would characterize as his first 'classical' formulation, can the totalization be? [38] Can it include every historical fact? History names the process of constituting historical facts, and, particularly, of their selection. A history that included everything would amount to chaos:

> In so far as history aspires to meaning, it is doomed to select regions, periods, groups of men and individuals in these groups and to make them stand out, as discontinuous figures, against a continuity barely good enough to be used as a backdrop. A truly total history would cancel itself out – its product would be nought. (257)

Meaning works through a form of metonymy, distinguishing between elements in terms of significance and insignificance, and that is why it must always be partial in relation to any text it interprets. (We might compare this to the way in which, in Sartre's later text, the synecdoche of the singular-universal insistently slides into the singularity of the event). Totalization in the first *Critique*, Lévi-Strauss suggests, can only create its meaning by selection through such metonymic devices of exclusion, that is, by founding itself on an – ethnocentric – absence. Historical consciousness dehistoricizes by shifting diachrony into a single synchronic totality:

> And so we end up in the paradox of a system which invokes the criterion of historical consciousness as a means for distinguishing the 'primitive' from the 'civilized' but – contrary to its claim – is itself ahistorical. It offers not a concrete image of history but an abstract schema of men making history of such a kind that it can manifest itself in the trend of their lives as a synchronic totality. Its position in relation to history is therefore the same as that of primitives to the eternal past: in Sartre's system, history plays exactly the part of a myth. (254)

History, far from constituting a privileged form of (historical) knowledge, is simply the myth of modern man, and merely amounts to a method of analysis. For all its stress on history and totalization as process, Sartre's argument is structured through the creation of a form of synchronicity. Lévi-Strauss demonstrates this through his well-known discussion of the function of the category of time.

Like all models of knowledge, he suggests, history requires a code to analyse its object, and for most historians this code consists in chronology. The use of chronology in historical writing, or in literary history, gives the illusion that the whole operates by a uniform, continuous progression, a linear series in which each event takes its place. History is thus a process of a continuous unfolding. But in fact, Lévi-Strauss argues, the process model of history is an illusion, for even dates do not work like that. [39] Dates only work by being a member of a class. In itself, a date tells us nothing: it only takes on meaning when it is part of a series. However that class does not necessarily correspond to other sets of dates, periods, millennia, ages, etc.

> History is a discontinuous set composed of domains of history, each of which is defined by a characteristic frequency and by a differential coding of *before* and *after*. It is no more possible to pass between the dates which compose the different domains than it is to do so between natural and irrational numbers. Or more precisely: the dates appropriate to each class are irrational to all those of other classes. (259–60)

So-called historical continuity is therefore often fraudulently constructed out of discontinuous sets which each have different temporalities. [40] History can neither be total, nor a simple series of facts, nor a continuity. The fact that it must always involve codification and therefore also interpretation means that 'historical knowledge has no claim to be opposed to other forms of knowledge as a supremely privileged one' (263). Historicity is a mode of knowledge for some societies but cannot *ipso facto* claim to be the fundamental basis of knowledge for all of them – a point that was to be re-emphasized by Foucault in *The Order of Things*. It is thus far from the case that the search for intelligibility comes to an end with history as such. [41]

Lévi-Strauss therefore makes three major criticisms of Sartre's concept of history. [42] In the first place, he contests its equation with any anthropological definition of 'man'; in the second, he argues that Sartre's description of history as making up one 'History' with one meaning is only achieved through the exclusion of all other histories with other meanings: the totalization can only totalize if everything which remains other to it is excluded. Sartre's definition is therefore tautological: it is one history because it is (only) one history. Specifically, Sartre creates a single history by excluding all histories except that of the West; his history as totalization can therefore only work through a determined ethnocentricity. In the third place, even in its own terms, the concept of history as a continuous development, a progressive totalization of totalizations, is dependent on a notion of chronology which assumes a synchronic homogeneous notion of time. But even historical chronology works through discontinuous sets, the elements in each class being defined only differentially in relation to the others in its class. This final criticism amounts to the challenge that Sartre's history can only ever be theorized as totalization insofar as it has been conceptualized as a synchronic form. While the criticism that Lévi-Strauss' structuralism emphasizes the synchronic at the expense of the diachronic has assumed the status of a critical truism, this in fact repeats the substance of his critique of Sartre, namely that the latter attempted to transform history into a space of synchronicity. Indeed totality in both *Critiques* presupposes a homogeneous temporality: the singular universal could only ever work by presupposing what Althusser would call an 'essential section'. Lévi-Strauss himself, like Althusser and Foucault, was preoccupied with the conceptualization of forms of heterogeneous temporality that consistently elude and trouble all theorization of history as a homogeneous diachrony.

Lévi-Strauss' attack, together with Sartre's own theoretical difficulties which have already been charted, was effective enough to be quite devastating to the project of the *Critique* – which was never completed. Sartre took four years to respond, and when the reply eventually came even his most sympathetic admirers agreed that it did not succeed in answering the main criticisms. [43] Lévi-Strauss' objections to Sartre's theory of history on the grounds of its ethnocentrism was certainly to the point, demonstrating that one lesson of Sartre's Herculean attempt to make history truth, and to give it one meaning, was the relation of such history to Western cultural imperialism.

At the same time we should also recall that, as Levinas puts it, 'the best thing about philosophy is that it fails'. [44] To the extent that Sartre's ontology does not succeed in totalizing history, it remains open to its irreducible otherness. Perhaps this is one reason why, despite the Eurocentrism of his intended historical schema, Sartre himself could certainly not be accused of ethnocentrism in his politics; already the first *Critique* contains substantial analyses of the political and psychological structures of colonialism and racism, even if they have to be, as always, 'dissolved *in History*' (I, 716). But this still allows Sartre to argue, for example, for the legitimacy of the use of violence by colonized peoples against their oppressors, thus anticipating Fanon's dictum that colonization was achieved by violence and must therefore be overcome with it. Aronson sees Sartre's turn to the cause of resisting colonial oppression as an act of 'self-flagellation' and a product of politico-theoretical despair, but this passes over the historical and political context in which Sartre, and *Les Temps modernes*, played a leading role in the opposition to the Algerian war. [45] In retrospect these concerns now seem a much bolder move, constituting an important political lead which was to be continued in the resistance to the war in South-East Asia in the sixties and early seventies. But Sartre's courageous intervention against French and other colonialisms could not have a corresponding theoretical impact so long as he retained his historicist Marxist framework. For his unitary theory of history has the effect of disallowing radical attempts at rewriting or retrieving other histories excluded by the West. Although it was taken by many as an attack on history as such, it was the critique of Marxist historicism initiated by Althusser that enabled new political possibilities in this direction.

Chapter 4

The scientific critique of historicism

Before Sartre had even replied to Lévi-Strauss' criticisms, Althusser had published *For Marx* (1965), a work which, together with the later volume *Reading Capital* (1968), far from defending Sartre's Marxism from the structuralist challenge, completed the move against it, and offered a new interpretation of Marxism from which humanist existentialism and Hegelianism had been resolutely purged, with Sartre's voluntarism replaced by a more mediated form of economism.[1] It is easy to represent Althusser's intervention purely in terms of structuralism, but to suggest that this was its only significant intellectual context is misleading. If his work needs to be considered in the context of the contemporary politics of the Communist Party, as several commentators have stressed, it also requires reference to work done in the history of the sciences, particularly that of Gaston Bachelard in the history of physics and chemistry, his pupil Georges Canguilhem in the life sciences, and Jean Cavaillès in mathematics. All four, together with Althusser's pupil, Michel Foucault, worked within an epistemological tradition which was critical of the positivism which, up to that time, had dominated the history of the sciences.[2]

To represent Althusser's work purely as a 'structural Marxism' therefore passes over the fact that there were distinct intellectual traditions in France whose difference was particularly pronounced in their respective philosophies of history. Much of what has been considered to be poststructuralism's wild disregard for history can be accounted for by the fact that it was operating within this – largely unknown outside France – anti-empiricist and anti-positivist tradition. In 1978 Foucault suggested that post-war French philosophy divides according to a line 'which separates a philosophy of experience, meaning and the subject from a philosophy of *savoir*, rationality and the concept': in other words, Sartre and Merleau-Ponty, against Cavaillès, Bachelard and Canguilhem, or the return-to-Hegel of Kojève in the thirties, versus the return-to-Kant initiated in the philosophy of the sciences by Léon Brunschvicg in the late nineteenth century.[3] Long before Sartre developed his own form of Marxist-Hegelian history, Bachelard had been working in a critical relation to Hegelian historicism.

What was new in Althusser was that for the first time this epistemological tradition was developed for a Marxism. Against Sartre's claim to establish Marxism's truth philosophically, Althusser reasoned that if Marxism is a science, then the history of Marxism ought to conform to the kind of history that had been developed for the sciences. The question then simply became whether it did or not. Or so it seemed. The difficulties in which Althusser subsequently became enmeshed were the result of his ignoring Canguilhem's warning that although the history of science takes science for its object, it is not itself a science, and therefore cannot claim to be value-free (or, in Marxist terms, non-ideological). As Gregory Elliott has recently emphasized, although Althusser always presented himself as the figure of the rigours of orthodoxy against the eclecticism of the existentialists, in his own work he was just as catholic, allying Marxism with non-Marxist philosophy, even if it was a history of science to which, he claimed, 'French philosophy owes its renaissance in the last thirty years'. [4]

II BACHELARD AND THE HISTORY OF SCIENCE

Against the Hegelian synthesis of all kinds of history within the same developmental schema, Bachelard argued that the history of science cannot be assimilated into the progressive evolutionary form commonly ascribed to other kinds of human history, and nor can it be mapped on a one-to-one basis against the history of its age. [5] In certain pure sciences, mathematics for instance, although discoveries may enable changes and developments of a material kind, their occurrence cannot *ipso facto* be explained by being related to the allegedly determining political and economic history of their immediate era. As Lévi-Strauss was to argue, different histories have different temporalities: the time scales of the sciences do not work at the same pace as other forms of history: they have their own dynamic, their own rhythm, their own times, sometimes fast, sometimes slow, that do not operate by the ordinary round of the year; Bachelard was fond of pointing out that from a scientific point of view the ten years from 1920 to 1930 were as long an era as the previous five hundred. This unevenness of development means that there can be no general history of science as such: it is uneven but it cannot be combined.

Many sciences moreover share the characteristic that a major discovery means that all other models and theories are simply out of date and have to be discarded. From the point of view of the present, the past has to be excised.

> Contemporary science is able to designate itself, through its revolutionary discoveries, as a *liquidation of a past*. Here discoveries are exhibited which send back all recent history to the level of a prehistory. [6]

Here we do indeed find an example of a 'liquidation' of history which, it will be recalled, is exactly the accusation that Terry Eagleton makes against poststructuralism; but the actual example in Bachelard demonstrates how much more complex the issue turns out to be. Science's negative relation to the past emerges as one of its most distinctive and significant aspects, one which marks a complete break with the cumulative structures of the arts and social sciences. It means, in particular, that the temporality of science cannot be accommodated to the rhythms of traditional historiography, which has not, however, prevented positivistic historians of science from writing its history solely in terms of precursors and anachronistic anticipations of modern ideas in early thinkers, as if science unrolled smoothly and inevitably from year to year. [7] The problem with this approach is that it overestimates the extent of narrative continuity in the history of science which, according to Bachelard's examples, works rather by sudden disruptions, discontinuities, and entire reorganizations of its principles. [8] Science is forever remaking its own history. [9] As early as 1934 Bachelard had argued that the revolutionary changes in physics, such as relativity theory and microphysics, meant that science itself was currently defined by its reaction against the past, and had become a 'philosophy of the non' – non-Cartesian, non-Euclidean, non-Newtonian, and non-Baconian. [10] These major transformations cannot be mapped onto the model of a continuous history, for its stress on putative anticipations fails to account for the way in which the whole form of knowledge can be transformed and a new understanding created. Bachelard's work on the formation of scientific disciplines led him to argue that the proper form of historical analysis should focus not upon an empirical history but upon the cognitive or epistemological status of concepts that distinguish a new science from an old one. Those concepts have not evolved from the old ones, for it is precisely their radical difference that constitutes the new science, the new 'positivity', produced by what he termed an 'epistemological rupture'. Bachelard himself preferred to give examples of such ruptures rather than theorize how they took place. [11]

Althusserians subsequently placed much emphasis upon the 'epistemological break', and were in turn castigated for being unable to explain how it occurred. But this neglects the force of Althusser's emphasis on Marxism as itself a theoretical practice with its own history of epistemological self-correction, a possibility derived from the work of the mathematician Jean Cavaillès, who stressed the degree to which the history of mathematics, particularly set theory, could be accounted for by the dialectical development of the concept. Much of the emphasis on set theory in Lacan and others, as well as the similarity of certain of their ideas to those of Gödel, whose work Cavaillès utilizes, can be attributed to his influence: indeed it would be possible to argue that the whole emphasis in post-war French thinkers on a non-contradictory heterogeneity in which incompatible or incommensurable elements are juxtaposed against or as part of each other is derived as much from set theory as from Freud. [12] Cavaillès developed these ideas into a theory of science as such, which, he argued, changed not through empirical discovery but through the theoretical reworking of its own concepts in the 'pure' sciences. [13] This view, whereby science progresses through the dialectic of its concepts rather than by testing its hypotheses against 'experience', was developed significantly by both Bachelard and Althusser. If it enabled the latter the crucial theoretical move of being able to reject the classical empiricist conception of knowledge, it was also to put him in the position of even castigating as 'historicist' any attempts to account for theoretical discourse in terms of its historical conditions of production – perhaps one of the major ways in which he differed from Canguilhem and Foucault.

Bachelard and Cavaillès agree that the distinguishing characteristic of modern science is the degree to which it has become separated from common-sense knowledge so that consciousness and its concepts are now opposed: [14]

The break between ordinary and scientific knowledge seems to us so clear that these two types of knowledge could not have the same philosophy. Empiricism is the philosophy which corresponds to ordinary knowledge. There empiricism finds its origin, its evidence, its development. By contrast, scientific knowledge is bound up with rationalism and, whether one wishes it or not, rationalism is allied to science, and demands scientific goals. [15]

The use of scientific instruments in particular means that scientific perception is constantly at odds with the experience of everyday perception. [16] Because scientificity is achieved through a break with common-sense forms of thinking, termed 'epistemological obstacles', Bachelard, like Lévi-Strauss and Althusser after him, argues that any philosophy such as existentialism that is founded on the basis of the truth of the experience of the knowing subject is bound to involve illusory or ideological forms of thought. [17] For this reason, Bachelard refers ironically to Sartre's phenomenology as a belated form of alchemy. [18]

But if the new science is produced through a rupture with the 'errors' of the old, the tenacious hold of common-sense forms of thought means that any given text may simultaneously embody aspects of the old and new ways of thinking, theoretical and ideological frameworks that Bachelard, and Althusser after him, term 'problematics':

Instead of the parade of universal doubt, scientific research requires the establishment of a *problematic*. It takes its real departure from a *problem*, even if it is badly set up. The scientific I is then a *programme of experiments*, whereas the non-scientific I is already a *constituted problematic*. [19]

Bachelard tries to think through the problem of how epistemological obstacles operated both before and after scientificity. In particular, he suggests that the educational system has a marked effect on the production and reproduction of scientific knowledge, and criticizes it for the ahistorical way in which it teaches scientific problems, theories, experiments and proofs. [20] While pedagogy continues the myth of an elementary or easy science, language itself can also produce difficulties. The nomenclature of science does not refer to definitive concepts:

> It is ceaselessly adjusted, completed, varied. The language of science is in a state of permanent semantic revolution. [21]

Obstacles such as these lead Bachelard to formulate a theory of 'material psychoanalysis' which offers a 'psychoanalysis of objective knowledge' to account for and think through the problem of epistemological obstacles. It is also supposed to have a therapeutic effect of a 'brutal, surgical' separation of unconscious and rational convictions in order 'to cure us of our images or at least to limit their power'. [22]

This separation between scientific and common-sense knowledge in turn produces a significant effect on Bachelard's thinking about history. For, as Lecourt describes it, he attempts

> to elaborate a system of concepts which will make it possible to think the intrication of *two histories*: that of the scientific and the non-scientific in the practice of the scientists. Hence this project culminates in *Le rationalisme appliqué* with the project of an epistemological history which is presented as a dual history; a 'ratified history' (or history of the scientific in scientific practice) and a 'lapsed history' (or history of the interventions of the non-scientific in scientific practice). [23]

This means that science can have two histories, which constantly intertwine but never resolve, with one evaluated as positive, the other as negative and therefore silently suppressed even though it may remain determining. [24] Instead of upholding one at the expense of the other, Bachelard offers the possibility of a deconstructive history which would reinscribe that which had been excluded; this could also enable a differential history of science and ideology, accounting for the perpetuation of ideology after the production of science. To do so, Bachelard, as Althusser was to do later, invokes the use of psychoanalysis for the study of history and ideology.

The notion of the epistemological break, while offering a theory of scientificity and even of ideology, implied a very different view of history from that of Sartre. In some sense, it went to the other extreme, for from a totalizing history it projected a form of history in which there was no attempt to link different histories at all. Bachelard assumed the necessary division of the scientific from the non-scientific, even if *de facto* he was continually encountering their imbrication and finding himself in the position of trying to keep them apart. Lecourt has pointed to the absence of 'a concept that would enable him to think together several histories with different statuses; in short, the concept of a *differential* history'. [25] Such a general concept was to be provided by Althusser's theory of relative autonomy within a structure in dominance.

III ALTHUSSER AND THE SCIENCE OF HISTORY

Althusser's rereading of Marx can thus be as usefully considered in the context of theories of the history of science as of structuralism; a certain conflation between the two has been possible because both were opposed to humanistic and phenomenological theories of knowledge in general and to historicism in particular. Within the general framework of his attack on the humanistic Hegelian tradition of Western Marxism, Althusser's specific objection to Sartre's attempt to mediate Marxism with existential subjectivity was that such a move went against the crucial discoveries which had founded Marxism in the first place; in an extension of Lévi-Strauss' argument, he maintained that the notion of 'man' that Sartre used was derived from a particular ideological definition of the human subject which represses Marx's insight that the human subject is not the centre of history, together with Freud's that the subject is not centred in consciousness. For Althusser both history and the subject are equally decentred: his attack on Sartre's claims for a unitary history (however complex its textual elaboration may have proved to be) was therefore accompanied by a critique of the notion of the unitary human subject that constitutes it. [26]

One way of characterizing Althusser's intervention would be Martin Jay's observation that he effectively destroyed the Lukácsian notion of totality. [27] Another would be to say he attempted to theorize the very position that Sartre had fought to get out of. If Sartre's argument depended on a logic of history as totalization but broke down when he could not combine the praxis of the individual with the general logic of 'totalization without a totalizer' except through the proliferation of his own writing, Althusser, by contrast, exploited the possibility of history as a 'process without a subject', a history characterized by radical breaks and discontinuities, distinct from each other and not totalizing. It was this aspect of Althusserian theory, perhaps more than any other, that led many orthodox Marxists to consider that Althusser was not really a Marxist at all. [28] The accusation that poststructuralism neglects history undoubtedly harks back above all to the work of Althusser who, more than anyone else, appears to have attempted to eliminate history.

Notwithstanding their philosophical and political differences, there are nevertheless certain similarities between Althusser's and Sartre's projects when viewed in relation to orthodox Marxism. Althusser shared Sartre's opposition to Stalinism's emphasis on economism and technical determinism, dissociating himself from it not through an assertion of individual agency but through a reformulation of the Marxist thesis of determination by economic relations – redefined as a causal rather than a historical relation. [29] At the same time Althusser argued that Sartre had not isolated the central problems of orthodox Marxist theory, and as a result continued to work with some of its more questionable preconceptions. In particular, in spite of his attempt to avoid positing history as an *a priori* transcendent law, in the published first volume of the *Critique* he had still utilized an organicist teleological model of history which assumes that the end is already implicit in the beginning, and that history rolls forward to a determined end. Both Stalinism and Sartreanism assume that history is an emancipatory process of self-realization, even if the forces of production in the one are replaced by the praxis of the self-conscious human subject in the other. Althusser termed such a view 'historicism': an abstract philosophical scheme that imposes an overall process of transformation upon historical events. [30]

At first glance, it might seem as if Althusser himself gave up history and tried science instead. Like Sartre, he sought to constitute Marxism as a form of truth, but attempted to prove its truth not through the dialectic of history but rather as a science, authenticating Marx's 'immense theoretical revolution' epistemologically through a demonstration of its scientificity. [31] In order to claim a scientific status for Marxism as knowledge rather than ideology, or non-knowledge, Althusser invoked Bachelard's historical epistemology which allowed him to posit the idea of a radical discontinuity between the two, with Marxist science separated from earlier forms of non-knowledge in Marx's texts by an 'epistemological break'. This necessarily meant that Althusser endorsed Bachelard's arguments about empiricism and rejected the concept of history as a system of progression or evolution. [32] However Althusser found it difficult to maintain a Marxist theory of history while avoiding its customary Hegelian form. His basic argument, that Marx proposed a new conception of knowledge defined against Hegelianism, implied an accompanying revision of the Hegelian concept of history, which, as we have seen in the cases of Lukács and Sartre, had hitherto provided the dominant model of Marxist historicism.

Althusser's theory of history has been more widely attacked and denigrated than any other aspect of his work, largely because he dared to argue that, far from providing the unassailable foundation of Marxism, history was a problematic concept even in Marx's own texts:

this apparently full word is in fact theoretically an empty word, in the immediacy of its obviousness – or rather, it is the ideology-fulfilment which surfaces in this lapse of rigour. Anyone who reads *Capital* without posing the critical question of its object sees no malice in this word that 'speaks' to him: he happily continues the discourse whose first word this word may be, the ideological discourse of history, and then the historicist discourse. As we have seen and as we understand, the theoretical and practical consequences are not so innocent. (143)

Althusser argues that Marx's intervention did not merely amount to the historicization of the formal categories of the classical economists. If this was the case all he would have done would have been to Hegelianize Ricardo. Marxists often imply that Marxism simply involves the introduction of a historical framework – 'always historicize!' – but this assumption can only be made, according to Althusser, because of *'the confusion that surrounds the concept of history'*: [33]

> In reality, it is to introduce as a solution a concept which itself poses a theoretical problem, for as it is adopted and understood it is an uncriticized concept, a concept which, like all 'obvious' concepts, threatens to have for theoretical content no more than the function that the existing or dominant ideology defines for it. It is to introduce as a theoretical solution a concept whose status has not been examined, and which, far from being a solution, is in reality a theoretical problem. (93)

Historicism presumes that a concept of history can be borrowed for Marxism from Hegel or from the practice of empiricist historians without difficulty and without asking how such a concept is specific to Marxism: for Althusser the crucial question is to ask 'what *must* be the content of the concept of history imposed by Marx's theoretical problematic?' That problematic cannot be identical to Hegel's because both Hegel and Marx define historical time in terms of the social totality: insofar as their definitions of the social totality can be shown to differ, so also will their concepts of historical time. For Hegel 'historical time is merely the reflection in the continuity of time of the internal essence of the historical totality incarnating a moment of the development of the concept' (93). Historical time is the existence of the essence of the social totality and will therefore indicate its structure.

Althusser isolates two key characteristics of Hegelian historical time, 'its homogeneous continuity and its contemporaneity'. The first is well known: here time is the 'continuum *in which* the dialectical continuity of the process of the development of the Idea is manifest' (94). In this schema the science of history consists of the problem of the division of this continuum into the periods that constitute successive dialectical totalities. [34] The second characteristic, the contemporaneity of historical time, that is, the category of the historical present, is more complex but an essential element in the whole Hegelian model of history, indeed is its condition of possibility. [35] If historical time is the existence of the social totality then the relation between the two must be one of immediacy, allowing what Althusser calls an 'essential section', that is 'a break in the present such that all the elements of the whole revealed by this section are in an immediate relationship with one another, a relationship that immediately expresses their internal essence'.

This section is possible precisely because the unity of the whole is an expressive totality, that is 'a totality all of whose parts are so many "*total parts*" each expressing the others, and each expressing the social totality that contains them, because each in itself contains in the immediate form of its expression the essence of the totality itself' (94). Hegel's conception of historical time, then, reflects his conception of the intrinsic unity between all parts of the social totality, each a part of the whole and the whole present in each part, so that history too partakes of a self-reflective immediacy which paradoxically makes it ahistorical. Perhaps surprisingly, given his alleged 'structuralism', Althusser argues that the structuralist distinction between synchrony and diachrony rests upon this Hegelian version of historical time which is both continuous and contemporaneous with itself. [36]

Against this Althusser maintains that time, even chronological time, is not just an empirical entity, but a concept; that though history may be articulated in general with chronological time, each history has its own temporality, which can only be found by establishing the conceptual nexus of the history in question. In order to determine what an event is, we must know the concept of the history in which the event is to occur. For example, in order to understand the history of physics, we have to know the concept or problematic of physics in order to establish what an event in physics consists of. Of course a chronological narrative can be constructed, but the history of physics in fact has its own temporality in which the first event after Aristotle was Newton, the second was Einstein, the third black holes, etc. Now this specific temporality will have no homogeneous relation to, say, the history of literature. However, it can be articulated with other histories, indeed is articulated, according to the overall but decentred totality of the particular mode of production. Sometimes Althusser seems to imply that different histories may range through different modes of production, at other times it appears that they are specific to each, an effect of the overdetermination of the social formation. But in either case, unlike the Hegelian essential section, where each event can be shown to be in an essential articulation with the whole in a continuous and homogeneous spatio-temporality, a cross-section at any particular moment will show a heterogeneous array of presences and absences.

Althusser elaborates his thesis that Marxism is not a historicism at some length, presenting a critique of the historicist and humanist traditions which he takes back from Sartre to the beginning of the century, even to the Russian Revolution itself, and in which he also includes the 'absolute historicism' of Gramsci and the Frankfurt School. Above all, he criticizes the ways in which Hegel reduces the diverse historical totality of a society to a single internal principle, so that history occurs only through the principle of contradiction in the dialectic. For Althusser, the apparently simple contradiction is always overdetermined: the inversion of Hegel's single principle to a dialectic generating successive modes of production amounts to economism. [37] This objection holds equally for Sartre's Hegelian historicism, the effect of which is to reduce the multiplicity of different practices to a single practice, '"*real*" history' (136). Sartre's historicism shares the common tendency of all historicist interpretations of Marxism which transform 'the Marxist totality into a variant of the Hegelian totality': they all share the structure of the contemporaneity of a temporal presence and continuity which allows the possibility of an essential section. Paradoxically therefore, Althusser argues, humanist Marxism shares the same basic theoretical principles with the orthodox economist Marxism of the Second International which politically it was its aim to oppose: for whether passive or active, fatalist or voluntarist, both reduce Marxist analysis to a single theoretical problematic. All that has happened is that the relations of production have been turned into historicized human relations. [38]

IV THE LONELY HOUR

Althusser's procedure has been to show that, within a notion of history that seemed as if it could be invoked on its own as self-evident, there rests an entire presupposition about the conception of the social whole that is not derived from Marxist theory. The Marxist concept of historical time must instead, he argues, be thought through 'on the basis of the Marxist conception of the social totality' (97). That Marxist conception is, of course, the Althusserian one: in Althusser's reading of Marx the unity of the whole is precisely not that of the Hegelian – and Sartrean – expressive totality; rather it is constituted through overdetermination, through:

> a certain type of *complexity*, the unity of a *structured whole* containing what can be called levels or instances which are distinct and 'relatively autonomous', and coexist within this complex structural unity, articulated with one another according to specific determinations, fixed in the last instance by the level or instance of the economy. (97)

The Hegelian model of the coexistence of presence which allows the possibility of the 'essential section' is incompatible with this description, but Althusser continues to assume nevertheless that there is a totality and that it has 'the structure of an *organic hierarchised whole*' (98). This structure, made up of a succession of different levels or instances, is dominated by one form of production which forces the unity of any conjuncture, the non-economic structures determined 'in the last instance' by the economic (99). This last description is often misunderstood: the point is that the economic is never a simple causal function that operates alone:

> the economic dialectic is never active *in the pure state*; in History, these instances, the superstructures, etc. – are never seen to step respectfully aside when their work is done or, when the Time comes, as his pure

phenomena, to scatter before His Majesty the Economy as he strides along the royal road of the Dialectic. From the first moment to the last, the lonely hour of the 'last instance' never comes. [39]

The significance of the allusion to Freud in this famous passage is to suggest that to conceive of the economic as operating in isolation is as illusory as to imagine that the ego can operate without the unconscious: they are both the reciprocal products of the other. The 'last instance', the economic, never operates in isolation separate from all the other instances of the social totality: it is the lonely hour that never comes. If one were to pursue the analogy with Freud rigorously, Althusser is even suggesting here that the primacy of the economic (ego) is a delusion, and that the superstructure (unconscious) is the more fundamental determining force, or at the very least that they are equally overdetermined.

Whereas Sartre's totality was never totalized because it was always still in process and could never be closed, Althusser's totality is never totalizable because it is decentred and displaced in time. The different structured levels do not coexist in a temporal present which coincides with 'the presence of the essence with its phenomena'. [40] This means that the model of continuous and homogeneous time which Lévi-Strauss had also argued against cannot here be regarded as the time of history. This has nothing to do with turning diachrony into synchrony; the point is rather that

it is no longer possible to think the process of the development of the different levels of the whole *in the same historical time*. Each of these different 'levels' does not have the same type of historical existence. On the contrary, we have to assign to each level a *peculiar time*, relatively autonomous and hence relatively independent, even in its dependence, of the 'times' of the other levels.... Each of these peculiar histories is punctuated with peculiar rhythms and can only be known on condition that we have defined the *concept* of the specificity of its historical temporality and its punctuations (continuous development, revolutions, breaks, etc.). (99–100)

These histories, their temporalities defined according to the specific concepts of particular domains, are not, however, independent of the whole: they are dependent on it, but in a structure derived from the 'differential relations between the different levels within the whole ... the mode and degree of *independence* of each time and history is therefore necessarily determined by the mode and degree of *dependence* of each level within the set of articulations of the whole' (100). So if there are different histories, they must nevertheless be related to those other histories from which they differ but with which they articulate in a structure of relative effectivity. Such histories are constituted according to a Saussurian differential relation. Althusser therefore criticizes the *Annales* historians for merely arguing that periodizations differ for different times, and that each time has its own rhythms. This is not enough, for it is also necessary to 'think these differences in rhythm and punctuation in their foundation, in their type of articulation, displacement and torsion which harmonizes these different times with one another' – though it must be added that this begs the question of how such harmonization is achieved. [41]

For such times are not even necessarily the obvious ones, 'the visible sequences of events recorded by the chronicler', they may be invisible, 'a complex "intersection" of ... different times, rhythms, turnovers, etc.', only visible when their particular concepts are constructed and produced 'out of the differential nature and differential articulation of their objects in the structure of the whole' (101–03). As an example of what he means, Althusser refers to Foucault's 'remarkable studies', *Madness and Civilization* and *The Birth of the Clinic*, two instances in which the historian has had to construct the concept of their history.

> This is antipodal to the empirically visible history in which the time of all histories is the simple time of continuity and in which the 'content' is the vacuity of events that occur in it which one later tries to determine with dividing procedures in order to 'periodise' that continuity. Instead of these categories, continuity and discontinuity, which summarize the banal mystery of all history, we are dealing with infinitely more complex categories specific to each type of history, categories in which new logics come into play. (103)

This means that if one tries to take an 'essential section' there is no essence revealed which is the present of each level; indeed the break valid for one history would not necessarily correspond to that valid for any other which will live in a different time and in a different rhythm.

> The present of one level is, so to speak, the absence of another, and this co-existence of a 'presence' and absences is simply the effect of the structure of the whole in its articulated decentricity. (104)

Any determinate mode of production, therefore, will evidence such a form of historical existence in its social formation: dislocated, uneven, absent and present. There is, Althusser stresses, no 'single ideological base time' to which all these different temporalities can be related, no ordinary 'single continuous reference time' which they can be seen to dislocate (105). This differential account of history requires us to rethink a whole series of common notions such as unevenness of development, of survivals, backwardness, even, Althusser claims, the contemporary economic practice of 'underdevelopment' – notions that provide the very basis of Western ethnocentrism. It also means that there can be be no history in general, only specific structures of historicity. [42]

Nor is history an evolving totality; each mode of production is made up of differentiated histories. These differentiated histories form a specific historical totality, for each history operates within the general totality of the mode of production. The economic therefore determines each history or level to the extent that its history is structured differentially against the totality which is defined as a specific mode of production. If for Hegel historical time is the reflection in time of the essence of the historical totality, for Althusser it is a function of the structure of the totality arising from a particular mode of production. No totality has a necessary transcendence embodied within it; as for the later Sartre, the course of historical change is open and will work only through the overdetermination of particular historical conjunctures. Althusser suggests that although Marxist history is defined as a theory of the modes of production, Marx did not give us any theory of how the transition was effected from one mode of production to another, nor of how each mode of production was constituted. [43] Much of the effort of Althusserian Marxism was taken up with trying to produce such a theory, and it was the failure to produce it that perhaps was the main reason for its subsequent collapse. [44]

Althusser's influence declined in France after 1968, partly as a result of the role played by the PCF, of which Althusser was a member, in the events of May 1968, and partly as an effect of a number of critiques of his work, some of them by Althusser himself. In Britain by contrast Althusser's greatest impact occurred in the decade that followed: from the late sixties his work constituted something like a hegemonic 'theory in dominance'. [45] After 1978, however, the influence of Althusser declined rapidly after a series of books by two Marxist sociologists, Barry Hindess and Paul Hirst, who developed and extended the implications of those critiques already made in France. Their work made it impossible henceforth to invoke the work of Althusser in Britain without reference to the problems which they had articulated. [46]

With Hindess and Hirst criticism of Althusser's theory of history shifted to the problematic of the relation of the concept (increasingly assimilated to representation) to the real, thus reducing it to a question of epistemology. [47] Where, though, does this leave the concept of history in Althusser? Does it have its own specificity aside from the problems of the subject, representation, narrative and interpretation, with which many have now shown that it is necessarily involved? Does this mean, as Hirst suggests, that the only concept of history must in fact still be the Hegelian one?:

Teleology and spirituality are essential mechanisms of all philosophies of history. And, save for mindless antiquarianism or utter scepticism, there can be no history without a philosophy of history. It is in the philosophy of history that the past becomes a possible and rational object of knowledge. It is through the conception of historical time as a continuum that the past becomes a coherent object. [48]

For Hirst this means that there can be no Marxist 'science of history' that can be opposed to the essentialism and teleology of a philosophy of history. Althusser's mistake, according to Hirst, was to attempt to construct another philosophy of history; but any theory of history, he contends, cannot do without teleology, spirituality (the realization of the Idea), and the continuum. On the other hand, we would add that the lesson of Hegel's, Marx's, and Sartre's attempt also suggests that history cannot be coherently essentialist and teleological either. Hirst's straightforward characterization of Althusser's work as 'a failure' does not acknowledge the constant tension in the historical project itself. If Sartre's endeavour to ground the Marxist science of history suggests that the Hegelian totality and continuum can only work by a continual labour of excluding the partial and discontinuous, Althusser's effort to constitute a differentiated history shows that you cannot do it without a teleology. What both demonstrate is that any history as such has to think both, simultaneously. As long as history is assumed to operate according to the protocols of a conventional logic, where a contradiction simply means you cannot think it or do it as Hirst supposes, then it remains at the impasse he describes.

Althusser's significant contribution was to problematize the concept of history by addressing its presuppositions about temporality – an area which Hindess and Hirst altogether neglect. In order to make their claim that his decentred totality is still expressive and therefore essentialist, they have to ignore the arguments about temporality in the critique of the Hegelian essential section as 'the co-existence of presence', and thus fail to do justice to the way in which Althusser constructs, as Foucault puts it, 'a counter-memory – a transformation of history into a totally different form of time'. [49] If the Althusserian mode of production is made up of differential times and histories, 'a complex "intersection" of the different times, rhythms, turnovers, etc.', then each element cannot express the whole because the whole is only accessible as a concept, which is precisely not *expressed* at all. For the concept, 'like every concept, is never immediately "given", never *legible* in visible reality: like every concept this concept must be *produced, constructed*' – by the analyst. [50] This formulation enabled Althusser to theorize a decentred totality which allowed the possibility of differences without reducing each instance to the operation of an essence or a single principle, such as the dialectic. If his notion of the mode of production as such a totality could not be sustained in a differential relation to other modes of production (notions of residual and emergent forms notwithstanding), Althusser nevertheless offered a particularly interesting theorization of the problems involved in the concept of the historical, articulating the paradoxical conditions of any theorization of history. If he showed it to be an impossible concept, he continued to demonstrate that it remains a necessary one, and acknowledged that we must learn to live with that impossibility.

How does this take place? It is at this point that the subject of history re-enters; history may be a process without one, but the subject is nevertheless inscribed within history. Once again, as for Sartre, the subject operates at the pivot of the paradox. For the subject does not understand history according to its scientific formulation, but undergoes the process of inter-pellation at the level of ideology, and thus experiences it through the formulas of historicism. [51] History, which can now no longer be considered a concept as such, is therefore made up of the incommensurable relation between these two disjunctive set-ups. It therefore operates for Althusser both at the level of science and of ideology, not in terms of truth to falsity, but as an irresolvable dialectic between the differential relations of the mode of production and the historicism of the ideological notion of history. Hence his argument that 'the knowledge of history is no more historical than the knowledge of sugar is sweet'. [52] What then is the relation of science to ideology, of Althusserian history to its ideological historicist formulation? The gap between them, according to Althusser, is mediated by art. This statement is often regarded as a curious relic of the values of bourgeois culture. But it is also possible to see it as an attempt to formulate the way in which the sliding incompatibility of the two can only be perceived through an 'internal distantiation' in which the problem of that 'relation' is enacted by its *relation*, in the sense of the telling of a story – which is how we get history. If history is a process, Althusser remarks, '*there is no such thing as a process except in relations [sous des rapports]*'. [53] History is a matter of relations, and thus of writing reports.

Althusser thus suggests that history can only be thought through as a permanent contradiction: it is a totality, but that totality is a decentred structure in dominance in which each history's history is defined not through its identity with, or difference from, a general history but by being differentiated from every other history, on which it is necessarily also therefore dependent, in a kind of negative totalization. Within the realm of ideology, on the other hand, history is experienced by subjects as a purposive continuum, with themselves as its subject. Another way of putting this would be to say that Althusser demonstrated that according to the protocols of conventional logic, history is impossible. If you try to think of it as a closed totality you get into the problems of historicism; if you try to think of it as entirely differentiated, then it becomes meaningless since there is no necessary connection, positive or negative, to anything else, nor would any one history produce any effect on another. Any differential theory of identity must think both totality and difference simultaneously. [54] It is this structure which both Sartre's 'singular universal' and Althusser's relative autonomy within a structure in dominance attempt to formulate, and in both cases the in-between of such simultaneity emerges as the process of writing itself. [55]

V 'IF THERE IS HISTORY': HISTORY, HERMENEUTICS AND HISTORICITY

With Sartre and Althusser we encounter the two poles of post-war French return-to-Marxism. Although both could be said to be reacting against the ossification of Stalinism, the subjectivist and ultra-objectivist paths that they followed were antithetical. This schematic characterization, however, does not do justice either to the manner in which they attempted to keep both poles in play at once, nor to the way in which they came to concede the impossibility of the theoretical projects which they undertook. To dismiss them as failures on this account, however, would be merely reductive. Their real force can be discerned from the extent to which the problematics they set up have continued to exercise subsequent writers. Since Sartre and Althusser no one has attempted a new theorization of a Marxist history. We are not, therefore, now looking at another paradigm, another system. Rather than attempting to repeat and surpass the exalted projects of Sartre or Althusser in a new guise, later writers such as Foucault or Derrida learnt a lesson from history, and stopped to ask why such comprehensive theories, like so many of those which preceded them, could not hold together. For the grand narrative of History was always too big for its boots.

Instead, therefore, of excluding history as has so often been claimed, such thinkers begin, in a rather more conventional way, from the anti-historicist perspectives of Althusser, even, arguably, of Sartre. The generic label 'poststructuralist' is here useful merely as a shorthand to designate those contemporary writers who share not a hostility to history as such but a distrust of simple historicisms. Lyotard, for example, is best known for his scepticism towards historicist universal narratives, advocating instead the possibility of a multiplicity of heterogeneous, conflicting and incommensurable histories. [56] Foucault works from exactly the same tradition in the philosophy and history of science as Althusser: like him he utilizes Bachelard's concept of differentiated histories, which still stands as the major alternative, epistemic or otherwise, to historicism. If such a theorization of history, as diacritical and singular, articulated according to breaks and ruptures, was by no means new even with Althusser, it has been continued as a self-conscious derivation from him by Derrida. In *Positions* Derrida comments:

> Althusser's entire, and necessary, critique of the 'Hegelian' concept of history and of the notion of an expressive totality, etc., aims at showing that there is not one single history, a general history, but rather histories *different* in their type, rhythm, mode of inscription – intervallic, differentiated histories. I have always subscribed to this. [57]

Contrary to the claims of certain American commentators, Derrida's uncharacteristically emphatic endorsement here of Althusser's project with regard to the possibility of 'intervallic, differentiated' histories, suggests the problems involved in invoking Althusser as an 'answer' to Derrida; both are equally distrustful of any form of Hegelian historicism. This does not, however, mean that they then take up identical positions in relation to the problem of history.

Derrida has not been concerned to formulate a new philosophy of history; nor has he attempted to specify new methodologies in the manner of Foucault. Describing himself as 'very wary of the concept of history', Derrida has rather attempted to shift the problem away from the conceptual analysis of history as an 'Idea' which, perhaps more than anything else, has proved to be Hegel's most enduring legacy, towards an analysis of the interstices in the implications of the general system in which it operates. [58] In the first instance, therefore, he focuses not on history as such but on the related problem of hermeneutics and historical understanding: history here becomes a problem of meaning and interpretation – 'the age already in the *past* is in fact constituted in every respect as a *text*'. [59] This also involves an inquiry into the ways in which the critique of the sign affects historical representation, and the dependence of history on the genetic metaphor and on narrative. Important though these issues are, Derrida's major contribution has been his insistence that history is a metaphysical concept according to which the meaning of history always amounts to the history of meaning. As he himself puts it:

From the first texts I published, I have attempted to systematize a deconstructive critique precisely against the authority of meaning, as the *transcendental signified* or as *telos*, in other words, history determined in the last analysis as the history of meaning, history in its logocentric, metaphysical, idealist ... representation. [60]

The Derridean critique of logocentrism necessarily includes the concept of history insofar as it depends on notions of presence and meaning determined as truth. For all its frequent invocation as the 'concrete', history must by definition entail a problematic represencing of an absence; Derrida therefore argues that, even in its 'materialist' conceptualization, it cannot avoid a certain metaphysics. As early as the 1966 essay 'Structure, Sign, and Play', for example, he maintains that his analysis of the paradoxical metaphysics of 'the centre' is equally applicable to the historical notions of 'origin' and 'end'. History consists of

a concept which has always been in complicity with a teleological and eschatological metaphysics, in other words, paradoxically, in complicity with that philosophy of presence to which it was believed history could be opposed. The thematic of historicity ... has always been required by the determination of Being as presence.... History has always been conceived as the movement of a resumption of history, as a detour between two presences. [61]

Derrida's deconstruction of the notion of presence by the logics of the 'always already' and 'originary repetition' inevitably conflict with a history constructed in terms of a teleological movement from an origin, which can always be reawakened, towards the self-realization of an idea 'whose end may always be anticipated in the form of presence'. [62] The meaning of such a history will always be determined through appeal to a transcendental signified, whereas a deconstructive analysis will demonstrate the simultaneous effects of the lack of such an authority.

More radically still, Derrida works at the limits of any possible philosophy of history, arguing that it is not just that the problems of hermeneutics, specifically of interpretation and language, affect historical understanding, but that what in a broad sense he calls writing, or *différance*, determines history. At the very opening of *Of Grammatology*, for example, he sets out the thesis that writing constitutes the condition of emergence for all forms of historicity as such:

> Historicity itself is tied to the possibility of writing.... Before being the object of a history – of a historical science – writing opens the field of history – of historical becoming. [63]

'Language as the origin of history': on what basis does Derrida make the startling and radical claim that writing as transcendence constitutes the condition of all historicity? [64] In order to try to elucidate this controversial argument, we can return to the well-known remark in the essay 'Différance':

> if the word 'history' did not carry with it the theme of a final repression of differance, we could say that differences alone could be 'historical' through and through and from the start. [65]

Here we revert to the dialectic of the same and the other: as Derrida puts it, 'that the same ... is never the identical, means first that Being is history'. [66] It is only through difference, by which the same becomes other and produces a tissue of differences, that history could ever take place: for if full presence were possible, then there would be no difference, and therefore no time, space – or history. *Différance* means precisely that you can never get out of – and therefore have no need to get back to – history. It also means that if difference in its sense of non-identity sets up the possibility of history, then difference in its sense of delay means also that it can never be finally concluded, for such deferral will always inhibit closure. It is in this sense that Derrida argues that Husserl's *Origin of Geometry* sets up 'the possibility of history as the possibility of language' whereby 'difference would be transcendental': writing, in the general significance which Derrida gives it of a differential marking, must be the condition of any historicity. [67]

'History as *différance*' then means that history will itself always be subject to the operations of *différance*, and that *différance* names the form of its historicity. [68] The same conditions hold for totalization. Derrida argues that though history is given the form of a totality by Hegel, his *Aufhebung* shows that in order to achieve that totality it must constantly transcend itself in a movement of excess. History

> is the history of the departures from totality, history as the very movement of transcendence, of the excess over the totality without which no totality would appear as such. History is not the totality transcended by eschatology, metaphysics, or speech. It is transcendence itself. [69]

History, in fact, works by exactly the same structure of supplementarity as Derrida charts in *Of Grammatology*. Here Rousseau himself demonstrates in his oscillating interpretations a history that cannot be linear, nor operate according to a single temporality, disturbing instead 'the time of the line or the line of time':

> We may perceive here the strange workings of the historical process according to Rousseau. It never varies: beginning with an origin or a centre that divides itself and leaves itself, an historical circle is described, which is degenerative in direction but progressive and compensatory in effect. On the circumference of that circle are new origins for new circles that accelerate the degeneration by annulling the compensatory effects of the preceding circle, and thereby also making its truth and beneficence appear. [70]

Such a history cannot be represented by the movement of a linear progression of unfolding time. Its 'transcendence' marks the way in which it can similarly never be limited to a finite totality, nor, conversely, to an infinity: it exceeds itself. This process of supplementation, this '*overabundance* of the signifier' that always goes beyond itself, is the result of a lack, or absence at the centre or origin, which must always be supplemented. [71] Thus the argument that 'history' is what 'poststructuralism' lacks, itself repeats totalization's own structure of supplementarity according to which history functions both as an excess and a lack in the origin. Insofar as it sets up such a process of necessary and constant supplementation, we could say that the impossibility of totalization produces a writing-effect whose process of perpetual deferral unremittingly provokes more writing.

It is thus no longer a question of being able to produce a new concept of history, which, as Derrida puts it, '*is difficult, if not impossible, to lift from its teleological or eschatological horizon*'. [72] History cannot be done away with any more than metaphysics: but its conditions of impossibility are also necessarily its conditions of possibility. This means, as Rodolphe Gasché observes, that 'the mimicry of totality and of the pretension to systematicity is an inseparable element of deconstruction, one of the very conditions of finding its foothold within the logic being deconstructed'. [73] Derrida himself, therefore, does not in any sense abjure history (or totality) but rather attempts to reinscribe it by writing histories that set up supplementary figures whose logic simultaneously invokes and works against historical totalities. [74]

From this perspective, even Sartre's *Critique* looks rather different from the way it appeared in the early sixties when read in the context of Lukács' *History and Class Consciousness*. Today it seems to evince a growing recognition that totalization cannot be achieved without a movement involving the transcendence of itself. In Sartre's terms, a totalization needs a totalizer. It must always involve an excess beyond the totality without which the totality could never be totalized, which must mean that it can never in fact be closed. Lyotard points to exactly the same structure in Marx, who could likewise never complete *Capital*. [75] This endlessness of perpetual deferral, he argues, is later formalized in 'a tragic political party ... the negative dialectic of the *Aufklärung*; it is the Frankfurt School, demythologized, Lutheran, nihilistic Marxism'. [76] But instead of the perpetual threat of totalization, a spectre which the Frankfurt School anticipates endlessly, Derrida suggests rather that the problem in any structure is rather how it achieves closure. Even if this appears to have occurred, a deconstructive account will show how such a text had to dissimulate in order to cover over its own openings, or, to put it the other way round, it will show how history must always be organized by an attempted occlusion of its own conditions of historicity. [77] This means that it is not necessary to reject totalization as such – because such a rejection assumes its very possibility, whereas all attempts at totalization such as Sartre's demonstrate rather its impossibility. Peter Dews has recently claimed that 'post-structuralism can be understood as the point at which the "logic of disintegration" penetrates into the thought which attempts to comprehend it, resulting in a dispersal into a plurality of inconsistent logics'. So poststructuralism is itself the 'shattered mirror of the logic of disintegration'. [78] But poststructuralism precisely does not try to *comprehend* disintegration, for grasping heterogeneity together is exactly what all totalizing theories have unsuccessfully attempted to do.

Having elaborated the paradoxical conditions of historicity, of any history or totalization, Derrida himself has been particularly concerned to analyse those such as Husserl, Heidegger or Levinas, who have been involved in investigations of time and temporality. Although it would be possible to pursue the question of history in terms of such analyses of the forms of historicity, such an enquiry would take us on a very different path from that prompted by our original question, namely if poststructuralism can apparently be faulted by reference to a history which it neglects, where in Marxism can this history be found? Since Sartre and Althusser there have been a number of possibilities: for some, the absolute historicism of the

Frankfurt School has become increasingly attractive, although in its current manifestation in the work of Habermas we might say that history has been eclipsed far more effectively than by any comparable French philosopher. If Althusser gave us history without a subject, Habermas gives us subjects without history. Otherwise there have been two possibilities which effectively continue the lines of descent from Hegelian historicism and the history of science. The most notable representative of the latter has been Michel Foucault, who has remorselessly continued the critique of totalizing forms of history and the disavowal of a general philosophy of history in favour of strategic 'genealogical' analyses. The alternative to this has amounted to a reaffirmation of historicism almost as if nothing had happened. This has been the course of Perry Anderson, who after his Althusserian moment has returned to espouse the virtues of empirical historical studies, under the general aegis of a historicism anchored in the recasting of orthodox historical materialism by G.A. Cohen. [79] More influential in the realm of literary and cultural theory has been another overt defence of historicism – that of Fredric Jameson. It is to Foucault and to Jameson that we now turn.

Chapter 5

Foucault's phantasms

It is in the work of Michel Foucault that we find the most unrelenting offensive against historicist theories of history. But Foucault at least can hardly be accused of neglecting history as such. The demise of Althusserianism has meant that the extent to which subsequent writers, such as Foucault or even Derrida, continued to work within the problematic that his work had established, has tended to be overlooked. It was Althusser who, after Sartre, problematized the very concept of history and laid the basis for much subsequent theoretical investigation. In the post-Althusserian context of today it is nevertheless somewhat startling to find the Althusser of *Reading Capital* citing his debt to Foucault (along with Bachelard, Cavaillès, and Canguilhem) as one of 'our masters in reading learned works'. Perhaps even more unexpected, in the light of the fact that a popular British Marxist position on Althusser is that he simply turned history into theory, is the choice of Foucault's *Madness and Civilization* ('that *great* work') and *The Birth of the Clinic* as examples of the kind of history, focused on the necessity of the production of a concept, that he was advocating. [1] In certain respects Foucault always remained close to the general positions from which Althusser worked, particularly in relation to the influence of Bachelard and his scepticism towards progressivist and homogeneous histories. [2] All were concerned to establish the possibility of discontinuity in a history, as Althusser described it, no longer 'steeped in the ideology of the philosophy of the Enlightenment, i.e. in a teleological and therefore idealist rationalism'. [3]

But whereas Althusser followed Bachelard's and Cavaillès' preoccupation with the formal systems of the pure sciences and set theory, Foucault rather pursued Canguilhem's focus on the medical and biological sciences, which emphasized their cultural frame and the historical and institutional (both discursive and non-discursive) conditions of their emergence which, according to Canguilhem, 'chronicle-history' neglected. [4] From Bachelard and Canguilhem, Foucault derived his emphasis on the history of science as an epistemological study of the formation of concepts, a process of separation and discrimination which defines both the object and the problem that is being made intelligible. For Canguilhem the history of a concept will have its own specific temporality, demonstrating less a process of epistemological self-correction as in the pure sciences than the persistence of the problem within all the contradictory solutions and ideological values that have been given to it and which make up its history. [5] This struggle is the inevitable result of disciplines which have no claim to the validation procedures of the pure sciences and involve non-discursive as well as discursive practices and forms of knowledge. Here the history of such sciences does not consist in the gradual unfolding and emergence of scientific truths, but rather of a history of 'veridical discourses'. [6] Truth, like historicity, is derived from particular discursive practices; it operates internally as a form of regulation, as well as being the historical product of the battle between different discursive regimes. Foucault's contribution was to adapt this type of analysis from the life-sciences to the human and social sciences. Typically, his history takes the form of establishing a concept of something that chronological history would assume had no history, for example, madness, or sexuality.

In relation to the almost antithetical Marxist positions of Sartre and Althusser, Foucault does not, however, simply follow the latter rather than the former: he articulates through a historical perspective the problems that their work encountered and attempts to produce a new method of historical enquiry – though not a general theory of history as such – that is both theoretically coherent and politically effective with respect to the particular problems under examination. That History and Marxism as such are casualties of this process is one obvious reason why attacks upon Foucault have been particularly virulent. Foucault objects to historicism and Western humanism to the extent that they assume a continuous development, progress, and global totalization. To this he adds his own more individual list of suspect conceptual categories: the subject, class, ideology, repression, the science/non-science distinction, as well as any general theory of society, causality, or of history itself. It is interesting that despite this some writers are still prepared nevertheless to claim Foucault as a Marxist – perhaps less an indication of his Marxism than of his discursive power and the lack of alternatives within Marxism today. [7] Foucault emphasizes that his work does not lay claim to universal or general categories, nor is it even homogeneous, a presupposition that, as he has shown, has less to do with the work as such than the critical construction of its 'author'. Nevertheless we can say at least that his preoccupation with history has been consistent throughout: the articulation of repressed history in *Madness and Civilization* (1961), the historicity of history in *The Order of Things* (1966), the epistemic mutation of history and the theoretical difficulties of historiography in *The Archaeology of Knowledge* (1969), and the attempt to write a different kind of history, 'genealogy', that demonstrates the emergence of new forms of power in *Discipline and Punish* (1975) and *The History of Sexuality* (1976–84). [8]

Like many of those discussed in this book, Foucault endorses the ethico-political project of establishing forms of knowledge that do not simply turn the other into the same: as he put it in 1968, he wishes to find another politics than that which 'since the beginning of the nineteenth century, stubbornly persists in seeing in the immense domain of practice only the epiphany of a triumphant reason, or in deciphering in it only the historico-transcendental destination of the West'. [9] This focus on the link between the structures of knowledge and of power is increasingly related to an accompanying analysis of the discursive and technological mechanisms of repression and domination. These ethico-political concerns formed the basis of his early works on madness: as he announced in his first book, *Mental Illness and Psychology* (1954):

> One day an attempt must be made to study madness as an overall structure – madness freed and disalienated, restored in some sense to its original language. [10]

Madness and Civilization was such a study, but the assumption that it was possible simply to lift the repression and to let otherness speak for itself was questioned by Derrida in his well-known critique, 'Cogito and the History of Madness'. [11] It is in this context that we can see the importance of the so-called Derrida-Foucault debate which is often misrepresented, not least by Foucault himself, as a confrontation between 'textuality' and 'history'. But Foucault's own subsequent work shows that it could not really be a question of choice on these terms, for the simple reason that, as he himself is at pains to point out in *The Order of Things*, history is itself a discursive practice: while the latter cannot be simply equated with the textual, it cannot be crudely opposed to it either. The dispute between Derrida and Foucault was less a question of text versus history than an argument about history itself.

Derrida focuses on Foucault's claim that in *Madness and Civilization* he is writing a history of the Other. His critique centres on two related problems: in the first place if, as Foucault argues, the expulsion of madness by reason constitutes the possibility of history as such, so that this gesture of exclusion produces the fundamental structure of historicity, then the 'classical' moment of this proscription that he describes must be an example rather than an originary moment. In the second place, if reason is defined by its elimination of madness, and if history is a rational concept, the question then follows, how can you write a history of madness? Derrida comments: 'It is the meaning of "history" or *archia* that should have been questioned first, perhaps'. [12] Implicitly he is criticizing Foucault's understanding of the relation of the same to the other which posits madness as outside the sphere of reason. To regard the latter as systematically oppressing madness and forcing it to the margins – to literature, or the hospital – is simply to repeat, in reverse, the very structure that is being criticized. Derrida contends that if madness is constituted as madness, as other, by reason, then this means that reason is itself defined through it and therefore already contains and depends upon it. Madness cannot be considered to exist outside the historical conditions of its production – and could never therefore be 'restored ... to its original language' as Foucault hopes.

The problem for Foucault is that this argument involves more than just madness as such, for it really amounts to a questioning of the very possibility of critique. In his early work we can see that Foucault's position involves a remarkable development of Althusser's hints that art can function as a privileged category that provides an 'internal distance' from ideology by relating histories, writing reports. Something of the same special place of 'retreat' for art, especially literature and painting, is to be found in Foucault. David Carroll has recently emphasized the significance of 'a transgressive aesthetics or poetics of self-reflexivity' in his work. [13] Such self-reflexivity, far from involving a turning inwards as is so often generally supposed, comprises rather an edge or void from which a critical perspective can be opened up: a 'thinking of the outside'. So madness, or certain radical forms of writing, such as that of Sade, Bataille, Blanchot or Roussel, by transgressing the limits of order and turning back to reflect upon it, enable a space from which a critique can be made. This self-reflexivity operates at the limit of reason or history, eluding even the structure of the *epistemes*. In this schema, Foucault is therefore proposing a fundamental, enabling separation between writing and history. But after Derrida's essay, Foucault abandoned his claims that certain forms of literature could effect such a critical, reflective detachment. This led to two problems: is there then any space from which a critique can be established? and how does Foucault reformulate the relation of writing to history? In his subsequent work, the connection between the two would remain profoundly equivocal.

The seriousness of Derrida's intervention can be discerned from Foucault's subsequent repudiation of the central thesis of *Madness and Civilization* and the change of direction that his work took thereafter. This is apparent from his rethinking of the 'age-old distinction between the Same and the Other'. [14] While he retained his criticisms of rationality, Foucault substituted the idea of an otherness at work within reason for that of a repressed alterity existing outside or beyond it. If madness or the other is always inside, then this means that it is always already a part of reason or the same; but it will also be exactly the element that reason is unable to comprehend, and will therefore work disruptively. This reformulation shows why it was necessary for Foucault to free himself from what he later termed 'the repressive hypothesis' of liberation. It also provides the context in which to consider both the claim that for the later Foucault knowledge is absolutely determined, leaving him in the impossible situation of requiring something outside this for any prospect of critique, as well as the question of exactly how power and resistance are interdependent and to what extent they are separable. [15] Any answer to these problems must take Foucault's own resituating of the dialectic of the same and the other into account. Even so, it is not at all obvious how he relocates writing in relation to the history to which it had until then been opposed. If it had previously operated critically outside history's limits, offering the only available possibility of critical distance, how might writing work transgressively within it?

II DIFFERENTIATED HISTORIES

In *The Order of Things*, published three years after Derrida's critique, Foucault re-examines the links between Enlightenment rationality and history and poses the questions about the latter which Derrida had suggested that Foucault's work invites. In the Preface he resituated his earlier formulations as follows:

> The history of madness would be the history of the Other – of that which, for a given culture, is at once interior and foreign, therefore to be excluded (so as to exorcise the interior danger) but by being shut away (in order to reduce its otherness); whereas the history of the order imposed on things would be the history of the Same – of that which, for a given culture, is both dispersed and related, therefore to be distinguished by kinds and to be collected together into identities. (xxiv)

Foucault thus modifies his argument that reason simply excluded madness and initiated the possibility of history by suggesting instead that the histories of the Other and of the Same are necessarily implicated within each other. But at the same time he refuses Derrida's equation of historicity with difference as such, instead reformulating his former thesis so that now history itself takes part in the epistemic shifts that he traces.

Initially Foucault argues that the stasis of what he calls the 'Classical Order' gave way to 'History' – which took over both as the form of knowledge and as the fundamental mode of being for empirical phenomena. By the end of *The Order of Things*, however, he revises this somewhat conventional thesis to suggest that what was involved was not so much a move from a static to a historical view of things as the break-up of a common, unified historical time-scheme in which every phenomenon had had its place in the same space and chronology. In place of a unity of time came the notion of discrete temporalities, with a recognition of a historicity proper to each discipline or area of knowledge. Instead of a great historical narrative common to all, everything now had its own chronology and its own history. [16] The effect of this was to dehistoricize man himself. Whereas formerly he had been the subject of history, taking pride of place in God's historical scheme from creation onwards, now 'the human being no longer has any history: or rather, since he speaks, works, and lives, he finds himself interwoven in his own being with histories that are neither subordinate to him nor homogeneous with him' (368–9). Man was no longer the measure of all things. Two possibilities were developed to deal with man's new homelessness in the world, his exposure, as Foucault puts it, to the finitude of the event, which attempted to draw all these heterogeneous histories together again: either men sought for some fundamental law through which a new general history could be constituted, or historicity as such was defined in terms of 'man' – whether as progress, economic laws, or cultural totalities. The creation of man as centre was effected by defining him against other, now marginalized groups, such as women, the mad, or, we would add, the allegedly sub-human 'native'. This move formed the basis for the human sciences which, through their organization around the figure of man, once more brought about a unity to History. We shall examine the relation of this new humanism to the history of Western colonialism in a later chapter: it is not a question that Foucault himself elaborates in the course of what is claimed to be an 'ethnology of Western culture'. [17] Rather he points to the theoretical paradox involved, namely that the human sciences' very emphasis on historicity as a mode of being was equally applicable to themselves as forms of knowledge, and inevitably destroyed any attempt to formulate universal laws comparable to those of the natural sciences.

Here we can see a rather different perspective on the human alienation which Lukács describes; in Foucault's account, Marxism's attempt to reproduce the totality in itself falls within the terms of his argument by which totalizing theories of history are based on an anxiety derived from the break-up of its unity. Marxism's claim to the status of a science proper thus functions as a device to avoid the historicity through which it accounts for other phenonema. [18] *The Order of Things* by contrast points to the emergence of historicity as a mode of understanding, and argues that 'History', both as a form of knowledge and as the primary state of being of empirical phenomena – broadly speaking, the assumption of all Marxisms – *is itself a historical phenomenon*. This means that history cannot provide an unquestionable ground for knowledge, and that historicity cannot claim an *a priori* privilege as the fundamental mode of being either. As the two 'counter-sciences' ethnology and psychoanalysis have suggested, history is simply one possible discursive form of understanding – even if its problematic of temporality spills over into many others. [19]

In making this argument, however, Foucault is not concerned to dispense with history – rather to make history itself an object of historical investigation and to question its presuppositions. In particular, he challenges Hegel's equation in the *Phenomenology* of the evolution of history with the developing consciousness of man himself. Although this has been particularly influential for many forms of Western Marxism, it also represents a deviation from Marx's original claim that history is the effect of material conditions rather than of human consciousness. In this way Foucault could be said to be returning to Marx in removing the subject from the centre of history, were it not for the fact that he dispenses with the consolations of Marx's historicism also. In this situation he asks, how do we come to terms with the event, with continuities and discontinuities, in short with history as difference and not just the story of sameness? Foucault adopts a strategy, obviously indebted to Bachelard, designed to restore the otherness that History by definition must disallow: he produces an account of epistemic shifts, with prior *epistemes* presented as altogether estranged from the present. In order to come to terms with the past, the initial gesture must be to confront its strangeness, rather than to seek for similarities and continuities so that it can be equated with the present and thus, in effect, dehistoricized.

Following Althusser's suggestion that a historical problematic might be altogether invisible even to experiencing subjects, in *The Order of Things* Foucault analyses what he provocatively calls 'the historical *a priori*' according to which the knowledges of grammar, natural history and wealth, and their epistemic replacements, philology, biology, and political economy, were structured. [20] But as with Althusser's modes of production, so Foucault's attempt to elaborate a *'positive unconscious'* of knowledge was criticized by Sartre, and subsequently by many others, for being unable to give any account of change and for implying a total discontinuity between periods. [21] The objection that Foucault neglects history because he does not attempt to give reasons why the epistemic shifts he describes occurred is perhaps inevitable but also begs the question: for conventional historiography has in general done nothing but account for such shifts – which has meant that it has consistently failed to recognize alterity and incommensurability in its insistent search for continuities with the past. Without history as a form of mediation the differences return as the problem, and it was this which, according to Foucault, *The Order of Things* was really trying to address. [22] Here we might recall Derrida's criticism of Levinas's history 'as a blinding to the other, and as the laborious procession of the same'. [23]

In the face of a history which obscures such discontinuities, the first stage for Foucault, therefore, is to defamiliarize it by reconstituting it without the mythology of a continuous History which has turned difference into identity. It is often assumed that Foucault is simply the philosopher of discontinuity, merely substituting it where previously there had been continuity; but the discontinuous is emphasized only because so much stress is normally placed on the continuous. It is not just a question of exchanging one for the other. This has a methodological implication as well: all too often it is assumed that Foucault's stress on disruption can be taken as equivalent to randomness, as we have seen with Perry Anderson. However, it is more helpful to consider it in the context of Canguilhem, who emphasized that the life sciences, like the natural sciences, require their own specific mode of history; they show that historical method itself must be heterogeneous, in the sense that there is no single method applicable to the whole range of different histories. Even the history of discontinuities is itself impermanent and discontinuous. If certain forms of history stress continuity, try to account for change, the history of science by contrast must be disjointed, for it is made up of a series of corrections in which the errors of the past have to be simply discarded. Foucault, as we have seen, is also criticized on the grounds that he cannot give a cause for the shifts he describes, but this criticism itself begs the question insofar as it assumes a certain kind of history, which itself presupposes that there was a cause in the sense of a single uniform causality, rather than a disconnectedness in the scientific mode. In the context of conventional historiography, Foucault argues that the point is to analyse the different kinds of transformation, the complex 'play of dependencies', links and redistributions, rather than to provide yet another account of change, succession and its causes. [24]

The Order of Things, although in many ways Foucault's most influential work, remains, however, an oddity in certain respects: first, that in arguing for an *a priori* common to a (limited) number of knowledges, Foucault at times seems to be advocating a structural key between different levels within the *episteme*, thus restoring the form of the essential section so criticized by Althusser. Foucault has even been accused of returning, in this work, to the concept of a totality in the *episteme*; it has certainly been somewhat hastily assumed that the latter can be appropriated more or less as a new way of describing a historical 'period'. [25] This fails to recognize, however, the extent to which it articulates only the structure of certain specific forms of knowledge rather than some single overarching principle. The constant emphasis on its being the *Western episteme* suggests immediate problems for any assumption that it constitutes a totality. The *episteme* rather delineates what Foucault calls a 'cluster of transformations'; these, he suggests, enable the substitution of 'differentiated analyses for the themes of a totalising history':

They allow us to describe, as the *episteme* of a period, not the sum of its knowledge, nor the general style of its research, but the deviation, distances, the oppositions, the differences, the relations of its multiple scientific discourses: the *epistemic* is not *a sort of grand underlying theory*, it is a space of *dispersion*, it is an *open field of relationships and no doubt indefinitely specifiable*. They allow us furthermore to describe not the great history which would carry along all the sciences in a single trajectory, but the types of history – that is to say, of retentivity and transformation – which characterize different discourses ... *the episteme is not a slice of history* common to all the sciences: it is *a simultaneous play of specific remanences*. Finally they allow us to situate the different thresholds in their respective place: for nothing proves in advance ... that their chronology is the same for all types of discourse.... *The episteme is not a* general stage of reason, it is a complex relationship of successive displacements. [26]

This is very different from the integral paradigms of Thomas Kuhn to which Foucault's *epistemes* are sometimes compared. But if *The Order of Things* is thus concerned to analyse 'ensembles of discourses' that do not form a totality, it does not focus on the ways in which such forms of knowledges relate to the institutions in which and through which they are produced. In *The Archaeology of Knowledge* Foucault corrects this by addressing the difficulties of making knowledges intelligible as a part of their institutional, social and political practices.

III ARCHAEOLOGY

Foucault's distrust of conventional forms of history, as we have seen, is a consistent thread in his project, as is his insistence that his historical method is limited to addressing specific problems – often comparable to those posed by the social sciences – to historical documents and practices in order to make them intelligible. Only once, however, does he devote a whole book to the problem of historical methodology. In *The Archaeology of Knowledge* he develops his suggestion in *The Order of Things* that an epistemological mutation is taking place today with regard to the very concept and methodology of history. [27] The book is both an account of and an intervention in that process, veering between the descriptive and the prescriptive. It begins by delineating the epistemological shift: the old order could be termed 'History', a continuous and chronological historiography, including Hegelianism and related forms of Marxism, with its philosophies of history, its assumptions of a rational, progressive and teleological historical development, its desire to discover a meaning in history, its questioning of the relativity of historical knowledge, and its use of categories such as tradition, the history of ideas, the *oeuvre*, the author and the book. Against this Foucault contrasts the work of the *Annales* school which analyses long continuities in certain social forms:

> The old questions of the traditional analysis (What link should be made between disparate events? How can a causal succession be established between them? What continuity or overall significance do they possess? Is it possible to define a totality, or must one be content with reconstituting connections?) are now being replaced by questions of another type: which strata should be isolated from others? What types of series should be established? What criteria of periodisation should be adopted for each of them? What system of relations (hierarchy, dominance, stratification, univocal determination, circular causality) may be established between them? What series of series may be established? And in what large-scale chronological table may distinct series of events be determined? (3–4)

Foucault notes that, at the same time as the *Annales* school and others were constructing a history according to the long *durée*, in the history of science, philosophy, and literature, attention was turning in exactly the opposite direction, that is away from vast unities towards phenomena of rupture, discontinuity, displacement and transformation, towards different temporalities as well as architectonic unities. Here he instances in particular the work of Bachelard, Canguilhem, Serres, Guéroult, and Althusser. He argues that, given the proliferation of both discontinuities and long periods, the problem is now to constitute the series, its elements, its limits, and its relation to other series. In other words, rather than set these antithetical approaches against each other as one might have expected, Foucault suggests that they are part of the same mutation.

Foucault characterizes this epistemic shift in terms of the difference between what he calls 'total' and 'general' history, or, History and archaeology. He explains this as follows. Total, or, elsewhere, global, history assumes a spatio-temporal continuity between all phenomena, and a certain homogeneity between them insofar as they all express the same form of historicity – Althusser's essential section – whereas in general history the problem is precisely to determine the relation between different series: whereas a total history draws everything together according to a single principle, a general history analyses the space of dispersion and heterogeneous temporalities. Total history seeks to reconstitute the overall form of a society according to some fundamental principle, law, or form, be it metaphysical or material, while general history despite its name is by no means concerned to produce a general theory of history, nor even a cohesive or comprehensive view, but rather to conduct a historical investigation according to particular problems, opening up a field 'in which one could describe the singularity of practices, the play of their relations'. [28] Foucault specifies the difference between them by contrasting their relation to the document: the historians of total history have been engaged above all in the interpretation of documents, attempting to reconstitute the past, to give it an inner meaning (always available only to the historian), to recover a voice and allow it to speak. The historians of a general history, on the other hand, reject interpretation as such in favour of making the evidence of documents intelligible by posing questions to them, constituting through such questions what counts as the series of historical events, its elements, its limits, and its relation to other series, or what rules operated for particular discursive practices. [29] This stress on intelligibility is a useful corrective to the widespread current assumption – for which Foucault himself is also partly responsible – that history is just another form of interpretation. [30]

Unexpectedly, perhaps, Foucault traces the beginnings of this epistemic mutation in the thinking of history to Marx. [31] This implies a challenge that contemporary Marxism has yet to address. As we have seen, for some

Foucault can apparently be dismissed with ease as merely the philosopher of discontinuity, a description which is hardly adequate; for others, criticism takes the form that he simply relativizes history, but this is really no better, for history is itself a mode of demonstrating the relativity, temporariness, and temporality of phenomena. Unless it is possible to prove the identification of History with Truth, as Sartre tried to do, then the claim that a single univocal History is not relative only works by removing all other elements in the set to which it could be compared, thus making a set of one. Effectively, however, all this does is to turn all history into a single event – which, paradoxically, dehistoricizes it. [32] What has not been adequately considered is Foucault's characterization of an epistemological shift within the theorization of history itself. He suggests not only that it begins with Marx but that he himself forms part of this mutation, which means that, according to his argument, in order to dismiss him you would have to dismiss Marx also. Foucault thus does not merely set up an alternative history, but contends that that alternative is part of a displacement that is in the process of replacing the history that preceded it. It is therefore necessary to address not only his theoretical and methodological but also his historical arguments – something that his critics have singularly failed to do.

The Archaeology of Knowledge thus analyses the shift in historiography of which Foucault himself is the most powerful contemporary representative. As epistemic breaks go, however, it seems to be a slow one: Foucault attributes its hesitancy to a fundamental reluctance to think difference rather than the reassuring form of the identical: it is, he comments, 'as if we were afraid to conceive of the *Other* in the time of our own thought'. [33] Here we encounter the continuing dominance of the philosophy of the subject, which, according to Foucault, was specifically introduced in order to provide a 'shelter for the sovereignty of consciousness' against the intrusion of heterogeneity. Continuous history and the subject are thus dependent on each other. [34] Instead of centring his analyses on the knowledge derived from the experience of the subject, Foucault investigates the conditions of emergence of the subject as the basis of knowledge; he argues that at the same time as it was widely proposed as the one saving good of human civilization it also facilitated a more sinister operation. Just as History involved the legitimation as knowledge of certain forms of political power, so the production of the subject by the human sciences as an object of knowledge also enabled a new form of political control: 'The individual is not a pre-given entity which is seized on by the exercise of power. The individual, with his identity and characteristics, is the product of a relation of power exercised over bodies'. [35] In *Discipline and Punish* Foucault demonstrates how the individual is constituted through specific technologies of power; in the *History of Sexuality*, he shows the extent to which the human sciences, including medicine and the practice of psychoanalysis, facilitated the extension of control beyond the limits of the body in the construction of the inner realms of subjectivity, consciousness and experience. [36] Foucault argues that a whole series of movements since the nineteenth century, including various anthropologizing Marxisms, have developed complicitly with this so as to preserve the sovereignty of the subject against Marx's and others' decentrings: positivism, the Hegelian Marxism of Lukács, the Marxist humanism of Sartre, as well as various theories of cultural totalities such as that of the Frankfurt School.

Dispensing with the subject necessarily also means the end of the use of the category of ideology; in this context Foucault's later work counters Althusser's influential essay on ideological state apparatuses. Many of those now hostile to Althusser continue to endorse this essay, which offers a theory of institutional power dependent on the categories of the subject and ideology. Foucault is critical of such a theory not just because it is based on a science/non-science distinction which for him is simply the product of a particular discursive formation which claims access to the real, rather than involving any epistemological questions of truth or objectivity, but also because it produces the notion of ideology as a secondary mediation (as in Althusser's interpellation) in an inside/outside structure between the determinants of power and the individual subject. For Foucault, the tendency of theories of ideology to entrammel themselves in the categories of psychoanalysis, even with the eternal in Althusser's case, means that they themselves begin to utilize the very procedures of individuation that they ought to have been analysing. [37]

The questions of the subject and of ideology raise as their corollary the problem of what position of enunciation the historian can claim in relation to his or her own work. Foucault is particularly critical of the appropriating structure of totalization, Marxist or otherwise, insofar as it implies the superiority of the theorist who produces the totalization of knowledge; in the same way, he distrusts the use of history as an encompassing framework because it works as a power structure that enables the expropriation and control of the past according to the perspective and truth of the present. It elides the fact that the historian will always also be historically located and therefore cannot be in a position to produce a final totalization, a dialectical situation anticipated by Sartre. Foucault argues that just as there can be no general theory of history, but only particular answers to particular questions which make individual practices intelligible, so the intellectual can best hope to be specific rather than universal (universal in the sense of proposing transcendent values, systems, totalities, narratives or teleologies). [38] This does not mean that the intellectual therefore nihilistically celebrates dispersion, fragmentation or relativity: rather she or he is the person who, facing such dispersion but without conceding to the nostalgic desire for totalization, poses the questions and constitutes the series and continuities for analysis – and thus for transformation – while attempting to respect its heterogeneity.

This suggests why, contrary to the way in which certain commentators tend to represent them, it is clear that for Foucault, as for Lyotard or Derrida, total fragmentation would be as counter-productive – and as impossible – as total synthesis. [39] As Gayatri Chakravorty Spivak puts it: 'Theoretical descriptions cannot produce universals. They can only ever produce provisional generalizations, even as the theorist realizes the crucial importance of their persistent production'. [40] Such arguments will have no pretensions, by definition, to knowledge-claims that affect to rise above the historical conditions in which they are made.

IV HISTORY AND THE EVENT

Despite his programmatic emphasis in the *Archaeology* on the discursive formation as a means of making intelligible those knowledges that are formulated through their institutional components, Foucault turned away from this kind of historical enquiry because it was too 'clean, conceptually aseptic' – in other words, too apolitical. [41] Foucault therefore abandons analysis of *epistemes* for the more Nietzschean 'genealogy', which allows him to articulate conflict in terms of differentiated histories with their own conceptual specificities and their own times, while retaining the possibility of the formulation of aims and intentions:

> I would call genealogy ... a form of history which can account for the constitution of knowledges, discourses, domains of objects etc., without having to make reference to a subject which is either transcendental in relation to the field of events or runs in its empty sameness throughout the course of history. [42]

Genealogy develops the possibility broached in the *Archaeology* that in a general history different significances can be accorded to events, depending on 'their correlation with other previous or simultaneous events, discursive or not'. [43] Here it is the problem the historian poses that determines what constitutes an event and what status it has. Foucault's genealogy means that by asking a question, posing a problem, you set up a generality against which you constitute events and arrange them in a series. The construction of that generality does not pretend to be the only possible one – the same event could operate in all sorts of different ways in different series, temporalities, which would mean that, strictly speaking, it was no longer the same event, for it would have been dispersed in their different rarefactions. This is not supposed to suggest that events cannot be said to occur straightforwardly in the real but rather that when set up in any series, narrative, or history they are constructed as such events retrospectively by the historian.

If all history attempts to conceptualize the event, to wean it from its finitude, then Foucault like many of his contemporaries is concerned to respect its singularity. In the essay 'Theatum Philosophicum' (1970), written shortly after the *Archaeology*, Foucault attempts to avoid the snares of the problem of the relation of the event to the totality, or the particular to the general, that beset both Sartre and Althusser, by arguing that the event as event is only constituted through its repetition in thought as a 'phantasm': 'it makes the event indefinite so that it repeats itself as a singular universal'. [44] This argument, which Foucault derives from Deleuze, although at the same time he tellingly invokes Sartre's theoretical formulation designed to solve exactly the same problem, provides a way of avoiding the incommensurability of the relation of the event to the concept by allowing 'the disjunctive affirmation of both' – thus solving the problem that the concept, as a part of the language of generality, will inevitably travesty the event's singularity:

> *Logique du sens* causes us to reflect on matters that philosophy has neglected for many centuries: the event (assimilated in a concept, from which we vainly attempted to extract it in the form of a *fact*, verifying a proposition, of *actual experience*, a modality of the subject, of *concreteness*, the empirical content of history); and the phantasm (reduced in the name of reality and situated at the extremity, the pathological pole, of a normative sequence: perception-image-memory-illusion). After all, what most urgently needs thought in this century, if not the event and the phantasm? [45]

Well, it might be hard to see it as that important. Foucault's gesture, however, marks the radical scope of such an anti-essentialist project which exploits Plato's admission that there can not only be a good copy but also a bad one (*phantasma*) – characteristic of the secondary representations of the poets. Deleuze reverses Plato by validating this simulacrum of the good copy on the grounds that, precisely because it is a bad copy, it breaks down all adequation between copy and model, appearance and essence, event and Idea. As Plato realized, it is dangerous because its effect is to dethrone the Idea from its position of Truth. Moreover, because the bad copy by definition cannot claim to be copying anything but itself, it creates its 'original' retroactively, so that the copy precedes the original in a ghostly originary repetition. Descombes describes a comparable paradoxical structure in his account of 'originary delay': a first event cannot be the first event if it is the only event; it cannot be said to be a first until it is followed by a second, which then retrospectively constitutes it as the first – which means that its firstness hovers over it as its meaning without being identifiable with it as such. [46] Thus, the phantasm, rather than *constituting* the event, hovers over its surface like a cloud, as an effect of meaning not identifiable with anything in the event as such. Deleuze's best-known example of how this works is the battle: '"Where"', he asks, 'is the battle?' [47] What we call a battle consists of a vast, heterogeneous array of individual actions in the field – fighting, firing, charging, wounding – none of which constitutes 'the battle' as such. 'The battle' hovers over the individual actions like an incorporeal cloud, distinct from them, but at the same time making up a surface of their meaning-effect, a simulacrum that brings the event into being at the moment when language and event coincide.

Foucault recognizes in Deleuze's account of events as singularities, points or intensities on a surface ready to be actualized in any particular form or meaning, the potential for pushing further his own notion of history as a genealogical series. Such genealogy works by repeating the (non)event, as an event, in thought – in a structure comparable to Freud's 'deferred action' or 'retroactivity'. [48] No more than the latter does it seek to lay claim to 'the real' or Truth as such. Foucault inflects this model by focusing on the possibility of constructing the series so as to repeat the disruption and discontinuity of the (non-original) event. In Freud, the point is similarly not just the question – on which most attention gets focused – of whether the event 'really' happened (a good copy) or was subsequently fantasized by the experiencing subject (a bad copy), but rather that it is repeated as a disruptive event that fissures ordinary forms of psychic continuity and therefore gains analytic attention in the present. [49] The same structure can be utilized by the historian so that the writing of history can itself become a disruptive event and consequently a form of political intervention.

V FOUCAULT'S PHANTASMS

If Foucault proposes the philosophy of the phantasm as a way for the historian to produce the meaning-effect of the event while still doing justice to its singularity, it also offers a way of thinking through some of the paradoxes that we have encountered in the problematic conceptualization of history. From Sartre to Foucault history has repeatedly emerged as a contradictory concept, both totalizing and detotalizing, essentialist and non-essentialist. [50] Such contradictions can be productive: the attempt to reject historicism absolutely results either in an utter particularism or in a surreptitious return of historicism in a different form. Only an understanding that recognizes that an irresolvable tension works within the historical schema itself will be in a position to make its contradictory claims productive. This possibility is outlined by Foucault himself as early as *The Order of Things*. He comments:

> The more History attempts to transcend its own rootedness in historicity, and the greater the efforts it makes to attain, beyond the historical relativity of its origin and its choices, the sphere of universality, the more clearly it bears the marks of its historical birth, and the more evidently there appears through it the history of which it is itself a part... inversely, the more it accepts its relativity, and the more deeply it sinks into the movement it shares with what it is recounting, then the more it tends to

the slenderness of the narrative, and all the positive content it obtained for itself through the human sciences is dissipated. (371)

History becomes the impossibility between this Scylla and Charybdis – in Lyotard's terms, it contains within its own project an incommensurable differend. It can only be described in terms of its organization according to an economy of logical tensions or strictures, of demands and constraints. It is, as Derrida comments, a question of showing:

> that history is impossible, meaningless, in the finite totality, and that it is impossible, meaningless, in the positive and actual infinity: that history keeps to the difference between totality and infinity. [51]

Thus both historicism or entirely differentiated histories are in themselves impossibilities: history will always involve a form of historicism, but a historicism that cannot be sustained. It is thus a contradictory (quasi)concept – a phantasm – in which neither the elements of totalization nor difference can be definitively achieved or dispatched. [52] This means that history can be theorized not so much as a contradictory process but as a concept that must enact its own contradiction with itself: 'this difference is what is called History'. [53]

In this context, we may recall that Althusser, rather than simply criticizing the notion of history as a totality as Foucault often tended to do, argued for the rearticulation of different histories within a decentred totality, on the assumption that history cannot do without one. Was it simply incoherence on his part when he suggested that his 'science of history', even though it allows for differentiated histories, still demands to be considered within a general concept of history? We have seen the ways in which Sartre's *Critique* shows how totalization cannot work without a movement of self-transcendence, a repeated interpolation of an excess beyond the totality which paradoxically then means that the totality can no longer be a totality. Although Sartre's inability to effect self-totalization is often presented as a failure, the movement of history that he describes is increasingly enacted through his own writing. Such a shift is not immediately discernible in Foucault. His Deleuzian notion of the phantasmatic event constituted a brief attempt to reformulate the relation of the particular to the general as a problem of history. But he made little effort to develop this outside his own definitions of the genealogical method, while his shift into the problematics of power seemed to lead him into a labyrinth from which it was virtually impossible to extract himself.

The philosophy of the phantasm may, however, help us to do justice to the event of Foucault himself. One of the oddities of Foucault's work is that it seems riven by an internal tension – for example, as Peter Dews notes, while on the one hand Foucault lays claims to a form of objectivity in his archaeology, and eschews interpretation in favour of 'intelligibility', on the other hand throughout his life he was also prone to endorse a Nietzschean insistence on the interminability of interpretation. For Dews this equivocation over the epistemological status of his own discourse is a sign of an uncontrollable oscillation: 'the shifting perspectives of Foucault's work', he writes, 'do powerfully illuminate, but at the same time fall victim to, the contradictory processes which they address'. [54] But such a self-undermining of the epistemological status of his own work is also characteristic of Lacan, and of Freud – indeed, Dews argues that this constitutes Freud's greatest strength. We might therefore wonder whether its appearance in Foucault, far from being the result of theoretical ineptitude, does not involve simulacra, or ghostly bad copies, similarly designed to undermine the claims of theoretical mastery, and to produce in his texts surface-effects of the kind of heterogeneity we might expect from someone who had contested the unifying function of 'the author'. With respect to history, the vacillations of Foucault's writing enact the impossibility of its simultaneous finitude and infinitude, the irresolvable conflict between history as meaning and history as difference, between history as a teleology and eschatology and history as the event, as finitude and mortality. Here we once more encounter the recognition that at a conceptual level the *idea* of history cannot be taken further: rather it can only be addressed through a tension in the writing itself. The early opposition between writing and history which enabled a critique from an outer limit has thus been replaced by a dissension within Foucault's own discursive practice. Instead of locating the other elsewhere in the transgressive writing of literature or madness, Foucault himself becomes Plato's banished poet, and enacts in his language a supplementary simulacrum of the delirium of history. As Maurice Blanchot has put it: 'And were not his own principles more complex than his official discourse, with its striking formulations, led one to think?' [55]

VI HISTORY AS POWER

In later work Foucault veers away from his most radical philosophical insights towards an analysis of discursive and extra-discursive systems of domination and exploitation, with increasing focus on the apparently more political question of power. But perhaps this shift is not so distinct: for the interaction of power and resistance, which mimes the mutual contamination and transmutation of Freud's death-drive and pleasure principle, also operates as a simulacrum of the ungraspable, vacillating manoeuvres of Foucault's formulations of history. Whereas Foucault was inclined to remark that in retrospect he considered that all his work had been about power, it seems almost equally possible that his analyses of power constitute a continuing meditation on the phantasm. Although in no sense a general theory, Foucault's notion of power reformulates the problem of agency and determinism which had beset Sartre and many others by focusing on the possibility of making intelligible the strategies and techniques of local operations of power without relying on the dialectic of ideology and the consciousness of subjects, or on their corollary, the assumption that power operates globally and homogeneously. The absence of the category of consciousness inevitably plays down the role of individual subjects and thus of individual agency and resistance as a result of specific acts of will. If this causes difficulties for some, Foucault's scepticism with regard to the tendency to inflate the effect of individual agency can only be compared to the position of many Marxisms in which resistance and revolution are hardly the privilege of the individual as such, but rather of collective class action. Those who forget the virtues of solidarity in order to protest against the downgrading of individual agency might recall that it has been intellectuals who have been most prone to inflate the significance of individuals – particularly intellectuals – to the same degree that their theories propose universal categories and claim universal effects. Moreover the exclusive focus on 'resistance' as a privileged political category is itself open to question. [56]

As with his genealogical history, Foucault's meditations on power are not themselves without problems, but reactions to them can also be too hastily dismissive, often because it is assumed that they are proposed as a general theory. For example, after the *History of Sexuality* much has been made of Foucault's analysis of power as a form of totalizing paranoia; [57] but the analyses in that book, of, for example, the shift from the Catholic confession box to the confessional psychoanalytic couch, are both culturally and historically specific, and Foucault's remarks about them need to be put in the same perspective. After all, if 'the system' really was bent upon the form of totalizing control that according to Foucault psychoanalysis, for example, enables, it is worth recalling that psychoanalysis has never been adopted by the state as such and that its activities remain confined to a few very limited districts in a handful of prosperous cities round the world. [58] Similarly, those who claim that Foucault removes the possibility of resistance as such miss the point: all that he downgrades is a theory of resistance centred on the individual subject as sovereign agent. He argues that to focus analysis in this way neglects the disciplinary forms and technologies through which power operates. The claim for a straightforward oppositional kind of resistance also assumes that subjects can resist from a position outside the operations of power, according to the dominant inside/outside model of conventional politics. This is the context in which to place Foucault's own recognition after Derrida's critique that he could no longer postulate madness or the other as outside, after which he maintained that the other is also always inside; he formulates the structures of power in exactly the same way, so that the forces of domination and resistance are caught up, sometimes indistinguishably, within each other. Acts of resistance may of course continue to be initiated through individual acts of will, but as for Sartre there is no guarantee that they will produce intended effects. An awareness of this structure does not mean that strategic intervention is either useless or impossible; but it does mean that analysis of how resistance actually operates, in what conditions it succeeds or fails, needs an altogether more complex model.

Foucault's account of power is thus difficult to the degree to which he argues that the exercise and resistance of power work in a disruptive rather than a dialectical relation to each other, suggesting that 'points of resistance are present everywhere in the power network'. [59] Where there is power, there is resistance: contrary to what is often assumed, it is the *absence* of resistance which is impossible. Power is a two-way process. Just as the exercise of power is heterogeneous, so is resistance; Foucault's point is simply that 'there is no single locus of great Refusal, no soul of revolt, source of all rebellions, or pure law of the revolutionary'. [60] Resistance does not operate outside power, nor is it necessarily produced oppositionally: it is imbricated within it, the irregular term that consistently disturbs it, rebounds upon it, and which on occasions can be manipulated so as to rupture it altogether:

> Just as the network of power relations ends by forming a dense web that passes through apparatuses and institutions, without being exactly local-ized in them, so too the swarm of points of resistance traverses social stratifications and individual unities. And it is doubtless the strategic codification of these points of resistance that makes a revolution possible, somewhat similar to the way in which the state relies on the institutional integration of power relationships. [61]

It is in this way that Foucault can return to the possibility of doing historical work that has political force through his notion of genealogy, which means, as he puts it, 'that I begin my analysis from a question posed in the present'. [62] The question enables the tactical use of historical knowledge in contemporary political situations which necessitate the posing of the question with which genealogy begins. [63] Such politics stress the local or the specific without assuming that they constitute the starting point for a global hegemony into which they will be subsumed. Foucault does not aim to produce 'a' politics any more than 'a' history. It is this factor which, perhaps above all, has enabled the critical use of Foucault's analyses of power in demarcated areas of analysis. Ironically, Foucault's most problematic 'theory' has generated the most successful and probing historical work among his followers.

VII CODA: THE NEW HISTORICISM

The relation of Foucault's politics to history leads to the question of the tactical use of Foucault himself in current forms of criticism; in addition to his extensive use by historians and sociologists, he is also associated with those movements that have become known as 'new historicism' and 'cultural materialism'. [64] The former is identified closely with Foucault, while the latter owes its allegiance to Raymond Williams, and really only amounts to a way of describing British ex-Marxists. New historicism is most concerned with the late Foucault, in particular with representations and mechanisms of power, the means through which cultural artefacts can be shown to be not passive reflectors of the history of their time but active producers of it. This charting of the circulating relations between aesthetic and other forms of production works best in those historical periods, such as the Renaissance, where there was no modern concept of Literature, thus allowing literary texts to be mapped against the political and other discourses of which they formed a part. New historicism emphasizes the way in which certain rituals and practices, for example of kingship, are equally a part of the processes and representation of power – whether at a beheading, a masque or in a poem. At the same time, it can also bring out the complex ways in which such forms of power also produce their own forms of resistance; as critics like Stephen Greenblatt demonstrate, these are not separable processes but are simultaneous effects of power. [65] The illustration of such a double logic working at a textual level often comes to seem remarkably close to a deconstructive analysis: in the same way as Derrida or de Man could be said to be deconstructing received readings that have institutional purchase, so the new historicists shift our understanding of institutionalized historical accounts.

However, the very historical focus poses the problem of agency and containment in a more immediate way that demonstrates some of the dilemmas that follow from Foucault's genealogical history. The real difficulty, as Greenblatt shows, is what status can be accorded the category of subversion or resistance: what is the historical status of the 'subversive' elements of a text? If the process of the construction of knowledge can be shown to work against itself, this can operate because the ideas of the dominant order are not in fact threatened by alternatives which, with hindsight, may appear radical to us now. As the cultural materialists concede, subversive thoughts are not subversive until they become a practice. [66] Can they be shown to have had historical effects? From the point of view of a radical politics, the onus on the critic, therefore, is to show the ways in which such subversions can be shown to have produced specific instances of change. Correspondingly, as Greenblatt argues, Renaissance ideas which might be subversive today are ignored in favour of 'radical' ideas which seem to echo our own. [67]

Both groups follow Foucault to the extent that they neither propose, nor utilize, a general theory of history as such; but unlike Foucault they simply tend to shelve the whole problem so as to avoid its theoretical difficulties. So, despite the Lukácsian resonance of its name, new historicism abandons both the notion of history as a readable background to literary texts, and the Marxist dependency on reflection, in its effort to recontextualize literary texts in a more immediate way with other forms of social production. For their part, the British cultural materialists quickly adopted a name which tactfully removes the suggestion of Marxism as such. In the context of the present discussion of history, moreover, it is highly significant that traditional 'historical materialism' has been jettisoned in favour of the anthropological 'cultural materialism'. The cultural materialists abandon the traditional Marxist use of history as a ground for truth in favour of bringing history into the present day in order to intervene in their own institutional and academic political context. In this case it becomes less a matter of addressing contemporary political problems than of resisting institutional power, namely those critical readings which have recently claimed cultural hegemony, and of providing instead alternative accounts which insist on heterogeneity and resistance in historical texts. An identification is then implicitly or explicitly made with parallel forms of political struggle in our own day. In other words, where yesterday's historian looked for the history of an oppressed working class, today's historian looks for marginalized groups, and those who have transgressed social norms. Whether they actually were subversive becomes irrelevant to the extent that they can now be retrieved to offer a potential that has a contemporary, that is twentieth-century, political relevance. To this extent we could say that the cultural materialists re-assert a form of reflection theory, where history has become a mirror in which contemporary political priorities have been substituted for the former certain ground of Marxist analysis.

The cultural materialists are inclined to separate the self-contradictory differences isolated by the new historicists into a more conventional political paradigm of opposing classes, of hegemony and subversion. Similarly, though Foucault is often invoked, there is a marked tendency to continue to utilize theoretical categories such as ideology, consciousness and the subject. Here it is salutary to recall Foucault's scepticism with regard to the 'perilous ease' with which politics quickly assumes positions that provide intellectual guarantees rather than specific analyses of particular relations or trans- formations; he reacts in the same way to political analogies, and correspon- dences, or to hasty links with current political practices. [68] To the last, Foucault himself remained suspicious of any 'progressive politics' if that meant that it continued to be linked to a (hidden) meaning, origin, or the subject. But if the cultural materialists, unlike the more fastidious new historicists, cheerfully ignore the theoretical consequences of Foucault's work for many Marxist concepts, in other ways they are closer to him insofar as they make clear in their work their own political priorities and commitments. Nevertheless it is worth recalling that Foucault never starts at the political, but rather begins with a contemporary problem and then addresses questions to politics about it. He argues that intellectual work need not always be measured against immediate political ends; rather the question to ask is what project is it undertaking, what problem is it analysing? It should always be possible for the intellectual to justify and to show the grounds on which any particular activity has been constituted. At the same time, it is too easy to condemn certain forms of work for being apolitical simply because they do not correspond to a certain paradigm of immediate political effectivity. Political interventions can also work according to different time scales. But if the cultural materialists tend to place a politics rather than a problem as the starting point of their enquiry, they do emphasize the deployment of specialized knowledges in the service of the popular political struggles of today. This suggests a closeness to Foucault's notion of genealogy that the more strictly academic new historicists, whose own politics remain more carefully hidden, ignore.

Chapter 6

The Jameson raid

> I have frequently had the feeling that I am one of the few Marxists left.
>
> Fredric Jameson [1]

The succession of Marxist and other critiques of historicism, which ended by problematizing the status of history and of Marxism itself, go some way to accounting for the paucity of Marxist literary theory in the past twenty years. An exception in the English-speaking world has been Fredric Jameson's *The Political Unconscious* (1981), considered by many to constitute a major work of theoretical innovation. In the USA it was taken by some as a refutation of poststructuralism; in Britain, by contrast, its reception was more muted, for the book in many ways already seemed somewhat dated on its appearance. Despite an intellectual climate that might have been expected to have been much more sympathetic to its project, it had comparatively little impact.

Why has *The Political Unconscious* been so influential in America, but much less so in Britain or Europe? [2] In order to answer this question let us follow Jameson's own prescription – 'always historicize!' The book's success in the USA came at a time when the tide of deconstruction seemed virtually unstoppable, and, apart from a few attempts such as those of M.H. Abrams or Harold Bloom, irrefutable. Jameson presented Marxism with some panache as the one form of criticism that could acknowledge Derrida's insights and yet go beyond them. At the same time, Jameson offered a return to the sort of ethical criticism which deconstruction was commonly taken to have disallowed: this appealed to a traditional understanding of criticism's value, as well as to male critics who felt increasingly upstaged by the forceful politics that feminism had made available to women. [3] These were two factors, internal to the discipline which, no doubt with many others, led to a resurgence of interest in Marxism which had hitherto suffered from comparative neglect.

In Britain, by contrast, where theory had always meant Marxism anyway, and where deconstruction remained a minority interest, Jameson's book answered fewer needs. His argument that Marxism is simply a form of interpretation, thus reducing so-called concrete history to hermeneutics, with the base-superstructure relation reformulated as 'allegorical', was hardly likely to go down well with a British Marxism always heavily dominated by the social sciences and a general distrust of the literary. Althusserian Marxism, furthermore, had already been a dominant part of British Marxist literary theory for years since Macherey's *A Theory of Literary Production* of 1966, and Eagleton's similar *Criticism and Ideology* of 1976. In this climate Jameson's book might have been more welcome had not Hindess and Hirst in the meantime published a series of interventions which, as Jameson himself was to put it later, appeared to have effected a melt-down in the Althusserian reactor. [4] The first thing to be said about *The Political Unconscious* from a British perspective, then, is that its reception was muted because, appearing in a post-Althusserian context, it gave the impression that it was announcing Althusser as a great discovery. However, as we shall see, if Hindess and Hirst may have momentarily seemed to have disabled Althusser, it was their work which, despite appearances, enabled Jameson's.

In fact both reactions, that Jameson went beyond Derrida, or that *The Political Unconscious* could be ignored because of Hindess and Hirst, were too hasty. Jameson's strategy was a good deal more subtle than the simple invocation of History and Althusser. But you could be forgiven for not noticing it, for nowhere does he really spell out the exact terms and implications of what he is doing, trusting instead apparently in the Machereyan not-said, or the political unconscious itself. Or perhaps such reticence derives from the fact that what he attempts to bring about is something which from the perspective of European Marxism is truly scandalous, namely, a rapprochement between the two antithetical traditions of Sartre and Althusser, incorporated within a larger Lukácsian totality. For reasons that should by now be clear, to try to assimilate such different theorists is an extraordinary project of Hegelian proportions and daring.

However, as Terry Eagleton has commented, Jameson is 'a shamelessly unreconstructed Hegelian', and this means that assimilation rather than differentiation has always been his intellectual mode. [5] Indeed Jameson's loyal expositor, William C. Dowling, goes so far as to suggest that his 'originality ... paradoxically does not lie so much in arriving at new ideas as in seeing the possibility of synthesis in the ideas of others'. [6] Jameson is equally prepared to risk assimilating non-Marxist theory, pressing it into the service of Marxist ends. He does so on the principle that, as he explains at the beginning of *The Political Unconscious*, Marxism is in a unique position because it does not have to reject other theories: in the best Hegelian fashion, it can utilize them dialectically in the process of transcending them. The fact they might be politically opposed to Marxism, and institutionally a great deal more powerful, never seems to matter – indeed it only provides a greater challenge to Jameson's omnivorousness.

For the most part, however, it has been different sorts of Marxism that

Jameson has specialized in bringing together. Although at the beginning of *Marxism and Form* (1971) he states that he has not attempted to 'reconcile' the various systematic constructions of the Marxists whom he analyses, by the end of the book he extends the possibility that they 'all ultimately complete each other, their apparent inconsistencies dissolved in some vaster dialectical synthesis'. [7] This has become the characteristic Jamesonian gesture, with which all theoretical differences evaporate into a dialectical sublime. Of course such 'ultimate' reconciliation tends to obliterate both the theoretical differences – and therefore to some extent the point – of the arguments of such thinkers, as well as, crucially, the political differences that such arguments presuppose and develop. Jameson's unrelenting synthesizing can at times look like a way of avoiding having to choose between political as well as theoretical options. The question then becomes whether we are dealing with an ability to synthesize derived from an intellectual power of a Lukácsian order, or merely a tendency to conflation that is the result of the fact that in the United States Jameson is far from the political realities with which European Marxists have to deal. [8]

The Political Unconscious remains noticeably circumspect in spelling out the politico-theoretical implications of what it is trying to do in synthesizing Sartre and Althusser, that is, Hegelian and structural Marxisms. [9] It is only cursorily mentioned that structuralism in general, and Althusserianism in particular, were developed explicitly against Sartre's existentialism: that is, to Sartre's humanism, Althusser's anti-humanism; to Sartre's Hegelianism, Althusser's anti-essentialism and attempt to extirpate all traces of Hegel from Marx; to Sartre's existentialist focus on the cogito and subjectivity, Althusser's decentring of the subject; to Sartre's individual agency as the motor of a totalizing history, Althusser's history without a subject or goal. But undeterred by such major differences, Jameson's project is to produce a dialectical resolution of the antinomies of post-war French Marxism, which he must magisterially subsume and rise above via a yet larger totalization.

One reason for attempting this manoeuvre is that Jameson has another adversary in mind: an apparently anti-Marxist poststructuralism, specifically that of Derrida, Lyotard and Foucault. Only in a context in which Althusser's work had hitherto made little impact could it have been possible to offer the unlikely Sartre-Althusser combination as a counter-force to surpass such thinkers. Nevertheless it was undoubtedly the case that Jameson's *Political Unconscious*, with its rallying slogan 'always historicize!', was taken by some in the United States to represent the long-awaited answer to post-structuralism and to Derrida in particular. So, for instance, Dowling claimed that Jameson was

> trying to neutralise the entire programme of contemporary poststruc-
> turalism by enclosing it within an expanded Marxism: in effect trying to
> swallow up the enterprises of Derrida, Foucault, *et al.* by showing that

they are incomplete without a theory of history that only Marxism can provide. [10]

Jameson's strategy is to empower Marxism against poststructuralism by rolling all Marxisms into one, assimilating them under the grand aegis of history, or rather, 'History itself'. His problem is that, while on the one hand he acknowledges the force of the recent arguments that question the status of history, he nevertheless attempts to retain the traditional truth-claims of historical materialism.

II MARXIST THEORY: CONFLATING THE UNCONFLATABLE

Whereas Jameson states very clearly in *The Political Unconscious* that he is introducing, recapitulating and reformulating Althusser, he makes his affiliations to Lukács and Sartre much less obvious, even though it is they from whom many of his basic assumptions and categories derive. Their residual influence is particularly evident in the emphatic emphasis which he continues to place on History as the fundamental ground for Marxism. Whereas orthodox Marxism rather stresses the contradictory relations of the economic as the motive force for conflict in the class struggle, Jameson follows Lukács and Sartre in substituting the more human History, which he tries to salvage by retrieving Sartre's historicism. [11] The problem for such a synthesizing project, however, is that, as we have seen, it is above all the question of history which divides Sartre from Althusser. While Jameson readily abandons the former's stress on subjectivity, individual consciousness, and the importance of freedom and the production of the authentic self, he retains his theory of history as the dominant form of totalization. Without allowing the real difficulties of Sartre's account, Jameson nevertheless does acknowledge the recent critiques of historicism even to the extent of following Althusser's concept of differential histories. But instead of defining each history in terms of the decentred totality of the mode of production, he retotalizes them all into a global narrative – the single story of what Sartre, and Jameson after him, call 'the human adventure'. [12] The major theoretical and political question therefore becomes: how does Jameson manage to conflate the unconflatable – Althusser with Sartre?

The answer, appropriately enough, is by mediation. Jameson admits that the Althusserian critique of the humanist Hegelian tradition of Western Marxism is on its own terms 'quite unanswerable', but is unwilling to evade it by the casuistical device of an E.P. Thompson, that is by taking refuge in a rejection of theory altogether. [13] This leaves him with two unthinkable alternatives: either to reject the Hegelian tradition as such or to attempt some form of synthesis. As a good Hegelian, Jameson takes the latter course: in fact as early as 1975 he had already reacted to Althusser by proposing a new '*structural historicism*'. [14] In *The Political Unconscious* he endeavours to synthesize him with Sartre through a series of theoretical moves, via narrative, mediation and totality. Narrative is used at various strategic points in the argument, but its initial task is to mediate between humanism and anti-humanism, between Sartre's stress on History as the totalization of individual agency and Althusser's account of history as a process without a subject. It is refreshing, at least, to find in Jameson one Marxist who unashamedly claims to bring back history rather than the subject: by characterizing narrative as 'the central function or *instance* of the human mind', he manages to avoid the psychologism of the subject while at the same time recasting history as a tale of human agents. [15] Narrative thus articulates the subjective with the objective, and this reconciliation apparently enables Jameson to dispense with the problem of the subject altogether. [16]

The first move facilitates the second: the introduction of mediation. Mediation represents a much greater challenge, for it was this concept of Sartre's which Althusser specifically attacked. Here instead of substituting a new category that subsumes the two in conflict, Jameson relies on a more devious strategy. In the *Critique* Sartre uses the concept of mediation to describe the reciprocal structure that allows the individual to become part of the fused group through a mediated reciprocity with another. [17] It thus constitutes the fundamental mechanism of intersubjectivity through which the individual becomes part of, and produces, the larger determining structure of totalization. Althusser contends that Sartre uses the typically Hegelian structure of mediation, along with origin and genesis, as 'magical ... post-stations', a way of filling in 'the emptiness between "*abstract*" categories and the "*concrete*" '.[18] This is very much the way in which Jameson himself employs mediation as an aesthetic category. But Althusser's most specific criticism is focused on the way in which Sartre uses it as a device to put the subject at the centre of the larger totalizations of history:

> i.e. the attempt to rediscover concrete individuals, the *subjects* of psycho-logical ideology, as the centres or 'intersections' of various progressively more external systems of determination, culminating in the structure of economic relations, systems which constitute a series of hierarchised levels.... Similarly, if men were the common supports of determinate functions in the structure of each social practice, they would 'in a manner express and concentrate' the entire social structure into themselves, i.e., they would be the *centres* from which it would be possible to know the articulation of these practices in the structure of the whole. At the same time, each of these practices would be effectively *centred* on the men-subjects of ideology, i.e. on consciousnesses. [19]

Here Althusser criticizes the way in which mediation enables Sartre to articulate his starting point in individual subjectivity with the impersonal structures of History so that at whatever level of the social and historical structure, the individual remains at the centre, expressing the totality. Consciousness thus functions in the same way as essence.

This is entirely absent from Jameson's account. He emphasizes only mediation's function as the relation between the part and the whole in general. Althusser, he claims

> grasps the process of mediation exclusively as the establishment of symbolic *identities* between the various levels, as a process whereby each level is folded into the next, thereby losing its constitutive autonomy and functioning as an expression of its homologues. (39)

This allows Jameson to claim that Althusser's real object of criticism was not so much the organic structure of the Hegelian essential section, whereby the same essence is at work in the part as constitutes the whole, as homology or isomorphism in which individual elements are epiphenomena of the economic base. Jameson even goes so far as to claim that Althusser is in fact at one with Hegel because the real object of critique in both instances is the category of 'unreflected immediacy'. This is followed by a long discussion of Goldmann's use of homology which really only addresses the problem of Jameson's fondness for making vertiginous leaps from the micro to the macro level in his own analyses. [20] The point, however, is that he has left out the substance of Althusser's attack on Sartre, namely that consciousness remains the basis for the structure of the totality.

In general terms it is possible to follow Jameson's argument that there is a close relation between Althusser's thesis of relative autonomy in his model of structural causality and Sartre's mediations, because they both place greater importance on the significance of cultural and political struggles at all levels. But Sartre's concept of mediation is really concerned with the problem of articulating individual consciousness with the forms of the social and of history. Moreover, whereas for Sartre each element is mediated in terms of the other, i.e. according to the category of totalization, for Althusser they are characterized by radical breaks and discontinuities, distinct from each other and not totalizing except at the conceptual level of the mode of production as a whole. The very real differences that become apparent illustrate the way in which Jameson's synthesizing can involve more of the persuasive rhetoric of a rough argument than a theory whose logical premises and moves have been demonstrated in detail. In a sense, however, he knows that he does not need to conduct a rigorous argument, for one has already been made for him. He can assimilate Althusser to Sartre by exploiting the critique by the British Althusserians Hindess and Hirst, in particular their argument that Althusser's structural causality remains, despite his best intentions, teleological and essentialist. Jameson, in other words, exploits a gap that had been opened up in Althusserian theory in order to subsume it into a larger totality.

III HISTORY AND 'THE REAL'

Hindess and Hirst's work was developed in a series of books in which ever greater areas of Althusser's work were successively rejected. Jameson uses only the first, *Pre-Capitalist Modes of Production* (1975), which goes some way to explain the relatively unproblematical manner in which he exploits their arguments in order to incorporate Althusser's intervention into his own framework. [21] As we have already seen, Hindess and Hirst argue that Hegel's expressive causality and Althusser's structural causality are in fact indistinguishable, since 'they both involve the expression of an inner essence' (277). Why? Because the structure in Althusser's description of the mode of production still functions as an inner essence of the whole – just because it is called a structure does not mean that it avoids an essentialist function. Thus Hindess and Hirst suggest that the idealist and teleological forms of Marxism cannot be broken with so easily, for they still operate at the level of transition and at the mode of causality. [22] We have already observed that Hindess and Hirst manage to arrive at this conclusion only by themselves conflating concept with essence, and by ignoring the arguments about temporality. Nevertheless, the contention that Althusser is in effect still teleological, that the mode of production is still an expressive causality, allows Jameson to effect the assimilation of Althusser to Sartre.

The concept of the mode of production offers a further opportunity. Hindess and Hirst raise the by now familiar problem of how such a concept can account for historical change, for in Althusser's description of history as modes of production such modes are theorized in terms of a static structural causality:

> In constructing his theory of history Althusser certainly avoids the Hegelian variant of teleology, a process with a purpose, but only at the price of falling into another, a structure whose end is its existence. (316)

In other words, by rejecting Hegelian expressive causality and substituting Spinoza's immanence, Althusser inevitably produced the problem of the form of transition between different modes of production, for, as Hindess and Hirst point out, 'the conceptualisation of the mode of production in the mode of structural causality precludes any concept of transition from one mode of production to another' (273). So much for the attempt to construct a theory of history as a non-teleological sequence. Balibar's proposed resolution of this problem through 'transitional' modes of production apparently fares little better, for all it shows is that history cannot do without a form of teleological causality derived from an unreconstructed notion of history:

> Transition is arbitrarily introduced into a problematic which should exclude it as a problem. Why? Because in 'real' history such transitions do occur. The untransformed notion of history enters here. (320)

In short it seems that there is a contradiction by which the anti-teleological is compelled to invoke the teleological. For Hindess and Hirst such contradictions simply demonstrate incoherence. Jameson on the other hand exploits this irresolvable antithesis between synchronic and diachronic models of history by declaring that the properly dialectical way of dealing with them is to synthesize them onto a higher level, a 'final horizon': 'these two apparently inconsistent accounts are simply the twin perspectives which our thinking (and our presentation or *Darstellung* of that thinking) can take on this same vast historical object'. [23] History thus becomes that which is *excessive* to conceptualization. We see here the basis of Jameson's strategy for retrieving 'History': whereas for Sartre such excess prevented totalization, in Jameson the structure has been neatly inverted so that it becomes the totalizing gesture itself.

This also enables Jameson to show how Althusser's decentred structure in dominance can be related to Sartre's totalization which is 'in a state of perpetual *detotalization*' – although both resist the open-ended position of the Frankfurt School for whom history detotalizes as indifferently as it totalizes. [24] In general totalizers and antitotalizers tend to represent their differences polemically as if they were simply antithetical. Jameson, however, recognizes that the two are interrelated: if the totalizers cannot finally totalize, so the detotalizers, while pointing to the impossibility of totalization, must still admit the necessity of the concept of totalization. [25] Therefore, while cheerfully admitting that there is an inherent contradiction in the claims of totality, Jameson nevertheless goes on to argue that it is as indispensable as it is unsatisfactory. [26] He suggests persuasively that a dialectical operation takes place between the theories and critiques of totalization; they are part of a symbiotic process and no totalizer is so totalizing that there is not some possibility of detotalizing and vice versa. This allows him to make the extraordinary but provocative alliance of Lukács and Sartre with Althusser, and, with the emergence of a certain negativity within totalization, even Adorno. The cost of such a confederacy is to concede what might schematically be called a poststructural reading of Sartre and Althusser. But once this concession has been made, it is quickly subsumed. Despite his brief admission of totalization's unfinalizability, Jameson is nevertheless impelled towards a final gesture whereby a transcendence is effected. This is accomplished by the invocation of a History that is beyond the concept – the Real, Necessity, 'the primacy of History itself'. But given that he has already conceded the status of history as representation, how can such an immediacy be posited?

Jameson once more relies upon Hindess and Hirst, who make two points: the first concerns the relation between the concept of 'history' and empirical history, the second the empirical status of history as an object. Once again, however, a certain blurring takes place. Just as earlier the concept was assimilated to essence, so here in the course of their argument they tend to slide from the question of the concept to that of representation so that the two become indistinguishable. While Bachelard had stressed that a scientific concept is not a representation as such but the constitution of a problematic, Hindess and Hirst shift from the question of the relation of the concept to the empirical, to that of representation to the real. The concept of concept becomes so weakened as to be virtually assimilable to representation, so that the concept merely represents the real, resulting in discussions about the difference between the 'thought' and the 'real' object. This slide leads to a more general critique of Althusser's epistemology on the grounds that it allows the 'real object history' to remain 'unchanged in its conception' – rather a startling accusation to make of the philosopher whose whole argument concerns the necessity of the production of new concepts. [27] According to Hindess and Hirst, the real problem is not so much epistemological, in the sense of the validation of the relation of knowledge to the real, as the fact that Althusser allows a category of the real object, of history as an object, at all. This is apparently then merely 'appropriated', unchanged, in thought. The long argument, from Bachelard onwards, that science is about the production and use of concepts, has been lost. Nevertheless, this allows Jameson his move.

For according to Hindess and Hirst, Althusser's definition of the science of history as a general theory of modes of production paradoxically leaves empirical history unchallenged.

> Althusser fails to break with the notion of history at the very moment of splitting from it. The means of destruction of the empiricist conception of history and of the philosophy of history engender a reprise in which history reasserts itself. Althusser does not say that there is no real object 'history', that the notion of a real concrete history is an illusion. He differentiates the thought object from the real object, but he does not deny the existence of the real object. Indeed, the effect of this distinction is to affirm it, to assign it a definite place in the Althusserian theory of knowledge. History in thought becomes an anti-historicist general theory of modes of production. But history as the real concrete, this survives untheorized and uncriticized. History is not therefore transformed. (318)

As Jameson recognizes, this argument opens a path of escape back to 'real' history, enabling his declaration that behind representation 'History is what hurts'. He can acknowledge Marxism's need to attend to the problematics of epistemology, representation, and interpretation, but in the end triumphantly retrieve a notion of 'real' history beyond them all. Once again, that which is excessive to any concept of history is brought in to subsume what it lacks.

If, however, at some level 'real history' does indeed escape, a Marxist history then is faced with the crisis that it must itself remain a form of representation rather than scientific knowledge. Hindess and Hirst's argument is premised on the assumption that Marxism in general is a science which can produce knowledge of its object. They suggest that since the object of history is whatever is past then by definition it cannot exist. The object of history becomes whatever is represented as having existed, now taking the form of 'preserved records and documents'. The historical object is therefore not a 'real concrete object' for it is only accessible through texts, and the writing of history involves the interpretation of those texts. [28] This leads Hindess and Hirst to what is perhaps the only example of a self-conscious rejection of history as such, on the grounds that it must be a representation rather than a real object. [29] Jameson, however, begins where Hindess and Hirst leave off, at this crisis of representation. [30] For him the problem is not so much that epistemology cannot be guaranteed for science, as the more Deleuzian problematic that history is not an object that can be known but a text that has to be interpreted. A concept such as history, so often invoked as the 'concrete', in fact involves a form of representation of reality inevitably subject to the effects of the recent analyses of representation in general. So Jameson warns his readers at the beginning of the *Political Unconscious* that:

> Above and beyond the problem of [historical] periodisation and its categories, which are certainly in crisis today ... the larger issue is that of the representation of History itself. (28)

This recognition distinguishes Jameson from many another Marxist or Marxisant who assumes that it is possible to criticize contemporary theorists in terms of a neglect of a 'history' that is positioned outside the framework of their argument. [31] Such a strategy is identified by Derrida as nothing less than the transcendentalizing gesture itself. [32] In fact Jameson, while realizing that the problematic of history and representation prevents any simple claim for its exteriority, nevertheless goes on to produce what is simply a more sophisticated form of the same argument.

He manages to finesse this little difficulty of representation by invoking a supratextual History as the Real or Absent Cause beyond it. He does this by utilizing the apparent chink in Althusser exposed by Hindess and Hirst, that is, that dualism of knowledge and being set up in Althusser's epistemology in fact still allows for a notion of a 'concrete' 'real' history, beyond representation. Although this cannot be known in any relation of immediacy, it can be discerned in its effects, a formulation which Jameson derives, without much justification, from Lacan's notion of 'the Real'.

> The sweeping negativity of the Althusserian formula is misleading insofar as it can readily be assimilated to the polemic themes of a host of contemporary post-structuralisms and post-Marxisms, for which History, in the bad sense – the reference to a 'context' or a 'ground', an external real world of some kind, the reference, in other words, to the much

maligned 'referent' itself – is simply one more text among others, something found in history manuals and that chronological presentation of sequences so often called 'linear history'. What Althusser's own insistence on history as an absent cause makes clear, but what is missing from the formula as it is canonically worded, is that he does not at all draw the fashionable conclusion that because history is a text, the 'referent' does not exist. We would therefore propose the following revised formulation: that history is *not* a text, not a narrative, master or otherwise, but that, as an absent cause, it is inaccessible to us except in textual form, and that our approach to it and to the Real itself necessarily passes through its prior textualisation, its narrativisation in the political unconscious. (35)

Thus Jameson can acknowledge the status of history as interpretation, as narrative, but still assert its ultimate transcendence beyond those as the 'real' itself. Acknowledging that a historical analysis will always have to invoke a representation of history rather than history itself, Jameson admits that Marxism cannot ground its argument on such a representation. However he then claims that, whatever the problems of representing it, the reality of history will always be felt in its effects, even if it is only ever accessible obliquely. Invoking Sartre's notion of scarcity, Jameson claims that 'history is what hurts'. In this way history can return as the 'absolute horizon' demonstrated by Marxist criticism – an 'absolute historicism' so absolute that it is not even subject to the effects of history. [33] History is now no longer meaning or even narrative, but a final cause beyond knowledge.

IV THE PREFACE: REALISM AND INTERPRETATION

Jameson's assimilation of Althusser to Sartre and his invocation of a 'Real' is given, then, a theoretical justification. Whereas Sartre enacts the impossibility of the idea of totalization – he has an idea of history but its realization has always to be deferred with more writing, in Jameson this same structure is formalized, so that Sartre's detotalizing excess becomes the very instrument of sublation. In other words, Jameson cleverly inverts the process by which the surplus broaches the totality by calling that surplus 'history itself'. The cost, however, is that history must be defined as a metaphysical absolute, and Sartre's shift from history as idea to its enactment in an economy of writing must be refused. Nevertheless, it re-emerges almost immediately as a historical inscription from the pressure of his own theoretical narrative. For despite its length and substance, Jameson invites his reader to skip the Althusserian section altogether, claiming that he is equally able to rely upon an argument at the level of hermeneutics. His strangely disposable theoretical argument, dismissed as merely a 'lengthy digression', takes him back to the point at which it started: the discussion of interpretation.

Theoretical analysis gives way to a persuasive rhetoric of subsumption.

Nevertheless Jameson's argument follows a procedure already familiar from the theoretical section. Instead of rejecting the claims of rival or antithetical theories, he acknowledges their full force, but only to subsume them onto the higher level of a further argument that thus becomes unassailable. As Samuel Weber has pointed out a cunning operation takes place here. For having shown the local ways in which other forms of criticism construct their objects of study and the 'strategies of containment' whereby they are able to project the illusion that their particular readings are somehow complete and self-sufficient, Jameson goes on to initiate his own 'strategy of containment' to comprehend those earlier strategies that he has exposed as only partial. [34] Their absences become the point of knowledge from which he produces his fullness, that which is lacking is transformed into an excess brought in from outside to effect a new totalization. So, while he appears to acknowledge the force of the critiques of the Marxist invocations of history as if it were the thing-in-itself rather than representation, Jameson is thus enabled to reintroduce the traditional claims of Marxism to science, knowledge, truth, and, as the book will demonstrate, to 'History' revealed through the political unconscious. This despite the fact that he opens the book with the assertion of the superiority of Marxist analysis not by reference to any founding notions such as history, truth, or science, but by an affirmation of the powers of Marxist criticism as a more advanced form of interpretation.

Let us follow the operation of this manoeuvre by returning to the Preface, where the rhetorical argument starts. Jameson begins by announcing that the moral of his book is that the slogan 'always historicize!' is, paradoxically, the one '"transhistorical" imperative' towards which all dialectical thought leads. History, it seems, must deny its own historicity in order to assert itself as the condition of Being and the unquestioned *a priori* of all forms of thought. Yet, in the same paragraph Jameson acknowledges that it is no longer possible, for him at least, to return to the 'reality' of history in traditional Marxist terms. This is the result of the crisis of History as representation, which Jameson here describes in terms of two alternatives:

> We are thus confronted with a choice between study of the nature of the 'objective' structures of a given cultural text ... and something rather different which would instead foreground the interpretive categories or codes through which we read and receive the text in question.(9)

Without giving any explicit reason for the grounds of his choice between the two – although it is a choice which is clearly determined by the sense that the first option has now been disallowed – Jameson then announces somewhat ruefully, in a curious reminiscence of the marriage ceremony, that:

> For better or for worse it is this second path we have chosen to follow here: *The Political Unconscious* accordingly turns on the dynamics of the

act of interpretation and presupposes, as its organizational fiction, that we never really confront a text immediately, in all its freshness as a thing-in-itself. Rather, texts come before us as the always-already-read: we apprehend them through sedimented layers of previous interpretations. (9)

Historical reality cannot be apprehended in any relation of immediacy, but can only be approached through its textual representation and interpretation; its absence bears the contradictory traces of the always-already-read.

As a result of this situation, Jameson is obliged to enter the rough and tumble of what he calls 'the intellectual marketplace today', and pit Marxist interpretation against all those other forms of interpretation – 'the ethical, the psychoanalytic, the myth-critical, the semiotic, the structural, and the theological' (not, we note, the feminist) – vying for critical supremacy through an interpretive will-to-power and rhetoric of persuasion: 'I will here argue', he announces, 'the priority of a Marxian interpretive framework in terms of semantic richness' (10). But if its interpretive power is richer, it is also more than this, for Jameson's form of interpretation makes one claim that goes beyond the limits of this Nietzschean model of interpretive communities struggling for power. [35] Even though Marxist criticism must now enter the market-place as interpretation rather than, as in the old days, through an invocation of its higher knowledge in the form of History and Truth, it is still a superior form of interpretation. For unlike all the others it does not actually have to compete with its rivals because, according to its dialectical logic, it can both incorporate and transcend them. [36] What at first, then, looked like an abandonment of traditional Marxist notions of History and Truth was in fact only a first move in bringing them back via the meta-claim of interpretive absolutism and history as transcendence. As Jameson himself puts it:

> Marxism cannot today be defended as a mere substitute for such other methods, which would then triumphalistically be consigned to the ashcan of history.... In the spirit of a more authentic dialectical tradition, Marxism is here conceived as that 'untranscendable horizon' that subsumes such apparently antagonistic or incommensurable critical operations, assigning them an undoubted sectoral validity within itself, and thus at once cancelling and preserving them. [37]

The grand assertion cited from Sartre's unfinished *Critique* might have given Jameson pause (but it doesn't). It seemed at first as if he had renounced the certitude and special claims of Marxism's privileged access to history in order to compete on an interpretive level as if Marxism were just another form of interpretation – a half-way position which certain other Marxists have somewhat gullibly followed. [38] But it then turns out that this retreat is only made in order to jump further than ever before so that Jameson can not only claim to offer the correct interpretation, but also the one that incorporates and transcends all others. The truth-claim is replaced by a meta-truth-claim. Marxism is thus both interpretation and yet not interpretation because it leads to the meta-claim that it has become truth. To sum up: in his Preface Jameson began by stating that there were two possible options, and reluctantly discarded the first in favour of the second; but he then moves from this second option into a third designed to recover the lost possibilities of the first. A form of sublation is thus preserved, but its logic returns us to Rousseau's circle that was 'degenerative in direction but progressive and compensatory in effect'. The emphasis now placed on the *always* of always historicizing begins to turn history into a process of repetition. Historical interpretation begins to enact the Rousseauistic structure of history as supplementarity.

We have already followed the theoretical moves which enabled Jameson's invocation of a 'Real' beyond interpretation. But, given that the theory is itself optional, how does he ground his claim for the totalizing power of Marxism's transcendence rhetorically? How can he move from an interpretive or semantic level to one which is not just an optional code among others? We have seen that Jameson has put forward the two possibilities for history in terms of an objective structure versus subjective interpretive categories. This is extended elsewhere in more explicit terms as:

> The so-called crisis of representation, in which an essentially realistic epistemology, which conceives of representation as the reproduction, for subjectivity, of an objectivity that lies outside it – projects a mirror theory of knowledge and art, whose fundamental evaluative categories are those of adequacy, accuracy, and Truth itself. It is in terms of this crisis that the transition, in the history of form, from a novelistic 'realism' of the Lukácsian variety to the various now classical 'high' modernisms, has been described. [39]

In this description the two forms of reality between which the critic is obliged to choose amount to an 'objective' historical reality, identified with 'realism', the habitual terrain for Marxist criticism of the Lukácsian historicist variety, including Jameson himself, and the newer mode of modernism that acknowledges the past as a problem for historical understanding, a representation inevitably mediated by its production in the present. What is odd about this discussion of reality as objectivity or as representation is its curious sense of familiarity. Stating that *The Political Unconscious* is not a work of literary history, Jameson suggests that the task of such an enterprise would be 'at one with that proposed by Louis Althusser for historiography in general: not to elaborate some achieved and lifelike simulacrum of its supposed object, but rather to "produce" the latter's "concept"', as, he adds, the 'greatest modern or modernizing literary histories ... have sought to do' (12). His example of a book that does this is Erich Auerbach's *Mimesis*. And it soon becomes clear that *Mimesis* provides the basis for his own assimilation of the choice between History as the Real and history as interpretation into the two literary modes of Realism and Modernism. If Jameson has lost the old form of reality, rendered in all the freshness of its historical being, Auerbach enables him to find another, deprived of that specific experience of historical reality, but which can still claim to go beyond all other forms of understanding in the name of history's untranscendable truth.

V CHAPTER ONE: REALISM AND INTERPRETATION

In the famous opening chapter of *Mimesis*, 'Odysseus' Scar', Auerbach distinguishes between two kinds of style in the literary representation of reality in European culture, typified by the difference between the *Odyssey* and the Bible:

> On the one hand fully externalised description, uniform illumination, uninterrupted connection, free expression, all events in the foreground, displaying unmistakable meanings, few elements of historical development and of psychological perspective; on the other hand, certain parts brought into high relief, others left obscure, abruptness, suggestive influence of the unexpressed, 'background' quality, multiplicity of meanings and the need for interpretation, universal-historical claims, development of the concept of the historically becoming, and preoccupation with the problematic. [40]

In these two forms of representations of reality we have a close analogue to the two choices with which Jameson describes himself as being faced. That first, now unavailable option of nineteenth-century realism, of history in its immediacy, 'in all its freshness as a thing-in-itself' can be compared to the realism of Homer, 'a realm where everything is visible', in which all phenomena are externalized in terms perceptible to the senses, set in the full light of the foreground. In the realism of Homer, everything is quite self-evident, its reality containing nothing but itself: 'the Homeric poems conceal nothing, they contain no teaching, and no secret second meaning. Homer can be analysed ... but he cannot be interpreted' (11). It is all very different in the Bible, in the account of the sacrifice of Isaac which Auerbach uses as his example. Here, the narrative gives only the minimum details necessary for the story; everything else is left in obscurity: 'time and place are undefined and call for interpretation; thoughts and feelings remain unexpressed, are only suggested by the silence and the fragmentary speeches' (9). The whole remains mysterious. Whereas in Homer reality is portrayed in all its immediacy, in the Bible reality is distant, obscure, and demands interpretation. The Biblical narrator, Auerbach suggests, was not primarily oriented towards realism in the first instance at all; if he succeeded in being realistic it was merely a means, not an end. For his single goal was an overall meaning, truth itself, and 'woe to the man who did not believe it!':

> Indeed, we must go even further. The Bible's claim to truth is not only far more urgent than Homer's, it is tyrannical – it excludes all other claims.... The Scripture stories do not, like Homer's, court our favour, they do not flatter us that they may please us and enchant us – they seek to subject us, and if we refuse to be subjected we are rebels. (12)

In the Bible, we find a close analogue to Jameson's second option which he follows in order to prove that all competing interpretations can be subsumed under the 'untranscendable horizon' of a Marxist interpretation. Surprising as this may seem, if we return to Jameson's text we find that this Biblical derivation is made perfectly explicit.

In the opening chapter of *The Political Unconscious*, Jameson repeats the argument about interpretation from the Preface that has already been outlined – except that here it is advanced in a rather different way. This time he begins with the contention that what he coyly calls the 'political interpretation' of literary texts is not merely a competitor or an optional extra to the other current methods available today but constitutes 'the absolute horizon of all reading and all interpretation' (17). This is then followed, as before, with two descriptions of different possible representations of history. But a significant change has taken place, for now Jameson no longer identifies with either of them. The first option is a form of historicism, an antiquarian attempt to reconstitute the past (still in all its freshness), which simply attempts to represent it as a thing-in-itself without any form of interpretation or understanding. This form of retrieving historical reality is conflated with the literary realism of the nineteenth century. Jameson then, as before, goes on to describe the alternative that foregrounds the problems involved in the interpretation and representation of the past, here identified with modernism. However, his original wedding to this second option seems now to have suffered a divorce:

> Today this properly antiquarian relationship to the cultural past has a dialectical counterpart which is ultimately no more satisfactory; I mean the tendency of much contemporary theory to rewrite selected texts from the past in terms of its own aesthetic and, in particular, in terms of a modernist (or more properly post-modernist) conception of language. (17)

This time, while acknowledging that the second, interpretive option invokes the problem of language, and thus of representation, Jameson no longer admits that this difficulty impinges on him. The two options are now described in terms of realism and modernism (or postmodernism, a problematic conflation that we will return to) – and Jameson claims that he himself stands outside them both. He has thus dehistoricized himself from the intellectual critiques of his own historical context with which he began in order to reintroduce, now beyond the problems of realism and the contemporary formulations of the problems of language and representation acknowledged in the Preface, the meta-interpretive claims of Marxism's transcendence as 'the absolute horizon of all reading and all interpretation'.

In other words, whereas in the Preface Jameson describes two possible options, identifies with the second but then claims to be able to transcend it, here he no longer acknowledges that either option has purchase on his own position because he has separated out his transcendence into a third. This third is identified as History, beyond all historicisms or relativisms, enabling him to go on to invoke what Auerbach describes as the tyrannical and exclusive claims of the Bible. This is Auerbach:

> The world of the Scripture stories is not satisfied with claiming to be a historically true reality – it insists that it is the only real world, is destined for autocracy. All other scenes, issues, and ordinances have no right to appear independently of it, and it is promised that all of them, the history of all mankind, will be given their due place within its frame, will be subordinated to it. (12)

And this is Jameson:

> Only Marxism can give us an adequate account of the essential *mystery* of the cultural past.... This mystery can be re-enacted only if the human adventure is one.... These matters can recover their original urgency for us only if they are retold within the unity of a single great collective story ... only if they are grasped as vital episodes in a single vast unfinished plot. (19–20)

It is here that in his account of this great narrative of the history of all mankind, Jameson appeals to the allegorical tradition of Biblical hermeneutics, the patristic and medieval system of the four levels of scripture, which offers him a mechanism for assimilating all other forms of history and interpretation into what he calls the 'collective logic of History' (30). The Augustinian method of patristic exegesis is structured in exactly the same way as Jameson's Marxism, to the extent that it is an interpretive method in which the meaning precedes the interpretation. [41] Just as the task for St Augustine was to interpret the Bible according to established Christian doctrine, so Jameson's Marxism begins with the doctrine that all history is one. The interpretive problem is not to discover other meanings in the past but to bring the recalcitrant material into line – the interpretation as such is not open to question. All interpretation is simply a matter of translation into a master code (58).

Jameson, therefore, can bypass his theoretical 'proof' as a mere digression because he also puts Marxism in the position of making a Biblical claim to truth. Nowhere is this clearer than on the final page of Chapter One, where he invokes Althusser's concept of history as structural causality, but places the stress on the formulation of Althusser's source, Spinoza, so that history becomes an 'absent cause'. The problem with – or perhaps the attraction of – this formulation is that, by invoking Spinoza in this way, it becomes impossible to distinguish between History and God: if they are not identical, then the two are set up in irresolvable rivalry with one another. This signals a further problem that arises from Jameson's appropriation of the Biblical truth-claim for History. For the invocation of the Biblical form of an *exclusive* claim to truth, which includes the history of all mankind in its purview, raises a logical difficulty or paradox. We have to ask whether Jameson's own argument must not necessarily be qualified by his suggestion that the absolute truth of the Biblical claim can be surpassed: once you have shown that an absolute truth-claim can be transcended, then any new absolutisms which you may propose in its place must also be open to the possibility of revision.

Moreover, has the usurpation of the Biblical truth-claim for Marxism allowed him to transcend the conditions of his own historical moment, as he claimed he could in his first chapter? That transcendence was achieved by Jameson's distancing his own interpretive strategies from the linguistic self-consciousness about problems of reference and representation in twentieth-century cultural and artistic form. A symptomatic effect of this move was the awkward and uneasy assimilation of modernism and postmodernism into one another in order to place himself beyond both. Yet in the Preface, as we saw, Jameson 'for better or for worse' conceded his own intellectual positioning within the contemporary world, and went on to admit that the book was not concerned with the challenge of:

> conceiving those new forms of collective thinking and collective culture which lie beyond the boundaries of our own world. The reader will find [in the Conclusion] an empty chair reserved for some as yet unrealized, collective, and decentred cultural production of the future, beyond realism and modernism alike. (11)

If we are permitted to think historically, we would have to ask what else could occupy this empty (no doubt professorial) chair beyond realism and modernism alike than postmodernism – the very critique of reference and representation that the central argument of *The Political Unconscious* is designed to transcend? At this point, with a little historicizing imagination, the reader may begin to reflect that although that part of Jameson's argument which seems to concede so much more comes first, in the Preface, the Preface is of course generally in fact the section that is written last. Either way it effectively undoes the entire meta-critical argument of the rest of the book.

Why does Jameson concede in his Preface the very certainty that the book sets out to establish? The answer can only be that he has recognized a problem with his category of the Real – and therefore with the notion of 'History itself'. Perhaps Jameson has been reading Foucault, who makes it clear that the real cannot escape as an unchanged object as Hindess and Hirst fear or as Jameson hopes, even to the extent of being inaccessible except in its effects, for the real is itself a category constructed as an ontology through discourse. This is not to say that there is nothing outside language. Rather it is to point out that even the invocation of a category beyond discourse must nevertheless *ipso facto* itself be a discursive category. A Real cannot therefore be invoked in spatial terms as existing somewhere outside discourse, to the extent that it is itself also a discursive construction. [42]

This realization leads Jameson into an immediate difficulty: he has already addressed the problem that a totalizing theory may be totalitarian, and that even theories of totalization that include negativity such as Adorno's or Foucault's tend to imply a political powerlessness. He argues that this is not a problem for him because the Real/History will always exist as a ground outside theory however totalizing it may be and will thus enable and effect a leverage upon it. Only necessity constitutes a truly untranscendable totality. [43] But if the Real is also a discursive construction it cannot function as a ground outside that enables a leverage of the inside. The totalization has now nothing exterior to it. The subsumption is so complete that Jameson has lost the excess that enabled totalization, for his own position of transcendence always depended on a supplementary point of enunciation outside ('beyond realism and modernism alike'). Without the Real, he is left inside unable to get out, caught up in his own writing, like the Bonaventura Hotel guest he so vividly describes: unable to find the exit, and becoming increasingly unsure that there really is one.

VI POSTMODERNISM – OR, THE CULTURAL LOGIC OF LATE JAMESON

The problem with which Jameson gets entangled in the Preface to *The Political Unconscious* is confronted again in the influential essay of 1984, 'Postmodernism, or the Cultural Logic of Late Capitalism'. [44] Here the meta-critical impulse has gone. As a result of the absence at the origin of history, the necessity of interpretation, that *The Political Unconscious* was designed to solve – but which it found itself repeating – Jameson now puts forward a rather different argument. Once again, however, it exposes the logical difficulties of the transcendent role for History that he has been trying to preserve.

In this essay Jameson now distinguishes postmodernism from modernism and identifies it with poststructuralism. Contrary to his assertion in *The Political Unconscious* – or to the arguments of Lyotard – he now subscribes to the view that a radical break occurred between modernism and postmodernism. In the late fifties/early sixties the hundred-year-old modern movement disintegrated in a 'final, extraordinary flowering' which left it 'spent and exhausted' (53). So much for modernism, now oddly transformed into a dead organism and historically placed well before the advent of contemporary theory with which it had formerly been assimilated. What followed, according to Jameson, became

> empirical, chaotic, and heterogeneous. Andy Warhol and pop art, but also photorealism, and beyond it, the 'new expressionism' ... Burroughs, Pynchon, Ishmael Reed, on the one hand and the French *nouveau roman* ... on the other, along with alarming new kinds of literary criticism, based on some new aesthetic of textuality or *écriture*. (54)

Contrary to the argument of a writer like Andreas Huyssen, Jameson thus assimilates poststructuralist criticism without question under the postmodern umbrella. [45] Indeed, later on he says quite explicitly, 'what is today called contemporary theory ... is also, I would want to argue, itself very precisely a postmodernist phenomenon' (61). Now this perspective on poststructuralism has an undoubted attraction because it enables him to historicize it, to give it a historical placing. And Jameson certainly has some interesting things to say about that. But what is most striking is his argument that postmodernism is not a style or a fashion but what in a Lukácsian spirit he calls the 'culture in dominance' of late capitalism. [46] It can be recognized in five constitutive features, the elaboration of which takes up the bulk of Jameson's argument.

These are well known and can be quickly summarized: a new depthlessness, where the depth models of intrinsic meaning, essence/appearance etc., are replaced by a conception of practices, discourses, textual play, surfaces and intertextuality; a return of history not as the 'real' but as representation, as pastiche, thus foregrounding consideration of the historicity of history; a new form of private temporality whose 'schizophrenic' structure Jameson links to textuality, *écriture*, or schizophrenic writing; the 'hysterical sublime' – a formula which he invents in order to describe the way in which, in Lyotard's terms, postmodernism involves the unrepresentable (with the enormous forces, or power, of the Kantian sublime now no longer nature but the forces of global capitalism); and a new form of 'postmodern hyperspace' which has managed to transcend the capacities of the individual body to locate itself, to organize its immediate surroundings, 'and cognitively to map its position in a mappable external world'. This stands, he suggests, as

> the symbol and analogue of that even sharper dilemma which is the incapacity of our minds, at least at present, to map the great global multinational and decentred communicational network in which we find ourselves caught as individual subjects. (84)

What is particularly interesting in this description of postmodernism as a culture in dominance is that, contrary to the argument of *The Political*

Unconscious, it is impossible for the individual to transcend it, to step outside it. As Jameson puts it elsewhere: 'The point is that we are *within* the culture of postmodernism to the point where its equally facile repudiation is as impossible as any equally facile celebration of it is complacent and corrupt'. [47] This relationship to contemporary culture is then allegorized in the long experiential description of the Bonaventura Hotel complex in Los Angeles. The totality has become the culture itself, and now seems to operate in an irresolvable oscillation between totalizing and fragmenting forces. [48] This time there seems to be no possibility of a subsuming gesture of transcendence.

From a theoretico-political perspective what is significant about Jameson's 'Postmodernism' article is that the traditional point outside the dominant culture which the Marxist or left-liberal critic customarily adopts is no longer regarded as possible:

> The cultural critic and moralist ... along with the rest of us, is now so deeply immersed in postmodernist space, so deeply suffused and infected by its new cultural categories, that the luxury of the old-fashioned ideological critique, the indignant moral denunciation of the other, becomes unavailable. (86)

It is because we are inside postmodernism, without the reassuring possibility of an outside, whether it be Althusser's 'science' or Foucault's 'self-reflexivity', that Jameson characterizes the final effect of the postmodern condition as 'the abolition of critical distance'. As the 'anti-aesthetic' the postmodern poses the most serious political – and intellectual – challenge to all forms of cultural politics on the left which conventionally assume the possibility of an aesthetic and therefore critical distance. This means that today, according to Jameson,

> Some of our most cherished and time-honoured radical conceptions about the nature of cultural politics may ... find themselves outmoded. However distinct those conceptions may have been – which range from slogans of negativity, opposition, and subversion to critique and reflexivity – they all shared a single, fundamentally spatial, presupposition, which may be resumed in the equally time-honoured formula of 'critical distance'. No theory of cultural politics current on the Left today has been able to do without one notion or another of a certain minimal aesthetic distance, of the possibility of positioning the cultural act outside the massive Being of capital, which then serves as an Archimedean point from which to assault this last. What the burden of our preceding demonstration suggests, however, is that distance in general (including 'critical distance' in particular) has very precisely been abolished in the new space of postmodernism. (87)

Even the muted murmur of Adorno's immanent critique, in the face of a situation which Jameson's own now so closely resembles, is no longer a possibility. We are, it seems, a long way from the confidence of Marxism's untranscendable and 'absolute horizon' from which Jameson claimed to be speaking in *The Political Unconscious*. It is almost as if complete paranoia has followed on from the most inflated delusions of grandeur. [49]

Postmodernism has somehow broken down the former situation in which science could comfortably be set against ideology and the world known and conceptualized accordingly. Totalization has now been effected not by the critic but by capitalism itself and postmodernism, its culture in dominance. At a theoretical level this abolition of critical distance is partly the effect of the questioning of the status of certain forms of knowledge, including history, and the category of the 'real', that Jameson had earlier attempted to counter. Here he acknowledges the force of Lyotard's and Foucault's arguments for the end of the possibility of critique as such – that is, the possession of a ground or certainty of truth from which to criticize other knowledges or truth-claims. Jameson's confession that this no longer allows him – or anyone else – the possibility of an absolute horizon, a meta-position of history as knowledge, is a striking admission of the impossibility of the earlier project of *The Political Unconscious*.

Jameson is left, somewhat nostalgically, positing an as yet unfulfilled return to science and knowledge sometime in the future through what he calls a 'global cognitive mapping'. The final totalization, Marxism's science fiction, here returns as utopian fantasy.

VII THE JAMESON RAID

Political arguments necessarily tend to project such utopian futures, although, as Terry Eagleton has commented, political futures will be based on a desire which, to the extent that it is based on a lack, as in Lacan's description of the subject, or Sartre's history, tends to be impossible to realize. 'But we can't stop desiring utopia' Eagleton adds, 'even if rationally we know that it will never come'. [50] All forms of radical politics need the future, just as all conservative politics require the past.

But there is also a danger that such utopian moments, if projected uncritically, may in fact perpetuate the very structures of the systems that they seek to displace, that they may project the past back into the future, not changing history but repeating it. Although Jameson concedes that repetition is itself the postmodern situation, he consistently refuses to acknowledge its dangers. [51] It is hard, however, to avoid the conclusion that his insistence on socialism's development as a global totality involves a form of neo-colonialism: 'we Americans, we masters of the world' know what is best for everyone else. [52] The attitude does not change whether the prescription be capitalism or socialism. [53]

Whereas in *Marxism and Form* Jameson had been prepared to concede that there was a time when 'history, in effect, had no single meaning', by *The Political Unconscious* Jameson's territorial ambitions have become more grandiose. [54] In an extraordinary recuperative gesture, part of which we have already cited for its relation to the Bible, he seizes even pre-history for Marxism in order to effect a vampiric resurrection:

> Only Marxism can give us an adequate account of the essential *mystery* of the cultural past, which, like Tiresias drinking the blood, is momentarily returned to life and warmth and allowed once more to speak, and to deliver its long-forgotten message in surroundings utterly alien to it. This mystery can be re-enacted only if the human adventure is one; only thus ... can we glimpse the vital claims upon us of such long-dead issues as the seasonal alternation of the economy of a primitive tribe, the passionate disputes about the nature of the Trinity, the conflicting models of the *polis* or the universal Empire, or, apparently closer to us in time, the dusty parliamentary and journalistic polemics of the nineteenth-century nation states. These matters can recover their original urgency for us only if they are retold within the unity of a single great collective story ... only if they are grasped as vital episodes in a single vast unfinished plot. (19–20)

The history of the world comprises a single narrative – but whose narrative? [55] And whose unfinished plot? Who constitutes the 'us' when Jameson proclaims that 'these matters can only recover their original urgency for us' – these matters being 'the seasonal alternation of the economy of a primitive tribe', as if there were no people in existence still categorized by this scarcely civilized terminology – as well as the 'dusty parliamentary and journalistic polemics of the nineteenth-century nation states' – as if there were not nations throughout the world still operating today under the determining effects of such polemics, and needing no 'great collective story' to recover any original urgency. There's no need to recover an original urgency if you live in a State of Emergency.

In short, whose history is Jameson's oft-invoked 'History itself'? No one apparently is allowed a history outside the 'us' – that is Western civilization and the Western point of view, which for Jameson seems to mean the USA. In its way, this recuperative project simply reduplicates the history of European colonialism, the great capitalist plot, in which the world outside Europe's borders, its other, was progressively engorged within its empires, with different cultures denigrated and other histories denied. In a recent article, 'Third World Literature in the Era of Multinational Capitalism', which he describes as a 'pendant to the essay on postmodernism', Jameson characterizes the Third World as a homogeneous entity that can be defined solely in terms of its experience of colonialism. [56] On the strength of this he proceeds to sketch 'a theory of the cognitive aesthetics of third-world literature' which begins with the declaration that 'all third-world texts are necessarily ... allegorical, and in a very specific way: they are to be read as what I will call *national allegories*. [57] Characterizing all Third World literature as different from that of the First World, but essentially the same in its difference, Jameson prescribes the single way in which it must be read, while at the same time warning his readers: 'Nothing is to be gained by passing over in silence the radical difference of non-canonical texts. The third world novel will not offer the satisfactions of Proust or Joyce'. [58]

This essay has been roughly but rightly criticized by Aijaz Ahmad, who deplores Jameson's patronizing attitude in general, his unproblematized use of the three worlds theory, his definition of the Third World as Other in terms only of its experience of colonialism, so that it becomes the passive object of a West that is the maker of history. [59] Jameson may deride the argument that links Hegelian forms of thought to nineteenth- and twentieth-century European history, but his own use of Hegel is striking in this context. First-World/Third-World relations are analysed according to the terms of Hegel's master-slave structure (though where this leaves the Second World is never made clear), while Hegel's description of agrarian societies (without history) and industrialized societies (with history), is assimilated to the difference between the first and third worlds. As Ahmad points out, Jameson soon begins to imply a primordial rather than historical difference between the two. [60] What Ahmad most objects to, however, is the way in which although on the one hand Jameson insists on difference, the Third World as Other, this very categorization necessarily leads him to insist on its homogeneity:

> The difference between the first and third world is absolutised as otherness, but the enormous cultural heterogeneity of social formations within the so-called third world is submerged within a singular identity of 'experience'. (10)

This is then contained within the narrative form of the national allegory. Thus the reduction of the Third World to a singular formation finds its corollary at the aesthetic level in the argument for a common allegorical narrative form for all Third-World texts. All Third-World texts? Is it rather, as Ahmad asks, 'that only those texts which give us authentic allegories can be admitted as authentic texts of third-world literature, while the rest are excluded by definition' (12)? Here we have an example both of the typical operation of exclusion through which totalization takes place, and of the way in which the Other is constituted as the same. The further effect of Jameson's insistent dialectical method becomes readily apparent when even the Third World's special narrative form turns out to be but the negative of that which he claims for the West, with the result that they end up as nothing so much than another version of Auerbach's two kinds of Western realism. [61] The Third World seems to offer a dialectical opposite to the postmodernism of the First World so that both can be transcended in the name of the utopian future of socialism. It becomes clear that Jameson needs the Third World more than it needs him. But even here it is not so simple. For postmodernism is itself defined by its globality, its penetration of the Third World.

Postmodernism, Jameson says, does not allow a point of critical distance. Although he readily admits to a totalizing form of thought, and constantly defines history as a single narrative and a single story, he is keen to retain this totalization as his own critical activity rather than projecting it as the unchangeable state of things. So he dismisses Adorno's negative dialectics for excising the possibility of resistance to the totalizing system, and in the same vein criticizes what he describes as Foucault's vision of the future as a system of total colonization. For the latter he claims:

> projects a fantasy future of a 'totalitarian' type in which the mechanisms of domination ... are grasped as irrevocable and increasingly pervasive tendencies whose mission is to colonize the last remnants and survivals of human freedom – to occupy and organize, in other words, what still persists of Nature objectively and subjectively (very schematically, the Third World and the Unconscious). [62]

But despite his attempts to distinguish his own totalizing tendency from Foucault's, it is hard to tell the difference between this curious description and that which Jameson himself gives of the state of postmodernism. Here

> the prodigious new expansion of multinational capital ends up penetrating and colonizing those very pre-capitalist enclaves (Nature and the Unconscious) which offered extraterritorial and Archimedean footholds for critical effectivity. [63]

Postmodernism has itself become the totalizing force, with the result that Foucault's fantasy totalitarian future has now apparently been realized: the colonization of the Third World ('Nature') is now complete with the 'penetration' of the global system of multinational capitalism into its furthest reaches. But what is the status of the claim that is being made here? Jameson seems to be implying that the Third World formerly offered a critical perspective and even a mode of resistance for Western Marxists (the position of its own inhabitants is left unclear and not discussed). This has now been lost. In the disorientation which the postmodernism of late capitalism brings 'we', according to Jameson, need once more to:

> begin to grasp our positioning as individual and collective subjects and regain a capacity to act and struggle which is at present neutralized by our spatial as well as our social confusion. [64]

But once again who is the 'we' here? Who is confused? Does the Third World constitute a possible site of resistance or not? Jameson oscillates between claiming that it does and that it doesn't.

At all events it is those in the West who are most obviously suffering the political and intellectual disorientation of the postmodern condition, and who, according to Jameson, need to regain their capacity to act and to struggle. How can this be achieved? The answer is through 'cognitive mapping': there is, Jameson declares, a 'need for maps'. Like the earliest explorations of the New World:

> The political form of postmodernism ... will have as its vocation the invention and projection of a global cognitive mapping, on a social as well as a spatial scale. [65]

But maybe the whole world won't thank Jameson for his new 'global cognitive mapping'; maybe the explorers won't be so welcome this time when they encounter what Jameson still calls the 'primitive tribe'; not everyone is grateful for the chance to play yet another part in the Europo-American story.

One advantage of cognitive mapping, however, is that it appears not to depend on the Third World as a dialectical opposite to the postmodern, which as Lyotard suggests, is a Western phenomenon even if it involves a global culture. [66] Complaining of his sense of bewilderment in postmodernist space and imprisonment in the present of postmodernism, Jameson notes specifically the

> loss of our ability to *position ourselves within this space and cognitively map it*. This is then projected back on the emergence of a global multinational culture which is decentred and cannot be visualized, a culture in which one cannot position oneself. [67]

The totalizing force is no longer class consciousness, nor even history, but capitalism itself. But the totality is ungraspable, and as long as it is ungraspable it cannot be resisted. Cognitive mapping, which is supposed to counter the disabling experience of postmodernist space, represents Jameson's equivalent, in the cultural dominant of postmodernism, to Lukács' class consciousness. But who can hope to do it? Class, says Jameson, now exists only at the level of fantasy. [68] It seems to be a matter for the individual decentred postmodern intellectual. If so, does the mind that constructs the map represent a point of exteriority from which it can begin to be positioned beyond the postmodern? It is probably not wise to push the metaphor too far. The argument that the inhabitant of postmodernist society needs a cognitive map, must reconstruct the 'mental map of social and global totality we carry in our heads' in order to regain some political purchase, is made via a somewhat unconvincing analogy with Kevin Lynch's thesis that city-dwellers become crippled if they are unable to map mentally the totality of their city. [69] The idea may have worked quite nicely as a way to account for the experience of Los Angeles, which evolved along the lines of its now vanished railways rather than the orthodox grid-plan of the American city. [70] But a comparison with London shows the tenuousness of the analogy; even cab-drivers who have trained for months to learn 'the knowledge' cannot carry the entire contents of the A-Z Map of London in their heads; moreover, the map which Londoners do use as a mental map is that of the Underground, which famously bears little correspondence to actual layout of the city above. Even a map does not *ipso facto* provide a point of exteriority or leverage, but can easily remain within what Jameson would call the ideological.

Is cognitive mapping, in fact, available to the First-World intellectual anyway? There seems to be some confusion here. In 'Third-World Literature', Jameson argues that 'national allegory' amounts to a form of cognitive mapping which, as a grasping of the social totality comparable to Lukács' class consciousness, is available only to the dominated classes. [71] In this case, it would be presumably unavailable to Jameson himself, as one of the self-proclaimed masters of the world. And yet, although national allegory can, it is implied, operate as a counterforce to the postmodern bewilderment experienced by the American intellectual, at the same time, as we have seen, postmodernism is itself defined by its penetration of the Third World, which no longer allows a foothold for critical effectivity. Once again Jameson finds himself caught up in the process which he describes, writing out his own critical position of enunciation.

Of late, his argument has begun to slide somewhat further, and the spatial struggle for the future has tellingly been projected back into history. In 'Postmodernism', Jameson told us that the bewilderment, loss of co-ordinates, and inability mentally to represent the whole, was a specifically postmodern phenomenon; postmodern hyperspace was thus a particular effect of late capitalism. More recently, however, he has suggested that this kind of disorientation was in fact the product of colonialism and that it can explain the specific aesthetic forms of modernism. But why stop with modernism? The conditions which Jameson describes, in which the 'spatial disjunction' of colonialism has as its 'consequence the inability to grasp the way the system functions as a whole', could be said to constitute the characteristic experience of capitalism itself. [72] Only in a feudal mode of production could the whole have been a part of immediate lived experience in this way. And even then....

Perhaps, as we have earlier suggested, postmodernism, in which the old imperial maps have been lost, is the condition not just of late capitalism, but also of the loss of Eurocentrism, the loss of 'History' as such. In Jameson's terms, postmodernism would then be orientalism's dialectical reversal: a state of dis-orientation. Which would mean that history can no longer be a single story, even though Western history continues to conspire with its 'vast unfinished plot' of exploitation, and Marxism, as Jameson confesses, continues equally to endorse global capitalism – on the grounds that it is the necessary preparation for global socialism. [73] But at the restless margins of the Third World which, let it be said, is neither Nature nor the Unconscious nor of course a homogeneous entity at all, Jameson's totalizing project of a single narrative also confronts a call that remains always excessive to it:

Come, then, comrades, the European game has finally ended.... It is a question of the Third World starting a new history. [74]

Chapter 7

Disorienting Orientalism

I COLONIALISM AND HUMANISM

But how to write a new history? When, as Césaire observed, the only history is white? [1] The critique of the structures of colonialism might seem a marginal activity in relation to the mainstream political issues of literary and cultural theory, catering only for minorities or for those with a specialist interest in colonial history. But although it is concerned with the geographical peripheries of metropolitan European culture, its long-term strategy is to effect a radical restructuring of European thought and, particularly, historiography.

This has not been a matter of setting up the critique of colonialism in opposition to European culture but rather of demonstrating the extent to which they are already deeply implicated within each other. European thought since the Renaissance would be as unthinkable without the impact of colonialism as the history of the world since the Renaissance would be inconceivable without the effects of Europeanization. So it is not an issue of removing colonial thinking from European thought, of purging it, like today's dream of 'stamping out' racism. It is rather a question of repositioning European systems of knowledge so as to demonstrate the long history of their operation as the effect of their colonial other, a reversal encapsulated in Fanon's observation: 'Europe is literally the creation of the Third World'. [2] We should not assume either that the anti-colonialism has been confined to our own age: sympathy for the oppressed other, and pressure for decolonization, is as old as European colonialism itself. [3] What has been new in the years since the Second World War during which, for the most part, the decolonization of the European empires has taken place, has been the accompanying attempt to decolonize European thought and the forms of its history as well. It thus marks that fundamental shift and cultural crisis currently characterized as postmodernism.

This project could be said to have been initiated in 1961 by Fanon's *The Wretched of the Earth*. The book is both a revolutionary manifesto of decolonization and the founding analysis of the effects of colonialism upon colonized peoples and their cultures. Throughout, the Third World is put forward as a radical alternative to the contemporary order of world power and its two rival ideologies of capitalism and socialism. Despite the influence of Sartre, Fanon has little time for the central contention of the *Critique of Dialectical Reason*, published only the year before, that men as self-conscious agents create the totality of history. He quickly points to what this means when put in the colonial context:

> The settler makes history and is conscious of making it. And because he constantly refers to the history of his mother country, he clearly indicates that he himself is the extension of that mother country. Thus the history which he writes is not the history of the country which he plunders but the history of his own nation in regard to all that she skims off, all that she violates and starves. (40)

If men make history, here Fanon shows how the men and women who are the objects of that history are condemned to immobility and silence. It is to these men and women that his own book is addressed. His criticism of Europe does not stop at the violent history of colonial appropriation. For the effect of colonialism, he suggests, is to dehumanize the native, a process which, paradoxically, finds its justification in the values of Western humanism. This humanism Fanon consistently attacks and ridicules. So, for example, in the Conclusion, he urges his readers:

> Leave this Europe where they are never done talking of Man, yet murder men everywhere they find them, at the corner of every one of their own streets, in all the corners of the globe. For centuries they have stifled almost the whole of humanity in the name of a so-called spiritual experience....
>   That same Europe where they were never done talking of Man, and where they never stopped proclaiming that they were only anxious for the welfare of Man: today we know with what sufferings humanity has paid for every one of their triumphs of the mind. (251)

As might have been expected, it was this aspect of Fanon's critique which particularly affected Sartre. In the *Critique of Dialectical Reason* Sartre rejects the humanist notion that there is an ahistorical essence of man, although the book is still founded on an attempt to put a very European 'Man' at the centre of history. Doubtless Fanon's intervention can be added to the list of reasons why Sartre's project foundered.

'Decolonization', Fanon comments, 'which sets out to change the order of the world, is, obviously, a programme of complete disorder' (27), and no more so than in the disorder it sets up in the values attached to European humanism. Sartre's remarkable Preface to *The Wretched of the Earth*, which, by contrast, is specifically addressed to the European reader, marks the opening move by a European in the critique of European culture from the perspective of its involvement in colonialism. Sartre does not try to come to terms with contemporary history by lamenting the decline of the West, nor does he merely acknowledge the violence of the history of European domination. The significance of Sartre's essay stems from the fact that he acknowledges that, although he himself had spent the past few years trying to correct Marxism's economism to a humanism, humanism itself, often validated amongst the highest values of European civilization, was deeply complicit with the violent negativity of colonialism, and played a crucial part in its ideology. The formation of the ideas of human nature, humanity and the universal qualities of the human mind as the common good of an ethical civilization occurred at the same time as those particularly violent centuries in the history of the world now known as the era of Western colonialism. The effect of this was to dehumanize the various subject-peoples: in Sartre's words, 'to wipe out their traditions, to substitute our language for theirs and to destroy their culture without giving them ours' (1).

Now, however, that disorder is being reversed. 'For we in Europe too are being decolonized', Sartre announces:

> that is to say that the settler which is in every one of us is being savagely rooted out. Let us look at ourselves, if we can bear to, and see what is becoming of us. First, we must face that unexpected revelation, the striptease of our humanism. There you can see it, quite naked, and it's not a pretty sight. It was nothing but an ideology of lies, a perfect justification for pillage; its honeyed words, its affectation of sensibility were only alibis for our aggressions. (21)

It was the recognition of this use of the human as a highly politicized category which led to the sustained critique of 'Man' by a broad range of post-war thinkers in the movement known as 'anti-humanism'. Few politico-intellectual projects have generated as much controversy, hostility, and, ironically but perhaps symptomatically, intolerance. What is striking is that few of those defending humanism ever ask where anti-humanism came from. The standard definition states that it is derived from the critique of Marxist humanism initiated by Lévi-Strauss and Althusser against Sartre and others such as Garaudy in the French Communist Party. But this account hardly tells us more than that the critique of Marxist humanism came from the anti-humanists. Taking Althusser's strategic homogenization of all humanisms into one on trust, it altogether neglects the Marxist-humanist attempt, by Lukács, Sartre, and others, to found a 'new humanism' which would substitute, for the Enlightenment's conception of man's unchanging nature, a new 'historical humanism' that would see 'man as a product of himself and of his own activity in history'. [4] But that very historical activity formed the basis for the critiques of both kinds of humanism by non-European writers such as Césaire and Fanon. This version of anti-humanism starts with the realization of humanism's involvement in the history of colonialism, which shows that the two are not so easily separable. For from the colonial perspective, humanism began as a form of legitimation produced as a self-justification by the colonizers for their own people, but later, as what Abdul JanMohammed has distinguished as the 'dominant' phase of colonialism shifted to the 'hegemonic' phase of neocolonialism, humanism was utilized as a form of ideological control of the colonized peoples. [5] This in turn set the structures of neocolonialism in place ready for decolonization. Fanon describes it as follows:

> The colonialist bourgeoisie, in its narcissistic dialogue, expounded by the members of its universities, had in fact deeply implanted in the minds of the colonized intellectual that the essential qualities remain eternal in spite of all the blunders men may make: the essential qualities of the West, of course. (36)

So those universal essential features which define the human mask over the assimilation of the human itself with European values; an identification perhaps clearest in the Marxist definition of history which states that if history is the product of human actions, then it only can be said to begin properly when 'primitive' societies give way to (European) civilization. To criticize humanism in this context therefore does not mean that you do not like human beings and have no ethics – the gist of certain attacks on 'anti-humanism' – but rather the reverse. It questions the use of the human as an explanatory category that purports to provide a rational understanding of 'man' – an assumed universal predicated on the exclusion and marginalization of his Others, such as 'woman' or 'the native'.

A good example of such a questioning can be found in Roland Barthes' short essay, 'The Great Family of Man'. [6] Barthes is discussing the well-known photographic exhibition which is organized around the fiction of the universality of fundamental human experiences. Barthes points to the way that 'The Family of Man' projects the myth of a global human community in two stages: first, there is an emphasis on difference – a multiplicity of exotic varieties of everyday activities of work, play, birth, death, etc. are compiled; but such diversity is only introduced so that it can be taken away again in the name of an underlying unity which implies that at some level all such experiences are identical, despite their wide cultural and historical differences, that underneath there is one human nature and therefore a common human essence. Barthes argues that such humanism, so reassuring at the sentimental level, functions simply to override differences 'which we shall here quite simply call "injustices" ':

> Any classic humanism postulates that in scratching the history of men a little, the relativity of their institutions or the superficial diversity of their skins (but why not ask the parents of Emmet Till, the young Negro

assassinated by the Whites what *they* think of *The Great Family of Man?*), one very quickly reaches the solid rock of a universal human nature. (101)

No one, of course, denies that there are universal facts, such as birth or death. But take away their historical and cultural context, and anything which is said about them can only be tautological. As Chandra Talpade Mohanty observes, 'that women mother in a variety of societies is not as significant as the *value* attached to mothering in these societies'. [7] Similarly, Barthes argues that the suggestion that work is as natural as birth or death negates its historicity, its different conditions, modes, and ends – specificities which matter to such an extent,

> that it will never be fair to confuse in a purely gestural identity the colonial and the Western worker (let us also ask the North African workers of the Goutte d'Or district in Paris what they think of *The Great Family of Man*). (102)

As his examples show, Barthes consistently places the claimed universal values of humanism in the ironic perspective of the facts of Western colonialism and racism. This is reinforced by what is perhaps the best known analysis of *Mythologies*, the *Paris-Match* cover of a young black soldier in French uniform saluting the tricolour. Barthes demonstrates how this photograph has a meaning, namely the reinforcement of a colonial ideology, the family of the French Empire: 'that all her sons, without any colour discrimination, faithfully serve under her flag, and that there is no better answer to the detractors of an alleged colonialism than the zeal shown by this Negro in serving his so-called oppressors' (116). [8]

As Barthes' analyses indicate, the French critique of humanism was conducted from the first as a part of a political critique of colonialism. Colonial discourse analysis, therefore, shows why 'anti-humanism' was not merely a philosophical project. The anti-humanists charged that the category of the human, however exalted in its conception, was too often invoked only in order to put the male before the female, or to classify other 'races' as sub-human, and therefore not subject to the ethical prescriptions applicable to 'humanity' at large. As Sartre put it: 'Humanism is the counterpart of racism: it is a practice of exclusion'. [9] This contradiction, according to Fanon, was resolved in the following way:

> Western bourgeois racial prejudice as regards the nigger and the Arab is a racism of contempt; it is a racism which minimises what it hates. Bourgeois ideology, however, which is the proclamation of an essential equality between men, manages to appear logical in its own eyes by inviting the sub-men to become human, and to take as their prototype Western humanity as incarnated in the Western bourgeoisie. (131)

A classic example of this kind of double logic would be John Stuart Mill's basing his argument for liberty on the prior division of the world into cultures of civilization and barbarism; or, at the level of aesthetics, the anthropologizing of Kant's notion of the universal claim in questions of taste into the basis for the claims by European critics that the perceptions and experiences represented by European writers achieve the status of universal human truths, without any knowledge as to whether this could possibly be so or not. [10] How universal would the Shakespearian 'human' values of the English have been to the people, say, of the city of Benin as they watched the sacking of their city in commemoration of Queen Victoria's 1898 Jubilee? Fanon gives us an answer:

> The violence with which the supremacy of white values is affirmed and the aggressiveness which has permeated the victory of these values over the ways of life and of thought of the native mean that, in revenge, the native laughs in mockery when Western values are mentioned in front of him. (33)

Every time a literary critic claims a universal ethical, moral, or emotional instance in a piece of English literature, he or she colludes in the violence of the colonial legacy in which the European value or truth is defined as the universal one.

The structuralist critique of humanism was produced in the context of the general refusal to acknowledge that such violence is intrinsic to Western culture and not simply accidental to it. Structuralism's so-called 'decentring of the subject' was in many respects itself an ethical activity, derived from a suspicion that the ontological category of 'the human' and 'human nature' had been inextricably associated with the violence of Western history. If the human is itself revealed as a conflictual concept it can no longer be presented as an undisturbed ethical end. As is well known, the preoccupation with the 'problem of the subject' was concerned to articulate the ways in which human subjects are not unitary essences but products of a conflictual psychic and political economy. One way of addressing this difficulty was to redefine the self through the model of the different grammatical positions which it is obliged to take up in language, which disallow the centrality and unity of the 'I' assumed by humanism. It is precisely this inscription of alterity within the self that can allow for a new relation to ethics: the self has to come to terms with the fact that it is also a second and a third person. The Foucauldian redefinition of the self according to its position within language, for example, showed how once engaged in any kind of linguistic activity it is displaced, decentred, and variously positioned as a subject according to different systems, institutions, forms of classification and hierarchies of power. As Spivak puts it, 'structuralists question humanism by exposing its hero – the sovereign subject as author, the subject of authority, legitimacy, and power', a critique which extends to the connection between the production of the humanist subject and the general process of colonialism by which Europe consolidated itself politically as sovereign subject of the world. [11] With the West's gradual loss of suzerainty the First World is now having to come to terms with the fact that it is no longer always positioned in the first person with regard to the Second or Third Worlds. As Sartre put it, 'Europe is springing leaks everywhere. What then has happened? It is simply that in the past we made history and now it is being made of us' (23).

A particularly symptomatic example of this strategic blindness and refusal to come to terms with the violence intrinsic to Western culture is the way in which Fascism and the Holocaust are often presented as if they were a unique aberration, a dark perversion of Western rationalism or a particular effect of German culture. Here the differences between the French and the Frankfurt school, which has remained curiously oblivious to the whole problem of colonialism, becomes most apparent. It took a Césaire or a Fanon to point out that Fascism was simply colonialism brought home to Europe. [12] Sartre spells out the implications of this argument:

> Liberty, equality, fraternity, love, honour, patriotism and what have you. All this did not prevent us from making anti-racial speeches about dirty niggers, dirty Jews and dirty Arabs. High-minded people, liberal or just soft-hearted, protest that they were shocked by such inconsistency; but they were either mistaken or dishonest, for with us there is nothing more consistent than a racist humanism since the European has only been able to become a man through creating slaves and monsters. (22)

Sartre, however, is in many ways more sanguine than the more fervent anti-humanists who were unwilling to recognize humanism as a conflictual concept, divided against itself. He demonstrates why a straightforward anti-humanism was always problematic insofar as it never recognized that the contradictory structure of the humanism made difficulties for the assumption that it could simply be opposed. For humanism is itself already anti-humanist. That is the problem. It necessarily produces the non-human in setting up its problematic boundaries. But at the same time, it can also produce positive effects. As even Althusser recognized, humanism found genuinely revolutionary echoes in Third-World struggles. [13] The question then becomes whether we should – and whether we can – differentiate between a humanism which harks back critically, or uncritically, to the mainstream of Enlightenment culture and Fanon's new 'new humanism' which attempts to reformulate it as a non-conflictual concept no longer defined against a sub-human other. For to some extent Europe itself fulfils this function in Fanon. As we shall see in the case of Edward Said, the contradictions of humanism continue to perplex anti-colonialist thought.

What is clear is that such challenges as Fanon's to the limits of Western ethnocentricity have had the effect of decentring and displacing the norms of Western knowledge: questioning, for example, the assumptions of

Western historicist history as an ordered whole with a single meaning, or of
Western nationalist discourse which, as Bhabha puts it, 'normalizes its own
history of expansion and exploitation by inscribing the history of the other
in a fixed hierarchy of civil progress'. [14] In addition to the rewriting of the
history of non-European histories and cultures, analysis of colonialism
therefore shifts the perspective of European history and culture so as to
interrogate the fundamental structures and assumptions of Western knowledge. The legacy of colonialism is as much a problem for the West as it is
for the scarred lands in the world beyond.

II SAID AND THE DISCOURSE OF 'ORIENTALISM'

The appropriation of French theory by Anglo-American intellectuals is
marked, and marred, by its consistent excision of the issue of Eurocentrism
and its relation to colonialism. Not until Edward Said's Orientalism (1978)
did it become a significant issue for Anglo-American literary theory. [15] Two
years earlier Said had complained quite justifiably that 'the literary-cultural
establishment as a whole has declared the serious study of imperialism off
limits'; it would not be too much to suggest that Orientalism broke that
proscription, and as such cannot be underestimated in its importance and in
its effects. [16] Nor would it be overstating the case to say that much of the
current pressure for the political, particularly in the US where there is no
recent substantial tradition of political criticism, has followed from the work
of Said. His injunction that criticism must be affiliated to the world of which
it is a part has exercised a powerful moral pressure. It has also enabled those
from minorities, whether categorized as racial, sexual, social, or economic,
to stake their critical work in relation to their own political positioning
rather than feel obliged to assume the transcendent values of the dominant
discourse of criticism. This in turn has contributed to the widespread
interrogation of the history and presuppositions of that dominant discourse
and, particularly, its relation to Western imperialism in both its colonial and
neocolonial phases.

In Orientalism Said argues that analysis of the politics of Western
ethnocentrism must begin with the question of representation as formulated
by Foucault. Foucault, it will be recalled, contended that knowledge is
constructed according to a discursive field which creates a representation of
the object of knowledge, its constitution and its limits; any writer has to
conform to this in order to communicate, to be understood, to remain 'in
the true', and thus to be accepted. Said shows how this also works for the
European constructions of knowledge about other cultures. Orientalism
argues that a complex set of representations was fabricated which for the
West effectively became 'the Orient' and determined its understanding of it,
as well as providing the basis for its subsequent self-appointed imperialist
rule. Disclosing a closely interrelated web of writings that stretch from

literary, historical, scholarly accounts to political, military, and imperial administrative ones, Said suggests that the former produced the Orient for the eventual appropriation by the latter.

As this might indicate, what *Orientalism* demonstrates above all is the deep complicity of academic forms of knowledge with institutions of power. As Said puts it: 'insofar as it was a science of incorporation and inclusion by virtue of which the Orient was constituted and then introduced in to Europe, Orientalism was a scientific movement whose analogue in the world of empirical politics was the Orient's colonial accumulation and acquisition by Europe'. [17] He therefore analyses the mode of operation and the detailed texture of cultural domination of an academic discipline that, he argues, constitutes nothing less than a science of imperialism. The question that follows is to what extent other knowledges are implicated in this or other sciences of domination, knowledges that enable exploitation and oppression of differing kinds. Does this stricture, Said asks, also apply to apparently progressive disciplines such as women's or black studies – or even, one might add, to the study of colonialism itself? The analyses of *Orientalism* force us to the recognition that all knowledge may be contaminated, implicated even in its very formal or 'objective' structures. To the extent that all knowledge is produced within institutions of various sorts, there is always a determined relation to the state and to its political practices at home and abroad.

The task then becomes not only the identification of the parameters of such knowledge, but just as importantly the theorization of how it is possible to produce knowledge of any other kind. An objection to *Orientalism* has always been that it provides no alternative to the phenomenon which it criticizes. [18] Said refuses to be drawn into this argument, on the grounds that there is no reason why there should be an alternative at all: the general, essentialist paradigms which constitute knowledge of 'the Orient' also constitute 'the Orient' as an object in the first place – to provide an alternative to Orientalism would be to accept the existence of the very thing in dispute. There may indeed be other knowledges, but they would take different, multifarious forms – unlike the Western creation of the Orient as a generalized 'other' which is constituted as the same everywhere and for all time (there could be no clearer instance, perhaps, of how the other is turned into the same).

On the other hand, the entirely correct refusal to offer an alternative to Orientalism does not solve the problem of how Said separates himself from the coercive structures of knowledge that he is describing. What method can he use to analyse his object that escapes the terms of his own critique? The absence of such a method constitutes the significant lacuna of the book, with the result that in many cases Said finds himself repeating the very structures that he censures. Typical of this kind of difficulty would be his criticism that Orientalism created an eternal unchanging platonic vision of the Orient –

'essentialist, idealist' (246) – having argued himself that as a discursive construction, Orientalism is characterized by an 'essence' that has endured 'unchanged' (42, 6). In the same way, he criticizes the early Orientalists for their tendency to dehistoricize the Orient by presenting it in terms of 'vision' rather than through the narratives of history, but then goes on to praise (the curiously popular) Auerbach, the model for his detached 'critical consciousness', for his ability to write a general history of Western culture that achieves 'true vision' (259). Or again, Said follows his critique of the notion of 'types' with the unexpected claim that Massignon and Gibb can be treated as representative types that epitomise general differences between 'the French' and 'the English'. [19] This problem can be seen to be more serious at a general level in relation to the whole project of the book in which, according to the logic of Said's own argument, any account of 'Orientalism' as an object, discursive or otherwise, will both repeat the essentialism that he condemns and, more problematically, will itself create a representation that cannot be identical to the object it identifies. In other words, Said's account will be no truer to Orientalism than Orientalism is to the actual Orient, assuming there could ever be such a thing.

At a theoretical level, these difficulties could be compared to those encountered in feminism: if 'woman' is the constructed category of a patriarchal society, how do you posit an alternative without simply repeating the category in question or asserting a transhistorical essence that the representation travesties? The difference, however, would be that whereas feminism is nevertheless reluctant to discard the category of 'woman' altogether, despite its problems, Said has no investment in saving the category of the Orient, and indeed declares that he hopes to effect its dissolution. The question then becomes what kind of representation can be posited – if at all?

Before it is possible to provide any counter-description to Orientalism or other comparable forms of colonialism, the problem of the critic's own methodology must therefore be addressed if he or she is to do anything more than simply repeat the structures that are being criticized. The problem returns of how to effect critical distance. If it is necessary, as Said demonstrates, to be inside such structures in order to make any argument at all, it is also, he argues, vital to be outside them in order to subvert them. But what kind of knowledge would this be? In 'Orientalism Reconsidered' (1984) Said admits that the question that remains unanswered in the book is:

> how the production of knowledge best serves communal, as opposed to factional, ends, how knowledge that is non-dominative and non-coercive can be produced in a setting that is deeply inscribed with the politics, the considerations, the positions, and the strategies of power. (OR 15)

Said's inability to provide any alternative forms of knowledge, or a theoretical model for such knowledge, results from his unwillingness to pursue this problem of methodology in any rigorous way. But if he does not pursue it, it pursues him: despite his opposition to totalization, once again the critic becomes entrammelled in his own writing. The theoretical difficulties which emerge in *Orientalism* are highly instructive for any attempt at the decolonization of European thought. Samuel Weber puts the problem succinctly: 'a social and historical critique which does not consider the conflictual structure of its own discursive operations will only reproduce the constraints it is seeking to displace'. [20]

III PROBLEMS OF METHODOLOGY

1 Representation and the real

Said's most significant argument about the discursive conditions of knowledge is that the texts of Orientalism 'can *create* not only knowledge but also the very reality they appear to describe' (94). At the same time his most important political claim is that as a system of learning about the Orient, Orientalism has close ties to enabling socio-economic and political institutions to the extent that it can be seen to have justified colonialism in advance as well as subsequently facilitating its successful operation. Said's wish to make both these points poses, however, a major theoretical problem: on the one hand he suggests that Orientalism merely consists of a representation that has nothing to do with the '"real" Orient', denying any correspondence between Orientalism and the Orient, looking instead for Orientalism's 'internal consistency' as a discursive object or field (5, 203), while on the other hand he argues that its knowledge was put in the service of colonial conquest, occupation, and administration. This means that at a certain moment Orientalism as representation did have to encounter the 'actual' conditions of what was there, and that it showed itself effective at a material level as a form of power and control. How then can Said argue that the 'Orient' is just a representation, if he also wants to claim that 'Orientalism' provided the necessary knowledge for actual colonial conquest?

Said posits a genealogy of Orientalism in which its essential characteristics can be found to repeat themselves throughout different historical periods up to the present day. But his argument that Orientalism is not just an idea or even a system of academic knowledge means that he also has to demonstrate its complicity with the exercise of power; at a certain point knowledge must be shown to articulate with the forces of colonial appropriation; the essentialist system of knowledge with history. The book therefore falls into two halves, the first concerned with the invention of the Orient by Europe, and its construction as a representation, the second with the moment when this representation, and the academic knowledge that was fabricated around it, became an instrument in the service of colonial power as the Orient shifted from 'an alien to a colonial space', and an academic attitude became an instrumental one, participating in and shaping oriental history for the first time. [21]

Said attempts to articulate this difficult difference through his idea that, in the later nineteenth century, essentializing 'vision' was increasingly susceptible to the pressure of 'narrative' or history (240). These are hinged together through a rather unexpected invocation of the psychoanalytic distinction between the latent and the manifest, so that the latent content continues unchanged, while any transformation is confined to the manifest, a model which at time seems to resemble less the operation of the dream work than Foucault's 'positive unconscious of knowledge' or even Saussure's distinction between *langue* and *parole* (206). But neither really solves the problem of how Orientalism both changed and stayed the same. A little later Said redefines his model by arguing that there are really two forms of Orientalism – that of the apparatuses of classical scholarship, constructing its object, and that of the 'descriptions of a present, modern, manifest Orient articulated by travellers, pilgrims, statesmen' (222–3) – which existed in tension with each other and finally converged: 'what the scholarly Orientalist defined as the "essential" Orient was sometimes contradicted, but in many cases was confirmed, when the Orient became an actual administrative obligation' (223). Said therefore attempts to solve his problem of how the representation articulated with the actual by creating two different kinds of Orientalism – while at the same time hedging his bets as to how much the representation did indeed correspond to the actual. He goes on to suggest that the tension between the two Orientalisms of the 'representation' and the 'real' first occurred with Silvestre de Sacy, that is, in the early years of the nineteenth century, thus producing a different history for Orientalism which up to this point has specifically been denied any contradiction or affirmation by a 'real' Orient until the colonial period of the late nineteenth century. This endeavour to solve the problem of articulation by changing the story fails, however, to solve the original theoretical problem of how a representation that it is claimed bears no relation to its putative object could nevertheless be put in the service of the control and domination of that object. But what becomes apparent is that while Said wants to argue that Orientalism has a hegemonic consistency, his own representation of it becomes increasingly conflictual. His refusal of a theory, his restless and sometimes contradictory shiftings of ground can be seen as an attempt to get out of this dilemma. The very vacillation from an inner dissension that he disallows in Orientalism re-emerges in his own writings.

Furthermore, if Said denies that there is any actual Orient which could provide a true account of the Orient represented by Orientalism, how can he claim in any sense that the representation is false? Having denied the general category 'Orient' altogether, he sidesteps this difficulty by positing another one in its place which we may call 'the human'. Unlike his theoretical mentor Foucault, who was specifically concerned to attack the human as an explanatory or experiential category, Said constantly appeals to the values of humanism and to the notion of the 'human spirit'. [22] His fundamental thesis is that Orientalism involves an attempt to eliminate 'humanistic values', and that 'Orientalist reality is both antihuman and persistent'. [23] 'Can one', Said asks, 'divide human reality ... and survive the consequences humanly?' [24] Criticizing the attempt to 'limit the human encounter between races' he invokes a general 'human experience', 'human history', 'human community', and speaks approvingly of a writer's ability 'to penetrate to the human heart of any text'. [25] In a perceptive review of *Orientalism*, James Clifford has pointed to the difficulties raised by Said's castigations of Orientalists for their tendency to negate the reality of human experience:

> Said characterizes the human realities thus elided with quotations from Yeats – '"the uncontrollable mystery on the bestial floor" in which all humans live'....
>
> It is still an open question, of course, whether an African pastoralist shares the same existential 'bestial floor' with an Irish poet and his readers. And it is a general feature of humanist common denominators that they are meaningless, since they bypass the local cultural codes that make personal experience articulate. [26]

The very possibility and power of making such a claim, Clifford adds, is itself 'a privilege invented by a totalizing Western liberalism'. Perhaps, given Yeats' links with fascism, he is in any case not the best example through which to cite the universal humanistic values of 'ordinary human reality'. This returns us to the problem of humanism itself.

'We are humanists', Said declares tautologically in a discussion of 'American "Left" Literary Criticism', 'because there is something called humanism, legitimated by the culture, given a positive value by it'. [27] In other words, the idea of the human which Said opposes to the Western representation of the Orient is itself derived from the Western humanist tradition. It was produced from the very same culture that constructed not just anti-humanist Orientalism, but also, as Said himself points out, the racist ideology of the superiority of the 'White Man' whose rhetoric of Arnoldian 'high cultural humanism' was defined against the intellectual and cultural depravity of the colonies (227–8). That anti-humanist Orientalism was the product of a humanist culture suggests a complexity that Said seems unwilling to address. If humanism is a conflictual concept, as Fanon argues, to what extent will Said's humanism itself remain marked by anti-humanism? Certainly it is possible to point to the way in which his own text repeats these contradictions which it leaves unresolved, once again highlighting the more general problem of his own relation to the theory that he utilizes. At times, as in those moments when he characterizes the reality of the East according to the terms of the universalist claims of European high culture, his analysis of Orientalism comes to seem remarkably close to an Orientalist work itself. This leads us back to our initial problem: how does any form of knowledge – including *Orientalism* – escape the terms of *Orientalism*'s critique?

2 The role of the intellectual

> What is the role of the intellectual? Is he there to validate the culture and state of which he is a part? What importance must he give to an independent critical consciousness, an *oppositional* consciousness? (326)

Said's constant questioning of the role of the intellectual assumes – against the evidence and argument of his own book – his or her ability to operate in a separate space independent from contemporary ideology, even without the customary benefit of the scientific knowledge of Marxism. But without it how is it possible, indeed is it possible, to achieve a critical distance? For Said, it comes, somewhat problematically, from 'experience', combined with a 'sceptical critical consciousness' (327). Attacking Orientalist scholarship for having been 'blind to human reality', Said goes on to praise those scholars who are both methodologically self-conscious and sensitive to the material before them, that is, to experience itself:

> I consider Orientalism's failure to have been a human as much as an intellectual one; for in having to take up a position of irreducible opposition to a region of the world it considered alien to its own, Orientalism failed to identify with human experience, failed also to see it as human experience. (328)

An ethic of fidelity to experience, of methodological self-consciousness, together with an identification with the common enterprise of promoting the human community is apparently enough to prevent the 'seductive degradation of knowledge' which *Orientalism* charts in such detail. The question, however, is whether the category of experience, together with that of a 'critical consciousness', both of which derive from traditions that have undergone detailed critical interrogation in the twentieth century, can be used in an unproblematical way. Setting aside the problem examined at length by the phenomenologists of its reliance on notions of consciousness and presence, is not 'experience' itself always experienced, analysed and given meaning through forms of knowledge that will themselves be already ideological? [28] It cannot be posited as prior to knowledge as such. Said's difficulty is that his ethical and theoretical values are all so deeply involved in the history of the culture that he criticizes, that they undermine his claims for the possibility of the individual being in a position to choose, in an uncomplicated process of separation, to be both inside and outside his or her own culture.

Indeed, insofar as such a culture is already contradictory, perhaps the very possibility of being inside or outside is already a part of that culture. This certainly seems to be Said's own position. He is, it is true, suspicious of culture as the totalizing system defined in nationalistic terms by Arnold and others. In a later essay he asks:

> To what degree has culture collaborated in the worst excesses of the State, from its imperial wars and colonial settlements to its self-justifying institutions of antihuman repression, racial hatred, economic and behavioural manipulation? [29]

And yet, however much he wishes to question its conditions and effects, it is noticeable that for Said culture always remains exclusively European high culture, to which is ascribed a special ability to effect resistance to the state:

> Culture becomes the opportunity for a refracted verbal enterprise whose relation to the State is always understated.... The realistic novel plays a major role in this enterprise, for it is the novel – as it becomes ever more 'novel' in the work of James, Hardy, Joyce – that organizes reality and knowledge in such a way as to make them susceptible to systematic verbal reincarnation. [30]

It is hardly a startling observation to suggest that the realist novel presents or subverts a particular – usually dominant – ideology. But what is more striking is this sense that the novels of James, Hardy or Joyce play 'a major role' in the relation of culture to the state. Although keen to emphasize institutional factors, Said nowhere comes to terms with the fact that such novels play what role they do almost exclusively through the state's educational institutions. Nowhere does he feel it necessary to consider the role or significance of anything that does not correspond to the most traditional notions of culture and literature. Said's culture, for all his reservations, resembles nothing so much as that of Arnold, Eliot or Leavis – there seems to be no irony intended at all when Said, the great campaigner against racism and ethnocentrism, laments in Leavisite tones the loss of culture's 'discrimination and evaluation' (292). There has, of course, been a long academic tradition in which high culture has been regarded as the crucial battleground – and in these terms the intellectual may indeed have a major interrogative role to play; but in the actualities of a world which is dominated by diverse forms of culture, such a role is distinctly muted. The long tradition of Brecht, Benjamin and the Frankfurt School which has interrogated the privileging of high culture has also argued that resistance is by no means confined to critical consciousnesses which stand comfortably, or even uncomfortably, outside it: resistance, like power, is part of culture itself.

3 The universal and the particular

Although Said's emphasis on Orientalism as a discursive structure is clearly derived from Foucault, he differs from him in one important respect. As we might anticipate from his retrieval of the category of the human, and his endorsement of the validity of individual experience as affording a theoretical and political base, Said rejects Foucault's downgrading of the role of individual agency. He comments:

> Unlike Michel Foucault, to whose work I am greatly indebted, I do believe in the determining imprint of individual writers upon the otherwise anonymous collective body of texts constituting a discursive formation like Orientalism. (23)

This is necessary from a theoretical point of view because, according to the value of experience, only the individual is in a position to adopt a critical stance with regard to the political and the social, or system and culture, all of which are anti-individualist and tend to override the values of the human. Apart from the fact that, as has already been mentioned, this contradicts the main thesis of *Orientalism* itself, it poses another methodological difficulty, namely how the individual can then be related to the social. As Said puts it:

> How then to recognize individuality and to reconcile it with its intelligent, and by no means passive or merely dictatorial, general and hegemonic context? (9)

Whether he proposes a reconciliation, or, as elsewhere, a dialectic, between the individual and the collective formation, this articulation of individual instance to the general poses a major uneasy question for Said – one which he admits was equally problematic for the Orientalists themselves.

This is entirely to be expected insofar as Said's move simply returns us to the age-old philosophical conundrum of the relation of the particular to the universal, and thus of free will to necessity. Foucault's contribution, like those of many recent theorists, was to get out of this by arguing against the terms of the opposition as such, moving into the realm of the phantasm (which might, as a bad copy, have been a promising way to have approached the problem of Orientalism's relation to its object). Said's revision of Foucault simply takes us back to the problem with which he had begun. So, in the most traditional, indeed theological, manner, Said wants to hang on to the individual as agent and instigator while retaining a certain notion of system and of historical determination. He must do the latter in order to argue for the existence of such a thing as 'Orientalism' at all, but on the other hand he must retain a notion of individual agency in order to retain the possibility of his own ability to criticize and change it. It seems that, once again, he must have it both ways. In fact, however, the two, far from being opposed, are rather mirror images of each other: positing a hegemonic Orientalism as a totality which has no reference – for there is no object to which it corresponds – nor inner conflict, but solely an intention to dominate, Said must then demand a counter-intention from outside the system for any resistance. This double bind, instead of being recognized as such, is given a theoretical corollary through an awkward meshing of Foucault's discursive system with Gramsci's organic intellectual, embodied in a methodological distinction between 'strategic location' – the author's position in a text with regard to the material he writes about – and 'strategic formation' – the relationship between texts and the way in which groups of texts acquire referential power. However, this *ad hoc* synthesis, like the invocation of Vico's statement that men make their own history (without Marx's crucial qualification), cannot provide an adequate theoretical solution to the perennial philosophical chestnut to which Said returns. Rather it repeats the difficulty which we have already encountered in his critique of historicism and the political effects of its Eurocentric universalism, where the rejection of totalizing systems for particularism appeared to risk substituting a total fragmentation for total synthesis. [31] The problem of how the generalizing historical representation or scheme can be articulated with the experience or reality to which it is opposed remains for him unsolved. For Said takes the totalization of the historicism to which he is opposed too much at its own word: as we have seen, the problem is as much how it can be closed, as how it can be opened.

Elsewhere, endorsing Foucault's distinction between the 'specific' and the 'universal' intellectual, Said proposes a role for the intellectual not as organic in the Gramscian sense, but as involved in particularities, in 'local, specific struggles'. [32] But unlike the Foucauldian singular or the Lyotardian event, which remain unassimilable to general categories, Said's particularity is specifically pitted against the totality. Moreover, as Spivak points out, the very category of 'the intellectual' is itself another universal. [33] Said's account therefore assumes the very totalities which he opposes, as is suggested by the grandiose claim implied in his *The World, the Text, and the Critic*. This title, which posits a separation between 'the world', 'the text' and 'the critic', as if the last two could at any time elect to avoid being part of the first, suggests a basic conceptual problem in its assumption of the possibility of an 'outside'. Said's model for the critic continues to be that he or she should occupy a space of 'critical consciousness' 'between the dominant culture and the totalizing forms of critical systems'. As with the book title, this assumes that the dominant culture and critical systems can be totalizing, homogeneous, monological (a supposition we have already found to be problematic), and that the only possible conflict can arise from the intervention of the outsider critic, a romantic alienated being battling like Byron's Manfred against the totality of the universe. There can be no internal conflict that can be exploited, no heterogeneity, no contradictory logics, no totalization that always requires supplementation, no writing that runs away with an unassimilable excess. By contrast Said suggests that his own theoretical perspective is 'hybrid' (23), which means that he does not adhere rigorously to any of the theoretical positions which he invokes. But how can this guarantee the degree of distance or subversion that he claims for his own 'critical consciousness'? By assuming that any 'method' must be univocal and totalizing, his own anti-method simply takes up the opposite pole of the antagonistic dialectic he has created. As we might expect, this means that he then inevitably acts out and repeats at a textual level the dualistic structures from which he is unable to free himself.

According to Said, criticism must distance itself from the dominant culture and assume an adversarial position. He censures the practitioners of universalizing historicism such as Perry Anderson because such a position depends 'on the same displaced percipient and historicist observer who had been an Orientalist or colonial traveller three generations ago' (OR 22). But to what extent does his own 'critical consciousness', standing outside both culture and theoretical, philosophical or political system, do more than produce another version of 'the same displaced percipient and historicist observer'? It is all very well to praise Noam Chomsky's 'independent radicalism' (OR 24), but when Said speaks of the critical consciousness as 'having initially detached itself from the dominant culture, having thereafter adopted a situation and responsible adversary position' (224), does not this beg the question? What are the grounds for the choice of a 'situation'? Individual experience? What are the principles from which a culture is seen to need an adversarial position? What is a 'responsible adversary position'? Is an 'oppositional' position necessarily the most effective politically? How dominant is a dominant culture? How would such choices relate to political objectives? Where could that 'outside' space be? From what position and theoretical postulates should the critic intervene – given that the critic is supposed to be as distant from theory as from the culture? Although it does not apply to Said's own politics, the possibility for the critic who imagines that he maintains a critical distance both from the dominant culture and theoretical practices can become restricted to a quietism of the most passive type, clutching to a hope that an individualistic criticism will make us better, more aware people. The substitution of an always problematic 'critical distance' for a politics becomes only too marked. Ironically, while Said writes trenchantly of the lack in the United States of a close correlation between literary and everyday politics and the weakness of Marxist criticism which becomes a mere academic exercise as a result, the general position for the critic which he postulates suffers from exactly the same dissociation which he criticizes. [34]

4 'Textualism'

As soon as Said has set up the traditional opposition of particular versus universal, individual agency as opposed to the determinations of culture or system, the problem remains by definition insoluble. To the totalizing culture the individual opposes a consciousness derived from experience: but how has that consciousness or experience been produced outside that culture if it is indeed totalizing? While Said objects that the singular is always totalized, his own position depends on the reverse – if, as a critic, he does succeed in being outside the system then it has not, by definition, been totalized. In relation to what, then, does he take his critical distance? His recent attempt to solve this theoretical difficulty by playing on the semantic tensions between the words 'filiation' and 'affiliation' does work as a local rhetorical strategy, and recognizes, furthermore, that the inside/outside opposition is best disrupted by a certain textual ambivalence. [35] The conceptual difficulty, in other words, is held in place by the binary structure of the linguistic terms. Even so, Said continues to situate any possibility for equivocation in the consciousness of the individual critic. Said's refusal to encounter head-on the philosophical and theoretical difficulties to which his project gives rise means that, as we have seen, the contradictions re-emerge in his own writings rather than in the analysis of the culture itself. For Said's theoretical difficulties – and his inability to solve them – begin at a textual and conceptual level.

In this respect, Said's crucial theoretical decision can be charted in relation to his long, revised essay on Foucault and Derrida, in which the latter's 'textualism' is rejected for the politics of the former. [36] If Said is then concerned to distance himself from Foucault's totalizing schemas by reintroducing the question of the human and individual agency, he nevertheless continues to assume the possibility of such totalizations. This non-conflictual totality should be contrasted to the Derridean account which draws attention to the ways in which totalizations never succeed in producing a perfect structure of inclusions and exclusions, with the result that the unassimilable elements determine (and disallow) any totality which seeks to constitute itself as a totality by excluding them. In other words, only by rejecting Derrida *tout court* can Said continue to entertain the very possibility of a closed structure, system or method. And only if it is closed does it require the intervention of the individual to open it.

This problem of closure is in fact fundamental to *Orientalism* itself. Said's hope is to illustrate the formidable structure of cultural domination involved in the duality of 'the Occident' and 'the Orient' and by doing so perhaps to eliminate it altogether. But if he shows how Orientalism works by this opposition he does not so much try to undo it as simply deny it, with the result that he repeats the inside/outside structures of dualistic thinking himself. His analysis of the Orientalists takes the form of a series of judgements, according to which each writer is identified in turn as complicit in the process of the intellectual subordination of the East by the West. [37] Said's remorseless drive to judge the texts of Orientalism into a straight-forward 'for' and 'against' division leads him to conclude that 'it is therefore correct that every European, in what he could say about the Orient, was consequently a racist, an imperialist, and almost totally ethnocentric' (204). Marx presents a more difficult case insofar as his economic analyses are consonant with Orientalist thinking but at the same time his 'humanity, his sympathy for the misery of people are clearly engaged'. However, instead of suggesting that Marx's analysis might be contradictory, perhaps even produc-tively so, Said closes all conflict down with the remark: 'Yet in the end it is the Romantic Orientalist vision that wins out' (154). This closure is sup-ported by a one sentence citation from *Surveys From Exile* that is supposed to disprove and efface all other indications of Marx's equivocation. You can only be for or against.

As the narrative nears Said himself, however, an interesting theoretical difficulty begins to emerge, for if Orientalism as a discursive structure is so determining on this long history of writers about the East, how can he escape himself? The Orientalists Gibb and Massignon are allowed a less easily resolved form of contradiction than that of Marx. With Massignon Orientalism has clearly become more ambivalent. This, however, is accounted for less in terms of any textual complexity or conceptual contradictions than by the 'individual genius' of the man rising above the impersonal pressures of ideology and tradition – which it is assumed cannot themselves be conflictual. Nevertheless, however much Massignon may have championed Islam against Europe, Said still criticizes him on the grounds that he misrepresented it. At this point, however, Said allows himself some self-reflection to ponder a little further on the more general issues that his argument raises:

> Much as one may be inclined to agree with such theses – since, as this book has tried to demonstrate, Islam *has* been fundamentally mis-represented in the West – the real issue is whether indeed there can be a true representation of anything, or whether any and all representations, because they *are* representations, are embedded first in the language and then in the culture, institutions, and political ambience of the representer. [38]

Said endorses the latter alternative – but without pursuing its implications for his point about the inevitability of the misrepresentation of Islam (itself anticipated by Islam's own prohibition on representation). If true representa-tion is an impossibility, on what grounds is he criticizing the Orientalists?

In fact the misrepresentation which he describes resembles nothing so much as the intervention of the individual against the system – the very situation which elsewhere Said claims for his own 'critical consciousness'. So, for example, Massignon is criticized because he emphasized the Sufism of al-Hallaj against the 'the main doctrinal system of Islam' (272). Similarly, Said considers Gibb's identification of certain internal dislocations within Islam as an assertion of power – not as an attempt to come to terms with the forms of Islam's complexity and the problem of representing it at all:

> Dislocation in Gibb's work identifies something far more significant than a putative intellectual difficulty within Islam. It identifies, I think, the very privilege, the very ground on which the Orientalist places himself so as to write about, legislate for, and reformulate Islam. Far from being a chance discernment of Gibb's, dislocation is the epistemological passageway into his subject, and subsequently, the observation platform from which in all his writing, and in every one of the influential positions he filled, he could survey Islam. Between the silent appeals of Islam to a monolithic community of orthodox believers and a whole merely verbal articulation of Islam by misled corps of political activists, desperate clerks, and opportunistic reformers: there Gibb stood, wrote, reformulated. (282)

Gibb, it seems, ironically occupies the exact position of the critic between culture and system that elsewhere Said appropriates for himself. In Gibb's case, however, it is taken to indicate not the desirable position of the critic but merely a contradiction in Gibb's work which indicates the power of an Olympian Western privilege. The dislocation of which he writes is not of interest with respect to Islam as such. Nor does it offer a critical possibility of any sort. But in what way does this structure differ from that in which Said places himself?

The Orientalist's misrepresentation apparently can be transformed into the critic's political intervention which dislocates the system. But *Orientalism* also shows how the Orient itself operates as a form of dislocation for the West. [39] If Orientalism involves a science of inclusion and incorporation of the East by the West, then that inclusion produces its own disruption: the creation of the Orient, if it does not really represent the East, signifies the West's own dislocation from itself, something inside that is presented, narrativized, as being outside. Here we can begin to account for the logic of why certain racial and gender theories were projected onto Orientalist stereotypes; [40] or speculate on the relation of anti-Islamic and Arab feeling to what Said describes as its dark shadow, anti-Semitism: in this context, the Jews come to represent the Orient within, uncannily appearing inside when they should have remained hidden, outside Europe: thus the logic of their expulsion, or extermination, becomes inextricably linked with Orientalism itself. [41]

What Said's analysis neglects, therefore, is the extent to which Orientalism did not just misrepresent the Orient, but also articulated an internal dislocation within Western culture, a culture which consistently fantasizes itself as constituting some kind of integral totality, at the same time as endlessly deploring its own impending dissolution. To some extent Said himself remains unselfconsciously within that European cultural heritage. We have already considered his tendency to focus exclusively on European high culture, but his involvement extends to more fundamental assumptions – assumptions which he himself describes and criticizes. So, for example, he praises Auerbach fulsomely for providing the summation of Western culture at its last moment of totality, while having earlier shown how the idea of European culture as a totality under threat of fragmentation is part of the Orientalist fantasy itself. The Orient, we might say, operates as both poison and cure for Europe: it constitutes both the greatest threat to European civilization at the same time as it represents a therapeutic for the lost spiritual values of the West, offering hope for the regeneration of Europe by Asia. This suggests the extent to which Orientalism represents the West's own internal dislocation, misrepresented as an external dualism between East and West. At the same time, the totalization of historicism, in its Orientalist form – for Orientalism is a genre of imperialist historicism – enacts the very process of its own impossibility in a significant doubling. For whereas for a Western historicism the problem centres on the resistant singularity necessary for the integration of the totality but problematic for its closure, the Orientalist image of the Other is both a triumph of that historicist rationality but, in its antithetical value, also effects its own alienation from itself. The problem of *Orientalism* is that without a concept of an inner dissension Said is constantly led simply to condemn Orientalism's projections of dissonance on to external geographical or racial differences – even as he himself repeats such a structure by identifying Orientalists as 'for' or 'against'. Meanwhile Orientalism's own internal divisions re-emerge inexorably in the series of theoretical contradictions and conflicts in Said's text.

Chapter 8

The ambivalence of Bhabha

If Said's *Orientalism* is directed against the hierarchical dualism of 'West' and 'East', other dualisms ceaselessly proliferate throughout his text: Orientalism as representation or real, for example, or as vision or narrative; or, in Said's own methodology, the opposition of universalism to particularism which repeats through many different forms. Of the many critiques of *Orientalism* Homi Bhabha's 'Difference, Discrimination, and the Discourse of Colonialism' (1983) stands out because it directly identifies this problem of ambivalence at the heart of the book and recasts it in a more positive, enabling form. [1] Bhabha seizes on the analogy with Freud's conflictual model of the dream, which Said himself makes briefly in passing, in order to argue that at the centre of Orientalism there is not a single homogenizing perspective but a polarity: 'it is, on the one hand, a topic of learning, discovery, practice; on the other, it is the site of dreams, images, fantasies, myths, obsessions and requirements' (DDDC 199). Orientalism is a discipline – of encyclopaedic learning, and of imperial power – and yet on the other hand it is also a fantasy of the Other. It is both a conscious body of knowledge (Said's 'manifest Orientalism'), and an 'unconscious positivity' of fantasy and desire ('latent Orientalism'). The problem of the book, according to Bhabha, stems from

> Said's refusal to engage with the alterity and ambivalence of these two economies which threaten to split the very object of Orientalist discourse.... He contains this threat by introducing a binarism within the argument which, in initially setting up an opposition between these two discursive scenes, finally allows them to be correlated as a congruent system of representation that is unified through a political-ideological *intention* which, in his words, enables Europe to advance securely and *unmetaphorically* upon the Orient. (DDDC 199–200)

Unlike others who criticized Said for constructing too hegemonic a picture of Orientalism's discursive formation, Bhabha points to the way in which Said himself shows that such a discourse is constituted ambivalently. Said resolves this ambivalence, however, in the most traditional literary-critical way by referring to a single originating intention; as he puts it, 'once we begin to think of Orientalism as a kind of Western projection onto and will to govern over the Orient, we will encounter few surprises'. [2] If Europe's intention towards the East was one of imperial possession, then Said can claim that the discourse of Orientalism is equally monolithic. Bhabha comments: 'There is always, in Said, the suggestion that colonial power is possessed entirely by the colonizer which is a historical and theoretical simplification' (DDDC 200). The assumed regularity between representation and object means that Said posits a binary opposition between power and powerlessness, which requires the supposition of an exterior controlling intention and leaves no room for negotiation or resistance, except from an exterior counter-intention (himself). Bhabha suggests that this is a reductive simplification: the representation of the Orient in Western discourse, which Said charts so patiently, evidences a profound ambivalence towards 'that "otherness" which is at once an object of desire and derision' (OQ 19). This equivocation indicates that colonial discourse is founded on an anxiety, and that colonial power itself is subject to the effects of a conflictual economy.

For Bhabha, Orientalism does not simply amount to a representation which may or may not correspond to 'real' conditions – a problem which cannot in any case be solved in purely epistemological terms. He takes seriously Said's claim that Orientalism is a 'discourse', and therefore utilizes the technical apparatus of discourse analysis. Orientalism may be a representation but it also takes part in an entire discursive field, any consideration of which, he argues, must include the question of enunciation, that is, of who is speaking to whom. It cannot be assumed that representations are just static entities which may or may not correspond to the 'real' – because they must always also form part of an address, whether written or spoken, with a specific addresser and addressee. Whereas Said, rejecting Foucault because his analyses allegedly offer no strategy of resistance, feels compelled to introduce a special, highly problematic, claim for the agency of individual subjects into his description of Orientalism as a discursive field, Bhabha shows how the question of enunciation demonstrates the operation of a subject already. Enunciation directs attention to 'the repertoire of conflictual positions that constitute the subject in colonial discourse' (DDDC 204). Bhabha analyses the conditions of this process of address in order to show the occurrence of a slippage which problematizes both the claim for a single political-ideological intention of the colonizer, as well as the straight-forwardly instrumentalist relation of power and knowledge which Said assumes.

Bhabha thus shifts Said's perspective, which emphasizes the representation of the Orient for consumption within a dominant Western culture, to focus on Orientalism's role when used as an instrument of colonial power and administration. In doing so he immediately solves Said's fundamental difficulty of how the representation articulates with the actual: the representation may appear to be hegemonic, but it carries within it a hidden flaw invisible at home but increasingly apparent abroad when it is away from the safety of the West. The representation of the colonial subject, for example, is not so much proved or disproved by actual colonial subjects, as Said suggests, as disarticulated:

> In occupying two places at once ... the depersonalised, dislocated colonial subject can become an incalculable object, quite literally, difficult to place. The demand of [colonial] authority cannot unify its message nor simply identify its subjects. (BSWM xxii)

Against Said, therefore, Bhabha argues that even for the colonizer the construction of a representation of the Other is by no means straightforward.

This is demonstrated through an extended analysis of the process of colonial stereotyping of subject peoples and their cultures – one way of describing the activity of Orientalism itself. Bhabha suggests that, contrary to what the very word 'stereotype' might imply, what is at issue is not a straightforward matter of the crudity of the stereotype as opposed to the complexity of the actual peoples being characterized. He argues rather that

> the colonial stereotype is a complex, ambivalent, contradictory mode of representation, as anxious as it is assertive, and demands not only that we extend our critical and political objectives but that we change the object of analysis itself. (OQ 22)

Highlighting Said's remarks about the vacillation evident in certain typical encounters between East and West, between Western contempt for the East's familiarity and delight or fear at its strangeness and novelty, Bhabha suggests that this 'median category' of recognition and disavowal is 'analogous' to the Freudian theory of sexual fetishism. In racial stereotyping 'colonial power produces the colonized as a fixed reality which is at once an "other" and yet entirely knowable and visible' (DDDC 199). As Baudrillard has suggested, as soon as the other can be represented, it can be appropriated and controlled;[3] but here such an impulse forms part of a larger structure which simultaneously disallows its authority:

> The fetish or stereotype gives access to an 'identity' which is predicated as much on mastery and pleasure as it is on anxiety and defence, for it is a form of multiple and contradictory belief in its recognition of difference and disavowal of it. (DDDC 202).

Colonial discourse does not merely represent the other, therefore, so much as simultaneously project and disavow its difference, a contradictory structure articulated according to fetishism's irreconcilable logic. Its mastery is always asserted, but is also always slipping, ceaselessly displaced, never complete.

Provocative though Bhabha's account undoubtedly is, it prompts the question of the curious historical provenance of a word like fetishism. When Freud proposed a theory of sexuality in terms of fetishism, the concept had already been employed by Marx in *Capital*, who had adapted it from its original meaning in which it was used to describe the artefacts of African 'native' religions: an 'inanimate object worshipped by primitive peoples for its supposed inherent magical powers or as being inhabited by a spirit'. [4] Bhabha's use of the term fetish to describe colonial racist stereotyping certainly brings the wheel full circle, but it is curious that he is himself silent about the historical conditions and provenance of the concept that he uses. He speaks of the need to examine colonial discourse in psychoanalytic as well as historical terms but does not risk any account of how they might be articulated (DDDC 201). Deleuze and Guattari's argument in the *Anti-Oedipus* that psychoanalysis works in non-European cultures, not because of the universalism of the categories of the mind but precisely because of colonial history, which has had the effect of imposing Western structures, would be one possibility for achieving such a conjunction. [5] Bhabha, on the other hand, would doubtless question their assumption that psychoanalysis simply repeats itself at the site of its colonial address.

This raises the larger question posed by Bhabha's work, namely his employment of the transcendental categories of psychoanalysis for the analysis of the historical phenomenon of colonialism. Bhabha uses psycho-analysis as a means of reading: it is obvious that his strategic use of Freud, so crucial for his account of ambivalence, produces important theoretical and political differences from Said's analysis of colonialism which is derived from Foucault's theory of discursive formations. Bhabha begins his account of colonial discourse by offering a Foucauldian description of its 'minimum conditions and specifications' as an apparatus of power. [6] But he goes on to suggest against Foucault that the colonial subject who is the object of surveillance is also the object of paranoia and fantasy on the part of the colonizer, thus immediately introducing psychoanalytic categories into the Foucauldian schema. In proposing a theory of racial stereotyping according to the psychoanalytic theory of fetishism, Bhabha elaborates a four-part 'anatomy' of colonial discourse which is very different to anything in Foucault; his concern is to argue that although there may be surveillance, fixity is not achieved:

> The construction of colonial discourse is ... a complex articulation of the tropes of fetishism – metaphor and metonymy – and the forms of narcissistic and aggressive identification available to the Imaginary. Stereo-typical racial discourse is then a four-term strategy.... One has then a repertoire of conflictual positions that constitute the subject in colonial discourse. The taking up of any one position, within a specific discursive form, in a particular historical conjuncture, is then always problematic – the site of both fixity and fantasy. It provides a colonial 'identity' that is

played out ... in the face and space of the disruption and threat from the heterogeneity of other positions. (DDDC 204)

Bhabha then concedes, however, that if the subject of colonial discourse is constructed according to such ambivalent categories this indeterminacy in the final analysis poses no threat to the strategic operation of colonial discourse: 'caught in the Imaginary as they are, these shifting positionalities will never seriously threaten the dominant power relations, for they exist to exercise them pleasurably and productively' (DDDC 205). Bhabha will later come to revise this position, demonstrating once again that he can avoid the problems that beset Said.

Said, it will be recalled, finally rejected Foucault on the grounds that his analyses offer no strategy of resistance. But Said's retrieval of the category of the individual is effected only to locate such resistance in the form of the consciousness of the individual critic, which hardly represents a great advance. The question, therefore, is whether the task of the critic is to locate evidence of historical examples of resistance, as is often assumed, or whether the analysis of colonial discourse can itself make political interventions in terms of current understanding and analysis. So Bhabha, for example, demonstrates against Said that the authority of colonial power was not straightforwardly possessed by the colonizer. Significant though this is, it is not the same as providing straightforward evidence of resistance:

Despite the 'play' in the colonial system which is crucial to its exercise of power, I do not consider the practices and discourses of revolutionary struggle as the under/other side of 'colonial discourse'. They may be historically co-present with it and intervene in it, but can never be 'read off' merely on the basis of their opposition to it. Anti-colonialist discourse requires an alternative set of questions, techniques and strategies in order to construct it [sic]. (DDDC 198)

Thus Bhabha's concern is to demonstrate an ambivalence in colonial and colonizing subjects by articulating the inner dissension within a colonial discourse structured according to the conflictual economy of the psyche. Without such instability of power, anticolonialist resistance would itself be powerless. It is not Bhabha's concern to focus on such resistance, but rather to show the hesitancies and irresolution of what is being resisted. The difficulty, however, politically speaking, is that such an analysis cannot but be equally applicable to colonized as to colonizer.

II THE MIMIC MAN

Bhabha thus seizes upon many of the theoretical difficulties encountered by Said as indications of processes that occur during the construction and exercise of colonial knowledge and power – perhaps not very reassuring for

Said but a brilliant theoretical insight on Bhabha's part. Colonialism is identified as the discourse which betrays a dissonance implicit in Western knowledge. Bhabha's subsequent essays all represent a refinement of the position first somewhat ambiguously sketched out in 'Difference, Discrimination and the Discourse of Colonialism'. In his Foreword to Fanon's *Black Skin, White Masks*, he writes of 'Fanon's search for a conceptual form appropriate to the social antagonism of the colonial relation' and of the 'colonial condition that drove Fanon from one conceptual scheme to another' (x). This description could equally well apply to Bhabha himself: in his essays we see him move from the model of fetishism to those of 'mimicry', 'hybridisation', and 'paranoia'. Bhabha's claims to describe the conditions of colonial discourse – 'mimicry is ...', 'hybridity is ...' – seem always offered as static concepts, curiously anthropomorphized so that they possess their own desire, with no reference to the historical provenance of the theoretical material from which such concepts are drawn, or to the theoretical narrative of Bhabha's own work, or to that of the cultures to which they are addressed. On each occasion Bhabha seems to imply through this timeless characterization that the concept in question constitutes the condition of colonial discourse itself and would hold good for all historical periods and contexts – so it comes as something of a surprise when it is subsequently replaced by the next one, as, for example, when psychoanalysis suddenly disappears in favour of Bakhtinian hybridization, only itself to disappear entirely in the next article as psychoanalysis returns, but this time as paranoia. It is as if theoretical elaboration itself becomes a kind of narrative of the colonial condition. Inevitably, of course, different conceptualizations produce different emphases – but the absence of any articulation of the relation between them remains troubling. Is this what Bhabha calls 'theoreticist anarchism' (STW 152)? Or is it a more considered strategy whereby Bhabha rejects a consistent metalanguage, refusing to let his terms reify into static concepts, thus eluding the problem that Said found so difficult to avoid, namely that the analysis ends up by repeating the same structures of power and knowledge in relation to its material as the colonial representation itself. If Bhabha exploits the structures of disavowal that he finds, it is first and foremost to undermine this possibility and to prevent the reifications of mastery.

At the same time, it is possible to detect a certain schema being worked through, almost unrecognizable in its dissimilitude. In this context it is useful to recall Bhabha's early description of colonial discourse in Foucauldian terms as an apparatus of power: from this perspective, each essay can be seen as illuminating specific moments in the ambivalent and cumulative apparatus of colonial discourse. The ambivalence of the latter means that by definition it cannot be approached in terms of a single illuminating concept; each article, therefore, addresses a particular structural figure in such an apparatus through a reading of a specific historically located text. Bhabha does not in any sense offer a history of colonial discourse, nor even a simple historical account of it – for such historicization marks the very basis of the Europeanizing claims he is trying to invert. Each text is both placed in its historical moment and gradually shifted from any single determination or linear development as Bhabha elaborates the complex problem of its reading.

Throughout the restless seriality of Bhabha's delineation of how historicization is produced through the different singularities and temporalities of processes that are never totalized but which do overlap, ambivalence remains a constant reference. Ambivalence necessarily also invokes the question of agency – the two problems which together had made up Bhabha's original grounds for complaint against Said. Initially Bhabha concentrates, like Said, on the conditions of the construction of knowledge by the colonizer, an operation governed as we have seen, by identification and disavowal. In 'Of Mimicry and Man', he develops Lacan's remarks regarding the concept of mimicry. [7] Mimicry offers Bhabha a new term for the construction of the colonial Other in certain forms of stereotyping – a colonial subject who will be recognizably the same as the colonizer but still different: 'not quite/not white' (OMM 132). Bhabha gives as his example the Indian, educated in English, who works in the Indian civil service and mediates between the imperial power and the colonized people. If it is in some sense reassuring for the colonizers that Indians become in certain respects 'English', the production of mimic Englishmen also becomes disturbing, for 'mimicry is at once resemblance and menace' (OMM 127). The mimic man, insofar as he is not entirely like the colonizer, white but not quite, constitutes only a partial representation of him: far from being reassured, the colonizer sees a grotesquely displaced image of himself. Thus the familiar, transported to distant parts, becomes uncannily transformed, the imitation subverts the identity of that which is being represented, and the relation of power, if not altogether reversed, certainly begins to vacillate:

> [It is] a process by which the look of surveillance returns as the displacing gaze of the disciplined, where the observer becomes the observed and the 'partial' representation rearticulates the whole notion of *identity* and alienates it from essence. [8]

The surveilling eye is suddenly confronted with a returning gaze of otherness and finds that its mastery, its sameness, is undone.

What is particularly interesting about this description is the way in which the whole question of agency gets moved from a fixed point into a process of circulation: the colonizer performs certain strategies in order to maintain power, but the ambivalence that inevitably accompanies the attempt to fix the colonized as an object of knowledge means that the relation of power becomes much more equivocal. Mimicry at once enables power and produces the loss of agency. If control slips away from the colonizer, the requirement of mimicry means that the colonized, while complicit in the process, remains the unwitting and unconscious agent of menace – with a resulting paranoia on the part of the colonizer as he tries to guess the native's sinister intentions. Though of course the native may well have violent thoughts of rebellion, we are not here, it should be stressed, talking about such orthodox forms of resistance, but a process which simultaneously stabilizes and destabilizes the position of the colonizer. This should be contrasted to Said's notion of Orientalism as a totalized image without a referent which requires an intervention from outside. For Bhabha mimicry itself becomes a kind of agency without a subject, a form of representation which produces effects, a sameness which slips into otherness, but which still has nothing to do with any 'other'. As Lacan puts it, it reveals 'something in so far as it is distinct from what might be called an *itself* that is behind'. [9] Compared to ambivalence, which describes a process of identification and disavowal, mimicry implies an even greater loss of control for the colonizer, of inevitable processes of counter-domination produced by a miming of the very operation of domination, with the result that the identity of colonizer and colonized becomes curiously elided. Mimicry is not, as it is for Derrida or Irigaray, a form of resistance as such, but describes a process in the construction of power which works instead more like the unconscious in Lacan, and could perhaps even be described, after Jameson, as 'the colonial unconscious'. [10]

III RESISTANCE

In 'Signs Taken for Wonders' mimicry, the displacement of authoritative discourse where ambivalence shifts to fantasies of menace, is itself displaced by the concept of the hybrid, the part object that articulates colonial and native knowledges and which can, it is now claimed, enable active forms of resistance. As a description of an object rather than a discursive concept, the hybrid can be shown to transform the conditions of its own creation. Bhabha defines hybridity as:

> a *problematic* of colonial representation ... that reverses the effects of the colonialist disavowal, so that other 'denied' knowledges enter upon the dominant discourse and estrange the basis of its authority. (STW 156)

If the effect of colonial power is to produce 'hybridization', this undermines colonial authority because it repeats it differently; other, repressed knowledges enter unawares and effect a transformation. Hybridity thus names a 'strategic reversal of the process of domination' which reimplicates colonial authority 'in strategies of subversion that turn the gaze of the discriminated back upon the eye of power' (STW 154). This returning gaze no longer produces disquiet and ambivalence just for the colonizer as Bhabha had argued earlier:

If the effect of colonial power is seen to be the *production* of hybridisation
... [it] enables a form of subversion ... that turns the discursive conditions
of dominance into the grounds of intervention. (STW 154)

For the first time, Bhabha here argues that the discursive conditions of
colonialism do not merely undermine the forms of colonial authority but
can actively enable native resistance. [11] In 'Difference, Discrimination, and
the Discourse of Colonialism', Bhabha, it will be recalled, had carefully
distinguished between colonial discourse and the practices of revolutionary
struggle. This new position adopted in 'Signs Taken for Wonders' might
therefore be regarded as an important theoretical and political advance.

On the basis of his new argument, Bhabha accordingly shifts his concept
of mimicry from being something which is simply disquieting for the
colonizer to a specific form of intervention:

Mimicry marks those moments of civil disobedience within the discipline
of civility: signs of spectacular resistance. When the words of the master
become the site of hybridity ... then we may not only read between the
lines but even seek to change the often coercive reality that they so lucidly
contain. (STW 162)

But with the claim for resistance and intervention, the problem of agency
returns: who is 'we' here, and when do 'we' do what we do? Is Bhabha
describing a forgotten moment of historical resistance, or does that resistance
remain inarticulate until the interpreter comes a hundred and seventy years
later to 'read between the lines' and rewrite history? And precisely what
reality can such a reading between the lines hope to change? Is it a question
of locating previously undetected moments of pre-nationalist subaltern
resistance that can now be produced and charted by the critic? Certainly
Bhabha's stress on reading seems to imply as much: 'What such a reading
reveals are the boundaries of colonial discourse and it enables a transgression of these limits from the space of that otherness' (OQ 19).

Although no doubt more acceptable to some to the extent that it offers a
politics legible in terms of populist categories, in many ways this claim for
forms of resistance marks a retreat from Bhabha's more original argument
about ambivalence into a more conventional political topos in which a
native otherness is constituted in a space outside the boundaries of colonial
discourse. Although the claim for active resistance (somewhat minimal in
this case) inevitably offers a certain political allure, it has to be said that
documentary evidence of resistance by colonized peoples is not at all hard
to come by, and is only belittled by the implication that you have to read
between the lines to find it. Setting aside the countless instances of explicit
military and political resistance, even the example of Christian missions,
with which Bhabha substantiates his argument, provides substantial evidence of quite spectacular failures: David Livingstone, for instance, in nine

years of missionary work prior to his becoming an explorer, made but one convert – who then promptly retracted. [12]

If Bhabha's description shifts from an ambivalence in colonial enunciation to a native resistance discernible when colonial texts and discourses are hybridized in the context of other cultures and sites, a more recent article, 'Sly Civility' (1985), usefully articulates these two poles with each other and, above all, retrieves the lost major theoretical insight. Ambivalence, it is now emphasized, works both at the point of enunciation and at the site of address, where it is (partially) resisted. So Mill's statements about the compatibility of British democracy with a despotic colonialism are shown to contain the contradiction which Bhabha implies is a central condition of the discourse of Western democracy. Similarly, he demonstrates how in the instructions of the East India Company, as the directions from London are transported for implementation in India, there is a slippage between their Western and colonial significance in the space between their initial enunciation and their destined address: once more, there is a loss of control in which an ambivalence reinscribes both colonizer and colonized in a different relation of power with the result that authority cannot be maintained. This means, however, that Bhabha finds himself obliged to make two contradictory arguments: while there is always an ambivalence at work within the discourse of colonial instruction, that ambivalence is at the same time the effect of its hybridization in the colonial context. Thus his own theorizations hover ambiguously on the borders of the divisions that he describes.

This points to a further difficulty in the notion of hybridization itself, insofar as it suggests the articulation of two hitherto undifferentiated knowledges – implying a pure origination of both Western and native cultures which Bhabha's earlier point disallows. Perhaps this is one reason why the hybrid, which seemed of such crucial theoretical and political significance in 'Signs Taken for Wonders', subsequently drops silently out of sight. Instead we are offered narratives of fixity that become uncertain, stories of original plenitudes – whether of the Bible, of nationalist discourse, or of colonial authority – that become ambivalent as soon as they are translated elsewhere: 'those substitutive objects of colonialist governmentality ... are strategies of surveillance that cannot maintain their civil authority once the "colonial" *supplementarity* of their address is revealed' (SC 74). In spite of the 'once', these narratives are given little historical substantiation; moreover as stories of the shift from certainty to uncertainty, they still go against the stronger suggestion that far from an original plenitude, ambivalence is constitutive of the colonial text as such: Bhabha instances the characteristic double logic at work in Macaulay's words: 'Be the father and the oppressor of the people; be just and unjust, moderate and rapacious' (SC 74).

Bhabha argues that, though what he calls the 'colonial supplementarity' of address is revealed through an account of the effects of a colonial context impinging upon the colonial text, it can best be analysed through the invocation of a psychoanalytic schema of the 'modern colonizing imagination' as a form of narcissism:

> If such passion be political, then I suggest that we should pose the question of the ambivalence of colonialist authority in the language of the vicissitudes of the *narcissistic demand* for colonial objects, which intervenes so powerfully in the *nationalist* fantasies of boundless, extensive possessions. (SC 75–6)

Bhabha suggests that the colonial demand that the other should authorize the self, reveals 'that the *other* side of narcissistic authority may be the paranoia of power'. Paranoia occurs when the narcissistic demand is refused, and is inevitably then 'reinscribed as implacable aggression, assertively coming from without: *He hates me*' (SC 78–9). But such projection is not simply a self-fulfilling fantasy: after all, the native really does hate the colonizing master. The colonizer's perception 'he hates me' is not the overinterpretation of paranoia, therefore, but an interpretation that is entirely correct. The problem, and the paranoia, comes in knowing when, how, and from whom: how to detect the difference between subservient obedience and the mask of what Bhabha calls 'sly civility'? But, it may be objected, if sly civility is indeed a prevalent strategy of the colonized then it suggests that what Bhabha calls 'the repeated fantasy of ... the litigious, lying native' (SC 79) is also less of a fantasy than he implies. [13] The native really does lie, albeit politely. Once again we find a crucial problem emerging: the more that Bhabha claims resistance, the less need there is for his psychoanalytic schema of fantasy and desire, narcissism and paranoia, in any analysis of the structures of colonialism.

IV PSYCHOANALYSIS AND COLONIALISM

If Bhabha exploits the ambivalence which Said denies but nevertheless demonstrates, his own work can be seen to come up against a provocative series of theoretical questions and difficulties. In the first place, the possibility of a general theory of colonial discourse, which Bhabha's analyses imply, is itself problematical: does it, for instance, always demonstrate the ambivalence which he claims or do his examples constitute particular privileged moments? If the latter is the case, what is their relation to the general text of colonialism? This can be related to a second question which would be concerned to ask who 'the colonizer', 'the colonized', or 'the native' actually is. Bhabha certainly develops Albert Memmi's argument that there is never a simple distinction between colonizer and colonized, but this only prompts the question of whether there can be such categories in general. [14] Similarly, although Bhabha gives an extremely subtle account which disallows straightforward intentionalist accounts of agency, this only reinforces the problem of whether resistance or compliance can be discussed in terms of the positing of a general colonial subject (singular, a somewhat neutralized male, out of time and space) within the demands of an overall schema of the conditions of colonial discourse.

These questions themselves point to a problem of interpretation, namely, what political status can be accorded the subversive strategies that Bhabha articulates? We have already encountered a similar difficulty in our earlier discussion of new historicism. It is formulated succinctly by Stephen Greenblatt in his discussions of the ways in which Renaissance texts both produce and contain powerful subversions of contemporary ideology. As the brief moment of scepticism is closed down by the text, Greenblatt comments:

> we may feel at this point that subversion scarcely exists and may legitimately ask ourselves how our perception of the subversive and orthodox is generated. The answer, I think, is that 'subversive' is for us a term used to designate those elements in Renaissance culture that contemporary authorities tried to contain or, when containment seemed impossible, to destroy and that now conform to our own sense of truth and reality. That is, we locate as 'subversive' in the past precisely those things that are *not* subversive to ourselves. [15]

By contrast, Greenblatt continues, those elements which we identify with Renaissance principles of order would, if we took them seriously, undermine our own contemporary assumptions (absolutism, hierarchies of class and gender, religious intolerance, etc.). They are not threatening, however, because our own values are strong enough for us not to take them seriously as alternatives. Greenblatt suggests that exactly the same holds for the subversive elements of Renaissance texts – which could be articulated only because they could be effortlessly contained. Bhabha, by contrast, argues convincingly that what is distinctive about such processes is that they are uncontainable, that they are outside the conscious control of the subject. The question this poses, however, is whether these apparently seditionary undoings in fact remain unconscious for both colonizer and colonized, who are nevertheless inexorably locked into a constant movement of destabilization which only Bhabha can articulate, or whether the colonized can detect such slippages in the speech of the colonizer and consciously exploit them.

Bhabha himself in fact vacillates between these two possibilities, perhaps understandably, for in the absence of any historical evidence of the effects of such operations, there does not seem to be any basis for choosing between them. But the question remains: how does the equivocality of colonial discourse emerge, and when – at the time of its enunciation or with the present day historian or interpreter? Sometimes Bhabha writes of colonial discourse only becoming ambivalent when enunciated at a certain moment of colonial history, thus implying that elsewhere, at home, it was not, or at the very least that its equivocal potential previously remained unactivated.

At other times he intimates that it was in fact always already ambivalent, which suggests that such ambivalence is always already inscribed at a textual level. This prompts the question of what, if anything, is specific to the colonial situation if colonial texts only demonstrate the same properties that can be found in any deconstructive reading of European texts.

In a similar way, Bhabha's use of psychoanalytic theories of the ambivalent constitution of the subject effectively disallows the claim for such ambivalence being specific to the colonial situation. To suggest otherwise would have to imply that, outside it, subjects are not ambivalent. This in turn points to the larger question of Bhabha's use of psychoanalysis in general. If a psychoanalytic model might at first sight seem somewhat unexpected in the colonial context, he has the precedent of no less an authority than Fanon for its use, particularly his *Black Skin, White Masks*, the title of which exactly catches the doubling of fantasy and disavowal of difference that constitutes Bhabha's stereotype. Bhabha's stress on ambivalence as constitutive of the colonial condition draws on Fanon's theory of Manichean dichotomy as the psychic pathology generated by the situation of a colonial governance which can only keep a society together through a validated violence. [16] Bhabha discusses some of the issues raised by the use of psychoanalysis in his Foreword to Fanon's *Black Skin, White Masks*, though he is more concerned to stress its advantages than its problems. It is psychoanalysis, Bhabha claims, which can best account for those perverse contradictions which colonialism brings out in the ideals of European humanism:

> The representative figure of such a perversion, I want to suggest, is the image of post-Enlightenment man tethered to, *not* confronted by, his dark reflection, the shadow of colonized man, that splits his presence, distorts his outline, breaches his boundaries, repeats his actions at a distance, disturbs and divides the very time of his being. This ambivalent identification of the racist world ... turns on the idea of Man *as* his alienated image, not Self and Other but the 'Otherness' of the Self inscribed in the perverse palimpsest of colonial identity. And it is that bizarre figure of desire, which splits along the axis on which it turns, that compels Fanon to put the psychoanalytic question of the desire of the subject to the historic condition of colonial man. (BSWM xiv-xv)

This, therefore, is the crucial justification for the use of psychoanalysis. However, though equally important for both, Bhabha's psychoanalysis is somewhat different to Fanon's, partly as the result of the influence of Lacan.

Interestingly enough, in *Black Skin, White Masks* Fanon does cite Lacan on several occasions, but without special privilege. Bhabha's more extended use of Lacanian psychoanalysis – the schemas of which sometimes seem almost given the status of truth or actuality – reposes the question of what it means to use Western psychoanalytic theory to analyse the colonial condition. [17] One difference between Fanon's and Bhabha's use of psychoanalysis is clear. Whereas Fanon, who was himself a practising psychiatrist, quite clearly uses psychoanalysis in a clinical context, Bhabha is much more undecided as to whether the structures of colonial discourse are 'analogous' to those articulated by Freud or whether, as is sometimes implied, they actually involve the psychic categories as described by Freud. Bhabha remains ambivalent on this question of the status of psychoanalytic concepts in his texts. For example, while the structures of desire are central both to Fanon and to Bhabha's exposition of his psychoanalytic model (as we have seen in the case of fetishism), when it comes to the structures of colonial discourse as such the question of sexuality and sexual difference is nowhere apparent in Bhabha's texts. By contrast Fanon attaches a crucial importance to the differences between male and female sexuality in his account of the sexuality of colonialism. [18] Bhabha's model nowhere broaches the question of a gendered colonial subject, but rather seems to regard the troubled structures of sexuality as themselves a metaphor for colonial ambivalence. Obviously he is not claiming to use psychoanalysis clinically; nevertheless, his generalized discussion of the desire of the subject in psychoanalytic terms without any consideration of sexuality as such prompts many questions: what, for instance, could be the ontological status of the 'desire of hybridity' or indeed of the 'desire of colonial discourse' (STW 157–8). In short, how can you talk about structures of desire in psycho-analytic terms outside the structures of sexuality? [19]

If Bhabha's use of psychoanalysis differs from Fanon's, his politics also contrast markedly. Surprisingly, perhaps, in his Foreword to *Black Skin, White Masks* Bhabha does not focus upon the problem of Fanon's own ambivalence between psychoanalytic descriptions and revolutionary imper-atives in his psychopathology of revolution, or his rejection of economic theories of revolution for psychological ones. [20] Bhabha rather castigates Fanon for being too ambivalent about psychoanalysis. Thus he goes so far as to characterize Fanon's more overtly political analyses as overly humanistic moments in which he is 'fearful of his most radical insights':

> In his more analytic mode Fanon can impede the exploration of these ambivalent, uncertain questions of colonial desire. The state of emergency from which he writes demands more insurgent answers, more immediate identifications.... These attempts, in Fanon's words, to restore the dream to its proper political time and cultural space can, at times, blunt the edge of Fanon's brilliant illustrations of the complexity of psychic projections in the pathological colonial relation. (xix-xx)

But if the exigencies of his participation in the Algerian War of Independ-ence deflected Fanon 'too hastily' from his most challenging theoretical advances, Bhabha is not suggesting a contrast between forms of politics and political analysis. Rather he proposes his own political strategy instead, a strategy of subversion that reutilizes the cultural confusion of the

Manichean colonial condition and the ambivalent tension of colonial demand and desire:

> It is from that tension – both psychic and political – that a strategy of subversion emerges. It is a mode of negation that seeks not to unveil the fullness of Man but to manipulate his representation. (xxiii)

Against the hasty humanist politics of the war of liberation, for Bhabha the psychoanalysis of colonialism becomes the privileged site of resistance:

> In shifting the focus of cultural racism from the politics of nationalism to the politics of narcissism, Fanon opens up a margin of interrogation that causes a subversive slippage of identity and authority. (xxiv)

While on the one hand Bhabha suggests that the ambivalence of colonial discourse allows its exploitation so that its authority can be undermined even further, on the other hand it seems also to be implied here that such slippage does not so much occur under the historical conditions of colonialism, but is rather produced by the critic. Psychoanalysis, in other words, is used by Bhabha predominantly because it makes possible a reading of the ambivalence operating within the processes of colonial authority. A psychoanalytic reading enables a contestation of the claims of any Europeanization. At the same time, in the face of the history of colonialism, what could be the political status of such intervention? Is it simply a question of historical reinterpretation? How is the historical situation placed in relation to that of the interpreting critic? But these questions do not mark the degree to which Bhabha's intervention disallows such residual but untheorized distinctions. The space of the critical activity is also that of the (re)construction of knowledges. As Foucault recognized in his genealogical notion of the phantasm, the historical 'event' is at once everywhere and nowhere, there and here, then and now.

Bhabha's own work is similarly difficult to place. Could his eclectic use of theory itself be an example of colonial mockery? A teasing mimicry of certain Western theorists and discourses that is like, but not quite? Here a comparison with Fanon is again useful. Sartre's introduction to *The Wretched of the Earth* raises the problem of the addressee of Fanon's text, and points to the discomfiture felt by a European in reading a book directed to another reader:

> And if you murmur, jokingly embarrassed, 'He has it in for us!' the true nature of the scandal escapes you; for Fanon has nothing in for you at all; his work – red-hot for some – in what concerns you is as cold as ice; he speaks of you often, never to you. The black Goncourts and the yellow Nobels are finished; the days of colonized laureats are over. An ex-native, French-speaking, bends that language to new requirements, makes use of it, and speaks to the colonized only. [21]

Bhabha's texts, by contrast, are not directed towards any specific addressee; nevertheless he manages to produce a comparable sense of discomfiture and disorientation. Fanon used the discourses of Marx, Sartre, and Freud, but turned them against the West through his many-voiced, non-standard French ostensibly directed only to the colonized reader, but, obliquely, also to the European through what Sartre called elsewhere 'a double simultaneous postulation'. [22] So Bhabha, whose discourse works to undermine its own monologic authority, constantly teases the reader with the difficulty of his texts, his oxymoronic phrases and indirect allusions. Indeed his use of disparate and conflicting theories produces just that kind of ambivalence which subjects the reader to the effects of colonial discourse's disconcerting uncertainty: is Western theory being employed rigorously, in its own disciplinary context, or does it function more by power of suggestion and analogy? Is it being used as a model, or is it a form of mimicry, hybridity, a ghostly and ghastly doubling that acts out the duplicity of Bhabha's own name? [23] Whereas Said reproduces what he has characterized as the limitations of his object, Bhabha reduplicates his object's positivities: in the opacity of his discourse, his descriptions of slippage and ambivalence begin to seem equally applicable to the rhetoric of his own writings which reproduce the forms and structures of the material that he analyses and thus simultaneously assert and undermine their own authoritative mode. To his reader, as he enacts what he describes, at times Bhabha's discourse becomes as incalculable and difficult to place as the colonial subject itself.

These difficulties can be related to the larger question of Bhabha's attempt to intervene against the structures of Western historicization. We have traced the complex, supplementary structures of historicism's own impossible totalization, and suggested that in Orientalism the production of a narcissistic image of the Other at the same time effects a comparable antithetical alienation of European selfhood. Bhabha asserts that his colonial discourse analysis allows the tracing of a different but analogous process, whereby the forms of Western rationality are shown to experience an ideological and semantic dislocation in the spatio-temporal displacements of colonialism. Such work also enables a strategic interrogation of Western knowledges which disorients all attempts to assert authority or to produce closure. Bhabha demonstrates how dissonant, non-syncretic theory can shift control away from the dominant Western paradigm of historicist narrative, temporality, and univocality – but also how any 'new history' must, necessarily, be almost unrecognizable as 'history'. If Said showed the problems implicit in any attempt to construct an alternative to Orientalism, for the same reasons we cannot expect that an easily recognizable form of a new history can be set up as a straightforward alternative to Western historicism. The problem of history becomes indissociable from the role of the investigator in the formation of knowledge and the traces of the historian as writing-subject.

Chapter 9

Spivak: decolonization, deconstruction

I HISTORY AND THE SUBALTERN

If Bhabha's work is strategically eclectic, that of Gayatri Chakravorty Spivak can only be described as heterogeneous. The remarkable and diverse range of her interests, which extend through (and no doubt beyond) Marxism, deconstruction, feminism, psychoanalysis, critiques of colonialism, of the institution and practices of pedagogy, demonstrates an extraordinary intellectual ambition as well as the ability to sustain a political and theoretical engagement simultaneously on multiple fronts. Unlike those who specialize in an individual field and are able as a result to produce a seemingly coherent account of their position, sustainable only by the very delimitation of its reference, Spivak's recognition of the extent to which different disciplines interrelate and implicate each other marks the difficulty and the challenge of her texts. Instead of staking out a single recognizable position, gradually refined and developed over the years, she has produced a series of essays that move restlessly across the spectrum of contemporary theoretical and political concerns, rejecting none of them according to the protocols of an oppositional mode, but rather questioning, reworking and reinflecting them in a particularly productive and disturbing way. As she puts it: 'I am a *bricoleur*, I use what comes to hand'. [1] This means that Spivak's work offers no position as such that can be quickly summarized: in the most sustained deconstructive mode, she resists critical taxonomies, avoids assuming master discourses. To read her work is not so much to confront a system as to encounter a series of events.

Spivak, according to Colin MacCabe, 'is often called a feminist Marxist deconstructivist'. [2] If so, she considers that, rather than reconciling the differences between the three, her task is to preserve their discontinuities. [3] This begins to account for the difficulty of her texts, and perhaps also for her unwillingness to offer any overall description of their situation. We shall here attempt to elucidate some specific strategies, focusing on the questions of history and colonialism. These sites disclose the place of the greatest and most provocative dislocation which she has provoked in the protocols of

Anglo-American academic knowledge, a disruption which extends beyond the formal limits of historicism. It is Spivak's constant attention to the colonial question that forces such discontinuities. While Bhabha's work has consisted of a rereading of the texture of colonial authority in terms which cunningly subvert any comparable impulse towards mastery, Spivak engages in a similar undertaking, but which, by presenting her own mode of operation more self-consciously, puts certain key theoretical difficulties at the cutting edge. Characteristically, she attempts a number of things at once, not out of disparateness or lack of focus but as the result of an awareness of the complexity of the undertaking in which she is engaged. Her strength can be measured by the fact that she constantly acknowledges the problems of carrying out such a project and puts them at the forefront of her interventions. Spivak moves the question of history into the historical present of its writing: overall she is concerned less with the process of historical retrieval or reinterpretation of colonialism as such than with a critique of the forms of neocolonialism in the contemporary academy – hence her focus on imperialism rather than the narrower historical form of colonialism. [4] If her own texts, like Bhabha's, frequently disorient the reader with their complexity, density and sudden shifts, that necessary discomfiture is also the subject which they specifically address. Her work is therefore best approached not through critical or historical labels, but in terms of the politico-theoretical difficulties which it raises.

Spivak's critique of contemporary forms of imperialism began in earnest in 1981 with the publication of the influential essay, 'French Feminism in an International Frame', the title of which immediately indicates the kind of double focus that she brings to bear. [5] In this text she focuses on the relation of history to pedagogy, criticizing the way in which nineteenth-century literary history is taught – not only for the consumption of those in the metropolitan cultures but also for subject-peoples abroad – without any consideration of imperialism and its cultural representation. This lacuna itself suggests the continuing ideological dissimulation of imperialism today. In the face of such practices characteristic of so-called empirical history, Spivak shows how analyses of colonial discourse, by contrast, demonstrate that history is not simply the disinterested production of facts, but is rather a process of 'epistemic violence' (RS 130), an interested construction of a particular representation of an object, which may, as with Orientalism, be entirely constructed with no existence or reality outside its representation. Where such history does not take the form of a representation, Spivak argues that it generally consists of a historical narrative, usually one written from the perspective and assumptions of the West or the colonizing power. She gives the example of the history of India which, she argues, in its British version constructs a 'continuous and "homogeneous" "India" in terms of heads of state and British administrators .... "India" can then be "represented", in the other sense, by its imperial masters' (CSS 127). The task of the critic is to ask who is represented, who is not, to show the dissimulation in imperialist history of the 'mechanics of the constitution of "facts"', to utilize the methods of literary analysis to demonstrate the indeterminacy of the distinction between truth and fiction in such histories, as well as to construct counter-narratives (RS 140). An example of such a counter-history would be Romila Thapar's research on the British construction of a race-differentiated historical demography of India in order to restore its own Aryan authority there. [6] In a similar way, through the use of archival material, Spivak herself shows 'the soldiers and administrators of the East India Company constructing the object of representations that becomes the reality of India' (RS 129).

Spivak's aim is to work against such imperialist representations and narrativizations of history not by demonstrating their disorienting ambivalence but rather, as she puts it, to 'produce a narrative, in literary history, of the "worlding" of what is now called "the Third World"' (TWT 243–4). She seeks to produce a new narrative of how the Third World was itself created as a representation, or as a set of representations, not only for the West but also for the culture whose representation was constructed. An example of the latter process would be 'the sudden appearance of an alien agent of "true" history in native space' (RS 144), namely the figure of the English Regional Collector riding about the Indian countryside. He is

actually engaged in consolidating the self of Europe by obliging the native to cathect the space of the Other on his home ground. He is worldling *their own world*, which is far from mere uninscribed earth, anew, by obliging *them* to domesticate the alien as Master. (RS 133)

The relation between administrator and native operates through an apparently unproblematical polarity. Here we can see that the cost of such counter-narratives must be to lose Bhabha's insight into the ambivalence of the authority, the textual complications, of the colonizer's representations. This raises an immediate and serious question, namely to what extent does Spivak create the very homogenized positions that she wishes to attack? To what extent does she require a totalization for the production of her own 'epistemic violence'?

Spivak shares the assumption with Bhabha that imperialism was not only a territorial and economic but inevitably also a subject-constituting project. As she puts it, if 'imperialism is a way to establish the universal normativity of the mode of production narrative', to turn the native into a proletarian, then 'to ignore the subaltern today is, willy nilly, to continue the imperialist project' (CSS 123). To make the place of the subaltern subject visible can therefore become a model for interventionist practice. The term 'subaltern' is drawn from Gramsci's 'On the Margins of History: history of the subaltern social groups'. [7] Gramsci uses 'subaltern' interchangeably with 'subordinate' and 'instrumental' in his class descriptions; [8] its sense of 'inferior rank', and, in logic, of a particular rather than a universal proposition, means that it is particularly well suited to describe the diversity of dominated and exploited groups who do not possess a general 'class-consciousness'. So, in Spivak's translation of *Of Grammatology*, the term is used in the discussion of the 'supplement' to imply the subversive potential of the marginal instance. [9] In invoking the subaltern Spivak is also influenced by the *Subaltern Studies* group, who employ the term for a history that seeks to describe the 'contribution made by the people *on their own*, that is, *independently of the élite*' – the dominant groups whether foreign or indigenous who have hitherto monopolized the historiography of Indian nationalism. [10] Charting and retrieving that contribution means that the subaltern quickly becomes identified with the (colonial) subject who is an insurgent and agent of change. Such a definition means that a critic or historian who traces the activities of such agents can also be termed 'subaltern' in relation to the dominant forms of academic historiography. The subaltern historian not only locates historical instances of insurgency but also aligns him- or herself with the subaltern as a strategy for 'bringing hegemonic historiography to crisis' (IOW 198) – which amounts to a good description of the strategic orientation of Spivak's own work. However, unlike those radical critics who become deluded with their own revolutionary rhetoric, Spivak also warns that the two forms of subalternity remain discontinuous, and cannot be simply identified: invoking Marx's eleventh thesis on Feuerbach, she recalls his famous distinction between the interpretation and the transformation of the world. [11]

Nevertheless subaltern history can operate within the discipline as a kind of insurgency with respect to conventional academic forms of history, particularly by working against the schemas of historicism and the silent extirpations of positivism that continue to fabricate the narratives of neo-colonialism; to that extent its project is consonant with the anti-essentialism of Western anti-humanism. Spivak criticizes the *Subaltern Studies* group, however, insofar as, somewhat contradictorily, their programme centres on the production of accounts which refigure (the truth of) peasant or subaltern consciousness. Although the retrieval of such consciousness is made in the context of a desire to chart the emergence, or failure, of a Marxist collective consciousness, Spivak is wary even of the strategic use of what is, after all, one of the prime categories which anti-humanism seeks to interrogate, observing that 'there is no doubt that poststructuralism can really radicalise the old Marxist fetishisation of consciousness'. [12] She therefore reorients subaltern history away from the retrieval of the subaltern's consciousness and will, an activity which, she contends, 'can be no more than a theoretical fiction to entitle the project of reading' (IOW 204), towards the location and reinscription of subject-positions which are instrumental in forms of control and insurgency.

The emphasis on subject-positions draws attention to the way in which the factors of class and, particularly, gender, create a heterogeneous field that problematizes the general notion of an undifferentiated colonial subject or subaltern – as indeed of a monolithic colonizing power:

> It is possible that it is not only 'the relationship between the three domination systems [class, racial/ethnic, and sex/gender]' that is 'dialectical' but that in the theatres of decolonization, the relationship between indigenous and imperialist systems of domination are also 'dialectical', even when they are variously related to the Big Three Systems cited above. Indeed, the relationship may not be 'dialectical' at all but discontinuous, 'interruptive'. (IOW 251)

Here Spivak begins to move back to the insights of Bhabha, problematizing the simple notion that a counter-history merely involves making subalterns the subject of their own histories. At the same time something of her own ambivalence emerges in the way in which the always qualified 'dialectical' is first broached and then shifted, though only in the tentative subjunctive, towards the 'interruptive'. This points to the problem of the uneasy status of Marxism in Spivak's discourse – a difficulty to which we will return. As far as subject-positions are concerned, however, though they may be complex and heterogeneous, the critic can seek to articulate their subject-effects. This then makes it possible to reinscribe positive subject-positions for the subaltern:

> What good does such a reinscription do? It acknowledges that the arena of the subaltern's persistent emergence into hegemony must always and by definition remain heterogeneous to the efforts of the disciplinary historian. The historian must persist in his efforts in this awareness, that the subaltern is necessarily the absolute limit of the place where history is narrativised into logic. (IOW 207)

The subaltern's relation to history could also be compared to Foucault's 'event'; once again we are working here at the limits of history, at the moment of its supplementary excess. As a form of analysis, subaltern history will always mark those points where conventional historiography shields its own cognitive failures, an analytic practice comparable to certain deconstructive manoeuvres. It will also involve the more difficult project of attending to those moments – in the case of the *Subaltern Studies* historians, according to Spivak, it is the figure of woman – where the historian remains complicit with the hidden assumptions of his or her own material.

Spivak as subaltern critic therefore not only engages with the continuing practices of imperialism, but is constantly vigilant with respect to the hidden ways in which nominally radical, or oppositional historians can often unknowingly, or even knowingly, perpetuate the structures and presuppositions of the very systems which they oppose. We will look at two important instances of this: liberal Western assumptions about the 'Third World Woman', and the reverse ethnocentrism of some critiques of imperialism.

II THE 'THIRD WORLD WOMAN'

In an influential article of 1984, 'Under Western Eyes: Feminist Scholarship and Colonial Discourses', Chandra Talpade Mohanty offered a powerful analysis of 'the production of the "Third World Woman" as a singular monolithic subject' in recent Western feminist texts in the social sciences. [13] Mohanty demonstrates the ways in which such Western scholarship constitutes women of the Third World as a homogeneous group, which it then uses as a category of analysis on the basis of certain sociological and anthropological universals which elide specific cultural, historical and economic contexts. This paternalistic assumption of an identical cross-cultural universal subordination, Mohanty argues, also privileges unquestioningly the values of Western feminism, while remaining unselfconscious about its own relation to the oppressive politico-economic power structures that operate between the West and non-Western countries. Western feminist discourse, in short, can not only be ethnocentric, but in certain contexts can itself be shown to be a contemporary form of colonial discourse. Mohanty concludes by suggesting

> some disconcerting similarities between the typically authorizing signature of such Western feminist writings on women in the Third World, and the authorizing signature of the project of humanism in general – humanism as a Western ideological and political project which involves the necessary recuperation of the 'East' and 'Woman' as Others. [14]

Like Mohanty, Spivak is only too well aware of the ways in which radical criticism, such as certain forms of feminism, even as it takes an interest in women of the Third World and Third World literature, unconsciously reproduces imperialist assumptions – such as the unquestioned promotion of feminist individualism as the greatest good, 'as feminism as such' outside any historical determination (TWT 244), or the anti-theoreticism which masks an equation whereby 'primitive' or 'intuitive' methods of analysis are assumed to be most appropriate for the texts of 'primitive' cultures:

> It seems particularly unfortunate when the emergent perspective of feminist criticism reproduces the axioms of imperialism. A basically isolationist admiration for the literature of the female subject in Europe and Anglo-America establishes the high feminist norm. It is supported and operated by an information-retrieval approach to 'Third World' literature which often employs a deliberately 'nontheoretical' methodology with self-conscious rectitude. (TWT 243)

Yet non-Western writing can also expose the limits of the sophisticated methodologies of Western high theory. Much of Spivak's recent work has been concerned to demonstrate the complexities of such texts and to offer examples of strategies of reading which can do justice to the subtleties and force of their operations. Alongside the production of a narrative of the 'worldling' of the Third World, therefore, she has attempted to wrench feminist interest away from 'the mesmerising focus of the "subject-constitution" of the female individualist'. The real object of her attack, in other words, is not so much French Feminism as American gynocritics, with its ideals of individuality and identity. Increasingly, however, all Western feminism is criticized as if it upheld such values.

According to Spivak, the appearance of the 'Third World Woman' in literature or in history marks exactly the same kind of paternalistic, colonizing process as Mohanty points to in the social sciences, whereby the native is constructed into a narcissistic, self-consolidating other for the Western feminist. [15] Against Mohanty, however, Spivak argues that a critique of this cannot just take the form of pointing to the socio-historical specificity of different contexts all equally labelled 'Third World' according to fundamentalist Marxist protocols. Instead, it must work out the heterogeneous production and constitution of women as sexed subjects, not according to the schemas of psychoanalysis but in terms of the diversity of subject positions which each individual is obliged to take up or refuse. [16] The subaltern as gendered subject, as we have seen, has 'a subject-position different from the subaltern as class-subject' (IOW 246). If the position of woman historically was to be caught between two forms of domination, patriarchy and imperialism, this means that they were assigned specific but probably contradictory subject-positions. Take the case of *sati*, for example, the practice of the self-immolation of widows on the funeral pyres of their husbands. The British intervention against this constituted the single exception to their adoption and utilization of Hindu law :

As the discourse of what the British perceive as heathen ritual is sublated ... into what the British perceive as crime, one diagnosis of female free will is substituted for another.... The dubious place of the free will of the constituted sexed subject as female was successfully effaced'. (CSS 124–5)

'What the British see as poor victimised women going to the slaughter is in fact an ideological battleground' (CSS 124): caught within the conflict of such assignations, there was no determinate position from which they could speak. This means that the gendered subaltern amounts to a historical trace that cannot easily be retrieved in the production of subaltern counter-histories. Even now there is no obvious place for her as signifier:

Between patriarchy and imperialism, subject-constitution and object-formation, the figure of the woman disappears, not into a pristine nothingness, but into a violent shuttling which is the displaced figuration of the 'Third World Woman' caught between tradition and modernisation.... The case of *sati* as exemplum of the woman-in-imperialism would challenge and deconstruct [Foucault's] opposition between subject (law) and object-of-knowledge (repression), and mark the place of 'disappearance' with something other than silence and non-existence, a violent aporia between subject- and object-status. (CSS 128)

The problem is not that the woman cannot speak as such, that no records of the subject-consciousness of women exist, but that she is assigned no position of enunciation: 'there is no space from where the subaltern (sexed) subject can speak' (CSS 129). She is allowed no subject position, or rather, the place of the *sati* certainly is an enunciative position, but she is not allowed to speak: everyone else speaks for her, so that she is rewritten continuously as the object of patriarchy or of imperialism. She is a signifier, whose distinction is that she is shifted from one position to another without being allowed any content. The historian might seek, probably in vain, for a record of an authentic voice corresponding to a Western notion of speech as the expression of a full subjectivity. But for Spivak, the literary critic does not attempt to retrieve records of what, according to our present assumptions, ought to have been there, but rather articulates a different kind of historical knowledge, namely the structure and assignment of subject-positions. [17] The subaltern woman is not simply constituted as an object, nor simply used instrumentally. Rather than speak for a lost consciousness that cannot be recovered, a paternalistic activity at best, the critic can point to the place of woman's disappearance as an *aporia*, a blind-spot where understanding and knowledge is blocked. Complicating the assumption that the gendered subaltern is a homogeneous entity whose voice can be simply retrieved, Spivak demonstrates the paradoxical contradictions of the discourses which produce such *aporia* in the place of subject-positions, showing that the *sati* herself is at best presented with the non-choice of the robber's 'your money or your life!' 'Voice' is of little use in this situation.

That 'the subaltern cannot speak' is in many ways Spivak's most far-reaching argument of all, posing radical questions to all orthodox and even subaltern forms of historicization. It can be compared to her concern, in the face of the apparently monolithic and ubiquitous signifier, 'Third World Woman', to 'trace the difficulties in fixing such a signifier as an object of knowledge' (RS 128). In Spivak's essay on the Rani of Sirmur, for example, she shows how the Rani only emerges as Rani, never as a named individual, at the moment 'when she is needed in the space of imperial production'. As a result,

Caught in the cracks between the production of the archives and indigenous patriarchy, today distanced by the waves of hegemonic 'feminism', there is no 'real Rani' to be found. (RS 146–7)

Once again, it is not a question, therefore, of being able to retrieve the lost subaltern subject as a recovered authentic voice who can be made to speak once more out of the imposed silence of history, because that subject is only constituted as a subject through the positions that have been permitted. 'After the planned epistemic violence of the imperialist project' it cannot be a question of producing texts that simply answer back from a nativist position (RS 131). There can be no such nativist alternative history any more than, for Said, there can be an alternative Orientalism. This is an argument that has been most difficult for Spivak's critics to accept. [18]

But Spivak is mindful of the intractable problems in which, as we have seen, Foucault became embroiled when attempting to retrieve the lost, true speech of the silenced other. This means that the Western academic has no easy alternative to offer:

The radical critic in the West is either caught in a deliberate choice of subalternity, granting to the oppressed either that very expressive subjectivity which s/he criticizes, or instead, a total unrepresentability. (IOW 209)

This certainly seems to present an impasse. But before rushing to criticize Spivak's position, it is worth pausing to consider once more to what extent an 'alternative' simply represents the narcissistic desire to find an other that will reflect Western assumptions of selfhood. In any attempt to turn the other into a self, the anti-imperialist perspective has to come to terms with the fact that the very project of imperialism was to do the very same thing, refracting 'what might have been the absolutely Other into a domesticated Other that consolidates the imperialist self' (TWT 253). Here Spivak instances a famous, typical example of the process by which the colonial subject functions only to consolidate the self of the colonizer: the career of Bertha Mason, the white Jamaican Creole wife of Rochester in *Jane Eyre*. The focus on this marginal figure demonstrates the importance of her function as subaltern in the novel:

In this fictive England, [Bertha] must play out her role, act out the transformation of her 'self' into that fictive Other, set fire to the house and kill herself, so that Jane Eyre can become the feminist individualist heroine of British fiction. I must read this as an allegory of the general epistemic violence of imperialism, the construction of a self-immolating colonial subject for the glorification of the social mission of the colonizer. (TWT 251)

The impact of Spivak's argument can be measured to the extent that as a text long subsumed into the institutional apparatus of the teaching of literature, today it has become hard to think about *Jane Eyre* without Rhys' *The Wide Sargasso Sea*, that it is impossible to forget that the moment when Jane achieves her independence by inheriting a fortune – from the West Indies – is also the moment in which she becomes complicit with the history of slavery.

As such a perspective on one of the earliest British feminist novels suggests, Spivak is particularly alert to ways in which radical critiques, albeit of patriarchy, can themselves become oppressive or imperialist when considered in a different context. This is particularly obvious in the case of individualism upon which so much Western feminism has been constructed – and which Spivak polemically extends to represent Western feminism as such. [19] Here 'the inbuilt colonialism of First World feminism toward the Third' (IOW 153) means that Western liberal feminism validates forms of behaviour which, possible only for the élite, can at the same time serve to oppress sub-proletarian women. While Spivak points to Mahasweta Devi's character Senanayak in the story of 'Draupadi' as an allegorical indictment of the First World scholar in search of the Third World, she illustrates the oppressive possibilities of First World feminism on women of the Third through a compelling analysis of Devi's story 'Stanadayini'. Here the heroine Jashoda precisely does not undergo that ideal of liberal feminist criticism – the development of a fully constituted individual female subjectivity. Jashoda's story is told as an affirmation against the assumption that, without such accession to consciousness, there is nothing to tell. It also complicates that most affirmative category of Western feminism, motherhood, relating how Jashoda provides the means for the 'liberation' of upper-class women from breast-feeding (IOW 256–7). For Jashoda it is not a question of acceding to consciousness, of a subjectivity or self, or even of speaking; it is her body that becomes the place of an uncomfortable knowledge when 'decolonization as failure of foster-mothering' is figured in a cancer of the breast. This, Spivak remarks, in stark contrast to Western notions of *jouissance*, constitutes 'an excess very far from the singularity of the clitoral orgasm' (IOW 260). Spivak's analysis of 'Stanadayini' thus demonstrates how the Third World text may intervene in current Western debates, question their terms and assumptions, and show up the limits of the space in which they operate. A narrative such as Devi's does not simply provide a haven of realism for the nostalgic critic at a time when First World literature has graduated into language-games; rather it can deconstruct First World discourse by inverting it and displacing it, thus initiating the process of the First World's own necessary decolonization. [20]

Instead, therefore, of rushing to speak for women of the Third World Spivak argues that the academic feminist:

must learn to learn from them, to speak to them, to suspect that their access to the political and sexual scene is not merely to be *corrected* by our superior theory and enlightened compassion.... in order to learn enough about Third World women and to develop a different readership, the immense heterogeneity of the field must be appreciated, and the First World feminist must learn to stop feeling privileged *as a woman*. (IOW 135–6)

In the place of the preoccupation with identity and the assertion of feminist individualism, Spivak offers the possibility of other perspectives and goals:

I see no way to avoid insisting that there has to be a simultaneous other focus: not merely who am I? but who is the other woman? How am I naming her? How does she name me? Is this part of the problematic I discuss? (IOW 150)

By shifting the question from 'who am I?' to 'who is the other woman?' Spivak offers a heterogeneity and discontinuity which demonstrates the extent to which, although as women women may be said to share a common situation, each instance of being a woman is historically specific. As Barthes argued, though birth and death may be universal facts, the meaning and significance of their experience is culturally determined. But such awareness must not be endorsed too quickly: Spivak stresses the pitfalls which it may involve if translated into new pedagogic practices. An interest in the other woman does not have to involve the instant commodification or territorial-ization of 'Third World Literature' or the 'pedagogic and curricular appropriation of Third World Women's texts in translation by feminist teachers and readers who are vaguely aware of the race-bias within mainstream feminism'. [21] Nevertheless, the paradox of Spivak's own work remains: it seems as if the heterogeneity of the Third World woman can only be achieved through a certain homogenization of the First.

III REVERSE ETHNOCENTRISM

In the same way as with the 'Third World Woman', Spivak argues that the concept of the 'Third World' has itself to be retrieved from its role as a convenient but hegemonic signifier that homogenizes the Third World into questions of nationalism and ethnicity. [22] But, once again, it is easy for the subaltern critic to be drawn into a simple reversal of this.

In the first place there is the problem of what Spivak calls the 'hyperbolic admiration or ... pious guilt that today is the mark of a reverse ethnocentrism' (CSS 121). This produces the double bind of 'considering the "native" as object for enthusiastic information-retrieval and thus denying its own "worlding" ' (TWT 245). Whether from the point of view of the patronizing Western enthusiast, or from that of the resisting colonized who seeks simply to reverse the opposition colonized/colonizer, reverse ethnocentrism is likely, as Fanon warned, to fall into a number of traps. [23] The kind of problem involved can be suggested by comparing it to a reverse sexism. If the man/woman duality as it is currently constituted is simply inverted, then, as many feminists have pointed out, the constitution of 'woman' is still determined according to the terms of the original opposition. In a similar way, those who evoke the 'nativist' position through a nostalgia for a lost or repressed culture idealize the possibility of that lost origin being recoverable in all its former plenitude without allowing for the fact that the figure of the lost origin, the 'other' that the colonizer has repressed, has itself been constructed in terms of the colonizer's own self-image. [24] Reverse ethnocentrism therefore, Spivak argues, amounts to a nostalgic assumption that

> a critique of imperialism would restore the sovereignty for the lost self of the colonies so that Europe could, once and for all, be put in the place of the other that it always was. It ... seems to me that it is this kind of revisionary impulse that is allowing the emergence of the 'Third World' as a convenient signifier. (RS 128)

The 'nativist' argument thus simply reproduces a Western fantasy about its own society now projected out onto the lost society of the other and named 'the Third World'. At one point Spivak even goes so far as to claim that her 'chief project is to point out the positivist-idealist variety of such nostalgia entertained by academics in self-imposed exile' (RS 132). No doubt guarding herself against the sentimental wistfulness of such diasporic intellectuals, she argues that it is only in the archives of imperial governance that the construction of the discursive field, of the colony as an object of knowledge for the West, can be articulated and produced without succumbing to the nostalgia for lost origins. [25]

Spivak suggests that it is possible to show through analyses of the discursive formations around specific fields, as in Lata Mani's work on *sati*, that all such arguments, whether from colonizer or colonized, tend to revolve around the terms which the colonizers have constructed. [26] To reverse an opposition of this kind is to remain caught within the very terms that are being disputed. Nationalist resistance to imperialism, for example, itself derives its notion of nation and of national self-determination from the Western culture that is being resisted. Nationalism is a product of imperialism, and often, as Spivak remarks, only succeeds 'in changing the geo-political conjuncture from territorial imperialism to neo-colonialism' (IOW 245). This means that, as Ranajit Guha argues in his introduction to the *Subaltern Studies* series, even post-colonial histories will always tend to pass over the role and examples of subaltern resistance not organized according to this particular ethos, so that in effect the élite culture of nationalism continues to participate with the colonizer. [27] This restriction of knowledge within the protocols of existing paradigms Spivak characterizes as the effect of certain forms of Western rationality. Against it she places, perhaps surprisingly, literature, positioned in an almost Althusserian mode of knowledge half-outside the dominant discourse:

> By contrast, emphasizing the literariness of literature, pedagogy invites us to take a distance from the continuing project of reason. Without this supplementary distancing, a position and its counter-position, both held in the discourse of reason, will keep legitimizing each other. Feminism and masculism, benevolent or militant, might not then be able to avoid becoming opposing faces of each other. (IOW 249–50)

Here Spivak comes close to claiming something like Foucault's madness or Said's 'critical distance', but elsewhere she puts it rather differently: 'textuality', she suggests, marks 'the unavailability of a unified solution' (IOW 78). In that sense it enables the deconstructive move which displaces as well as reverses an opposition, such as that between colonizer and colonized, and thus provides a position for the forcing of an effective critical leverage. Spivak warns, however, that such a displacement can only be produced by taking 'the investigator's own complicity into account' (RS 147). This is not just a matter for occasional reflection. The involvement of the subject in the object of investigation complicates any assumption such as Said's that the critic is in a position to detach him or herself from systems and cultures so as to produce an oppositional criticism.

In this context, Spivak's first concern is to ask what relation the Western quest for knowledge – even if now a reverse ethnocentrism, or that of a 'Westernized Easterner' – has to the object of that knowledge. What, for instance, does it mean to use European high theory in critiques of colonialism? Characteristically although she poses this question Spivak is unwilling either simply to endorse or refuse theory as such. She comments that 'it is of course understood that only the élite playing at self-marginalization can afford the impossible luxury of turning their backs on those resources' (CSS 121). The objection that 'élite' methodology should not be used for 'subaltern' material, already encountered in the case of certain Western assumptions about how to teach non-Western literature, is sometimes made by subaltern critics also, in which case it involves a category mistake and an epistemological/ontological confusion:

> The confusion is held in an unacknowledged analogy: just as the subaltern *is* not élite (ontology), so must the historian not *know* through élite method (epistemology). (IOW 253)

This can be related to the problem of 'possessive exclusivism' discussed by Said, according to which it is claimed that whites cannot discuss racism, men feminism, etc. The argument assumes that all political categories can only be sustained ontologically and epistemologically through experience.[28] Spivak's response is to suggest that the problem is really a political one which occurs only when an oppressive class controls the form of knowledge exclusively. She also concedes that when subaltern groups participate in the production of knowledge, even about themselves, they thereby begin to assume a position of privilege comparable to that of the dominant group. For subaltern studies, as for Marxism, the problematic assumption is that the historical subaltern's 'own idiom did not allow him to know his struggle so that he could articulate himself as its subject' (IOW 253). Against this, Spivak argues crucially that post-colonial intellectuals are obliged to 'unlearn' their privilege as their loss and to mark their theoretical positionality as any investigating subject ought. [29] This notion of the intellectual 'unlearning' his or her privilege seems, however, remarkably utopian. And the problem with the investigating subject marking his or her theoretical positionality is that it assumes the very homogeneity of the subject that Spivak, the anti-individualist, disputes.

IV MONITORY MODELS FOR THE INVESTIGATOR

The difference between twentieth-century Anglo-American positivism and European theory has been articulated in terms of the contending models of explanation and interpretation. [30] But the real distinction, according to Spivak, occurs with respect to the function of the critic; interpretation should also attend to the constitutive and complicating role of the investigator in the formation of knowledge. The residue of positivist assumptions that persists in Anglo-American theory means, however, that all too often 'the position of the investigator remains unquestioned' (CSS 120). One of the strongest features of Derrida's work, according to Spivak, is the way in which he focuses very specifically on his own role as an intellectual and questions his own production as a part of the discipline. This is the aspect of deconstruction which interests her most:

> the recognition, within deconstructive practice, of provisional and intract-able starting points in any investigative effort; its disclosure of complicities where a will to knowledge would create oppositions; its insistence that in disclosing complicities the critic-as-subject is herself complicit with the object of her critique; its emphasis upon 'history' and upon the ethico-political as the 'trace' of that complicity – the proof that we do not inhabit a clearly defined critical space free of such traces. [31]

Today, Spivak argues, it seems obvious to what degree nineteenth-century knowledge of India was produced by interested observers; this makes it possible to 'track the mechanics of the construction of the *self-consolidating* other – a history that is in some senses a genealogy of the historian. What is marked is the site of desire' (RS 131). She herself is therefore always concerned to introduce the question of the desire of the analyst, of the historian as well as her own, countering the tendency to neglect the investigator's own involvement by giving detailed descriptions of her own place, history and special interests during the course of her analyses. [32] The problem with this is that it can easily be mistaken for that very feminist individualism that elsewhere she argues remains so ubiquitous in the West.

As an Asian, educated in India and in the United States where she now works, Spivak describes herself as one who has been subject to a process of 'ideological victimage' ('"naturalisation" transformed into privilege', IOW 136) and who has, as the trajectory of her own writings shows, been obliged to pull herself out of certain hegemonic forms of Western critical thinking. [33] Such a position as an Asian woman in the Western academy also, let it be said, gives her unassailable political credentials – in the Western academy at least. Although Spivak constantly attempts to undo the homogeneity of the signifier 'Third World Woman', by announcing her position as investigator so insistently, she runs the inevitable risk of presenting herself as the representative of that very 'Third World Woman'. Her reaction to the difficulties of such a position emerges in the contending and sometimes conflicting languages of her work. Here psychoanalysis, though on occasion rejected for its Eurocentrism, provides, as it does for Derrida, a model and a cautionary example of the operation of the (un)knowing subject within the production of knowledge:

> As Sarah Kofman has shown, the deep ambiguity of Freud's use of woman as scapegoat is a reaction-formation to an initial and continuing desire to give the hysteric a voice, to transform her at least into the *subject* of hysteria. The masculist-imperialist ideological formation that operated that desire into 'the daughter's seduction' is part of the 'same' formation that constructs the monolithic 'Third World Woman'. As a post-colonial intellectual, I am operated by that formation as well. Part of our 'unlearning' project is to articulate that ideological formation into our *object* of investigation. Thus, when confronted with the question 'Can the subaltern speak?, and, can the subaltern (as woman) speak?' I am aware that our efforts to give the subaltern a voice in history will be at least doubly open to the dangers run by Freud's discourse. [34]

The subaltern cannot speak. Nevertheless the possibility here opens up after all of speaking for her – not in terms of retrieving a lost historical voice but as an effect of being constructed as a representative of 'the monolithic "Third World Woman" '. This suggests the politico-theoretical difficulties which the project of decolonization involves; one that cannot be solved by a theoretical method but only by a constant vigilance and a consistent transgression of the norms that facilitate, and control the production of knowledge. The first of these norms claims the separation, and occlusion, of the analyst from the object of investigation: psychoanalysis confronts the consequences of their complicity, and deconstruction uses it as a point of leverage: 'This is the greatest gift of deconstruction: to question the authority of the investigating subject without paralysing him, persistently transforming conditions of impossibility into possibility' (IOW 201). But also the reverse.

Spivak, for all her willingness to enter into the most complex areas of theory and philosophy, must therefore also be persistently concerned with the institutional place of the academic who, if supposed to unlearn his or her privilege, has also to learn his or her complicity in the production of knowledge. It is not just that there is no position strictly speaking outside the institution but that the history of institutionalization and the production of disciplines itself cannot be disentangled from the production of the West as 'the West'. [35] Such a programme also involves an awareness of the ideological function of academic authority in more mundane and less glamorous areas such as, for example, the production of textbooks for undergraduates. [36] It also entails consideration of the participation of the institution in contemporary processes of neocolonialism. Spivak constantly invokes and reminds her readers of the powers and economies that enable academic privilege: so, for instance, having discussed the effects of the international division of labour on the subjects of imperial territories in the nineteenth century, she adds: 'The lives and deaths of the paradigmatic victims of that division, the women of the urban sub-proletariat and of unorganized peasant labour, are not going on record in the "humanist" academy even as we speak'. [37] The production of counter-knowledges and of counter-histories from the past is never carried out without awareness of the same repeated effects of that imperial process which continue today.

Great stress has been placed in this discussion on Spivak's preoccupation with certain deconstructive methodological concerns but this has not been at the expense of her politics, for in a real sense her politics are implicated in them, directed as they are against the Western academy's forms of knowledge and its pedagogy. Spivak has a particular ability to project the extensive range of such issues simultaneously with the detailed texture of her historical, literary, philosophical, theoretical or political analyses. It is this which constitutes not only her own importance as a critic, but also demonstrates the extent to which the critique of colonialism involves a project that is not merely historical nor peripheral but rather attempts a radical restructuring of the traditional perspectives, norms and assumptions which form the basis of Western thought. She thus shows that the way to counteract Western history and Western historicism is not simply to produce alternative or counter-histories but to contest and inflect the more far-reaching implications of the system of which they form a part.

On the other hand, and this constitutes the lasting paradox of her work, despite the sophistication of the deconstructive positions which she so patiently establishes, at moments Spivak cannot resist reverting to the imperatives of an individualism, or the continuity of a Marxist narrative not always characterized by the qualified 'dialectic' of a 'Marx after Derrida':

so she upbraids her readers, for example, for taking so 'little notice of the politico-economico-technological determinant', of 'masculist-imperialist ideological formations', of the international division of labour, and the like. [38] This residual classical Marxism is invoked for the force of its political effect from an outside that disavows and apparently escapes the strictures that the rest of her work establishes. Spivak speaks of the 'strategic' use of essentialism and universals in certain situations, which describes, perhaps, the way in which class and the economic operate as implicit, undisturbed collectivities against which the anti-individualism and heterogeneity are driven. [39] For all the carefully constructed disparateness of her work, for all the discontinuities which she refuses to reconcile, Spivak's Marxism functions as an overall syncretic frame. It works, in fact, in exactly the same way as Jameson's – as a transcendentalizing gesture to produce closure. Spivak's supplementary history must itself be supplemented.

V THE EMPIRE WITHIN

Said's major theoretical achievement, the creation of an object of analysis called 'colonial discourse', has proved one of the most fruitful and significant areas of research in recent years. The concept of colonial discourse, necessarily still being debated, has been extended to other categories such as 'minority discourse', and is increasingly being used to describe certain power structures within the hierarchies of the West itself, particularly the relation of minorities to the dominant group (for example, by women of colour in relation to feminism). Colonial discourse provides a good illustration of how theoretico-political advances can effectively transform the work of a range of different disciplines. However, its own theoretical problems remain.

We have seen how Said's lack of methodological self-analysis also betrays his lack of an answer to the question of an alternative to Orientalism, even how to go about subverting it, how to be inside and outside at once. His refusal of the possibility of ambivalence, which he recognizes but transforms into the question of the transcendence of the system by the individual, means that he is effectively restricted to the very limited model of a detached, oppositional critical consciousness. What both Bhabha and Spivak have demonstrated, on the other hand, in the more Derridean mode that Said refuses, is that the critic can exploit the ambivalence of the discourse of Orientalism and position himself or herself in an equally ambivalent relation to the theoretical method that is being employed, so as to disconcert and disorient the reader from the familiar politico-theoretical structures which it seems to promise. In this way Bhabha and Spivak demonstrate the possibility of providing a critique in which both theory and detailed historical material can be inflected towards an inversion of the dominant structures of knowledge and power without simply reproducing them. This means that for them the possibility of criticism comes not from experience or conscious-ness as in Said, but rather from the exploitation of a certain methodological scission within the rationalist project. Such a strategy of supplementarity will always leave us with the uncertain irony of inaccessibility: are such texts sometimes simply out of control or are they intended to make the reader feel out of control, uncomfortable, and unsure where to place him- or herself? It is a condition of their own operativity that this question must remain unanswerable.

Crucial to this discomfiture has been the demonstration of the extent to which colonialism, in the British example, was not simply a marginal activity on the edges of English civilization, but fundamental in its own cultural self-representation. To date there has been comparatively little analysis of the construction of such a representation. Colonial discourse analysis is placed in the unique position of being able to examine English culture, literature, and indeed Englishness in its widest sense, from its determined position on the margins: not questing for the essence of Englishness but examining the representations it has produced for itself of its Other, against and through which it defines itself, together with the function of such representations in a structure of power in which they are used instrumentally. Perhaps more than in any other context, colonialism makes such strategies of power clearly visible; but the analysis of them is a complicated matter to the extent that it always necessitates that the analyser examine his or her own relationship to them – particularly when the analysis takes place in the context of British or American academic institutions. Its difficulty is that it can highlight the operations of neocolonialism in unexpected places, making trouble for the dominant theoretical positions which have until recently either ignored the question of the Third World or simply assimilated it within categories developed for First World economies or politics. Colonial discourse analysis, as Hazel Carby suggests in the case of black feminism, does more than make visible something which had previously been absent: it also challenges central categories and assumptions of mainstream Marxism and feminism in the same way that, as Fanon argued, the Third World constitutes the disruptive term for the European political duel between capitalism and socialism. [40]

What has also been particularly significant for Britain has been the demonstration of the relation of structures of colonialism to contemporary forms of imperialism, neocolonialism and racism. If the process of de-Europeanization has been going on since the nineteenth century, in the twentieth century decolonization has brought about a much more radical revision of Western culture. This has been dramatically augmented by the post-war phenomenon of immigration, but even here, as Salman Rushdie has suggested, it is possible to argue that the colonial situation has been simply reversed: instead of the Europeans occupying the colonies in order to take advantage of the labour power available, the indigenous inhabitants of the colonies have been brought to Europe to provide cheap labour power there. [41] If the imperial situation has thus been reversed, the power-structure remains exactly the same – something that the racism of the Right, which presents immigration as an 'alien wedge' supposedly threatening the basis of English culture and identity, chooses to ignore. What colonial discourse analysis can show is that this representation of the 'alien wedge' is itself the construction of the colonial culture, forcibly maintained as a part of Englishness itself, and only now apparently visible as what Rushdie has called the 'empire within'. [42] This construction of English culture, the connections between representations of Englishness, including 'English literature', and the forms of neocolonialism in contemporary Britain, all prompt urgent questions about culture and nation. This is the significance of Bhabha's recent shift from analyses of colonial discourse to a consideration of the complex structures of cultural and national identity. [43]

We shall be examining such work on a later occasion: in the meantime what should be emphasized is the degree to which analysis of colonialism has shown the extent to which such relations of power and authority are still endemic in current social and institutional practices. Here the question becomes not colonial discourse or even neocolonialism as such but racism. Colonial discourse shows the enactment of racism in its colonial moment. Analysis needs to be extended now to the discursive forms, representations and practices of contemporary racism, together with their relation to the colonial past and to nineteenth-century forms of knowledge such as evolutionism – including its own evolution into racial theories – showing in particular how they sustain and intervene in contemporary practices of the state which legitimize racism, such as immigration and nationality law or educational institutions.

These are the difficult political questions. They emerge from the analysis of colonialism because it combines its critique of Western history with one of Western historicism, showing the enactment of the links between the two in the colonial past and the neocolonial present. The effect of this has been to produce a shift away from the problem of history as an idea towards an examination of Western history's and historicism's contemporary political ramifications. For that history lives on: its effects are operating now. It is those events that the new logics of historical writing must address.

Notes

1 WHITE MYTHOLOGIES

1 Hélène Cixous and Catherine Clément, *The Newly Born Woman*, trans. Betsy Wing (Manchester: Manchester University Press, 1986), 70. Further references will be cited in the text. For Derrida's childhood memories of violence, fear and racism in colonial Algeria see 'Derrida l'insoumis', *Le Nouvel Observateur* 9th September 1983 (translated in *Derrida and Difference*, eds David Wood and R. Bernasconi [Warwick: Parousia Press, 1985], 107–27); Lyotard's writings on Algeria have recently been collected as *La Guerre des algériens: Ecrits 1956–1963*, ed. Mohammed Randani (Paris: Galilée, 1989).

2 For example, Rachel Bowlby, 'The Feminine Female', *Social Text* 7 (1983), 67. The question that follows is to what extent the concerns expressed here significantly affect Cixous' work.

3 The general argument, for example, of Gillian Rose's *Dialectic of Nihilism. Post-Structuralism and Law* (Oxford: Blackwell, 1984).

4 In *The Philosophy of History*, trans. J. Sibree (London: The Colonial Press, 1899), Hegel concludes his brief discussion of Africa with the comment, 'at this point we leave Africa, not to mention it again. For it is no historical part of the World; it has no movement or development to exhibit' (99). Marx, in 'The Future Results of the British Rule in India' (1853), comments:

> Indian society has no history at all, at least no known history. What we call its history is but the history of its successive intruders who founded their empires on the passive basis of that unresisting and unchanging society.... England has to fulfil a double mission in India: one destructive, the other regenerating – the annihilation of old Asiatic society, and the laying of the material foundations of Western society in Asia.

(*Surveys from Exile*, ed. David Fernbach [Harmondsworth: Penguin, 1973], 320); compare also Said's comments on 'World history', section II, below. For an Althusserian alternative to the orthodox Marxist view see Brian Turner, *Marx and the End of Orientalism* (London: George Allen and Unwin, 1978); Eric Wolf's *Europe and the People Without History* (Berkeley: University of California Press, 1982) attempts an anthropological account of the relation of European history to that of the rest of the world.

5 cf. Jacques Derrida, 'Le Facteur de la vérité', in *The Post Card: From Socrates to Freud and Beyond*, trans. Alan Bass (Chicago: Chicago University Press, 1987), 480–2n.

6 For a recent account of Hegelian Marxism in France, see Michael S. Roth,

Knowing and History: Appropriations of Hegel in Twentieth-Century France (Ithaca: Cornell University Press, 1988).

7   Alex Callinicos, *Making History* (Oxford: Blackwell, 1987), 177.

8   The same difficulties could be demonstrated for Habermas' attempt to shift the basis of the subject from consciousness to intersubjectivity – which necessarily means that he is even more dependent on presupposing a category of normativity that has to repress difference. Such a move forms part of a strategy designed to enable a reaffirmation of a progressive schema of world history. See Jürgen Habermas, *Theory of Communicative Action. Vol. 1: Reason and the Rationalisation of Society*, trans. Thomas McCarthy (London: Heinemann, 1985), *Vol. 2: Lifeworld and System: A Critique of Functionalist Reason*, trans. Thomas McCarthy (Cambridge: Polity Press, 1987). For a critique of the notion of normativity as a form of imperialism, see Jean-François Lyotard, *The Differend. Phrases in Dispute*, trans. Georges Van Den Abbeele (Manchester: Manchester University Press, 1988), 142–5, and, with respect to Habermas in particular, see my 'Not Revolutionary – But Communicating', *Oxford Literary Review* 11 (1989), 224–5.

9   Ernesto Laclau and Chantal Mouffe, *Hegemony and Socialist Strategy. Towards a Radical Democratic Politics* (London: Verso, 1985), 149–52. Jean-François Lyotard makes a similar point in relation to narratives of emancipation in *The Differend. Phrases in Dispute*, trans. George Van Den Abbeele (Manchester: Manchester University Press, 1988), 161.

10 Roland Barthes, *Mythologies*, trans. Annette Lavers (London: Jonathan Cape, 1972), 148.

11 Particularly apparent in the opening description of *The Communist Manifesto* (Moscow: Progress Publishers, 1952), 40–2.

12 Translated as Vincent Descombes, *Modern French Philosophy*, trans. L. Scott-Fox and J. M. Harding (Cambridge: Cambridge University Press, 1980).

13 Jacques Derrida, 'White Mythology' (1971), in *Margins – of Philosophy*, trans. Alan Bass (Chicago: Chicago University Press, 1982), 213.

14 Michel Foucault, 'Georges Canguilhem: Philosopher of Error', *Ideology and Consciousness* 7 (1980), 53–4. Foucault discusses his own relation to the Frankfurt School in 'Critical Theory/Intellectual History', in *Michel Foucault: Philosophy, Politics, Culture. Interviews and Other Writings*, ed. Lawrence D. Kritzman (New York: Routledge, 1988), 17–46; see also David Couzens Hoy, 'Power, Repression, Progress: Foucault, Lukes, and the Frankfurt School', in *Foucault: A Critical Reader*, ed. David Couzens Hoy (Oxford: Blackwell, 1986), 123–47.

15 Thus Peter Dews, for example, in *Logics of Disintegration: Post-Structuralist Thought and the Claims of Critical Theory* (London: Verso, 1987), consistently sets the Frankfurt School against poststructuralism in a simple relation of truth to illusion. For a more productive comparison, see Rainer Nägele, 'The Scene of the Other: Theodor W. Adorno's Negative Dialectic in the Context of Poststructuralism', in Jonathan Arac, ed., *Postmodernism and Politics* (Minneapolis: University of Minnesota Press, 1986), 91–111.

16 Max Horkheimer and Theodor W. Adorno, *Dialectic of Enlightenment*, trans. John Cumming (New York: Continuum, 1982).

17 *Dialectic of Enlightenment*, 6. Lyotard discusses Adorno's analysis of Auschwitz in *The Differend*, 86–106.

18 Foucault, 'Georges Canguilhem', 53. Further references will be cited in the text. Edmund Husserl, *Cartesian Meditations*, trans. D. Cairns (The Hague: Nijhoff, 1960), and *The Crisis of the European Sciences and Transcendental Phenomenology: An Introduction to Phenomenological Philosophy*, trans. D. Carr (Evanston: Northwestern University Press, 1970). Husserl was, of course, also important in different ways for both Sartre and Adorno.

19 For further discussion of this project in Foucault, see Chapter 5, below. With regard to Lyotard, Geoffrey Bennington notes that 'perhaps the most coherent view of Lyotard's work as a whole is that it strives to respect the event in its singularity, and has experimented with various ways of achieving that respect. Such a stress on a singularity which is not an individual is itself not individual to Lyotard, of course, and he has even suggested that it might be taken as a guiding thread of what in the English-speaking countries is known as "poststructuralism"' (Geoffrey Bennington, *Lyotard. Writing the Event* [Manchester: Manchester University Press, 1988], 9).

20 Edward Said, 'Orientalism Reconsidered', in *Europe and Its Others*, ed. Francis Barker *et al.*, 2 vols (Colchester: University of Essex, 1985) I, 22. Further references will be given in the text.

21 For an account of 'Third Worldism' see Nigel Harris, *The End of the Third World: Newly Industrializing Countries and the Decline of an Ideology* (Harmondsworth: Penguin Books, 1987), 11–29; see also Peter Worsley, *The Third World*, 2nd ed. (London: Weidenfeld and Nicolson, 1967).

22 In *Nationalism, Colonialism and Literature: Modernism and Imperialism* (Derry: Field Day Pamphlets 14, 1988), Fredric Jameson, on the other hand, recalls Lévi-Strauss' contention in *Tristes tropiques* that Islam amounts to 'the last and most advanced of the great *Western* monotheisms' (17). On Islam as an anti-colonial revolutionary force see Frantz Fanon, *The Wretched of the Earth*, trans. Constance Farrington (Harmondsworth: Penguin, 1967), 171; on Islamic fundamentalism, see Bruno Etienne, *L'Islamisme radical* (Paris: Hachette, 1987).

23 Emmanuel Levinas, *Théorie de l'intuition dans la phénoménologie de Husserl* (Paris: Alcan, 1930), and 'Jacques Derrida: tout autrement', in *Les Dieux dans la cuisine: vingt ans de la philosophie en France*, ed. Jacques Brochier (Paris: Aubier, 1975), reprinted in *Noms propres* (Montpellier: Fata Morgana, 1975).

24 Emmanuel Levinas, 'The Trace of the Other', in *Deconstruction in Context*, ed. Mark C. Taylor (Chicago: Chicago University Press, 1986), 346–7.

25 Emmanuel Levinas, *Totality and Infinity. An Essay on Exteriority*, trans. Alphonso Lingis (Pittsburgh: Duquesne University Press, [1969]), 21ff. Further references will be cited in the text.

26 Compare Michel Foucault's analysis of power in terms of war in *The History of Sexuality. Volume One: An Introduction*, trans. Robert Hurley (London: Allen Lane, 1979), 93, and in *Power/Knowledge: Selected Interviews and Other Writings, 1972–1977*, ed. Colin Gordon, trans. Colin Gordon *et al.* (New York: Pantheon Books, 1980), 123.

27 Emmanuel Levinas, 'Beyond Intentionality', in *Philosophy in France Today*, ed. Alan Montefiore (Cambridge: Cambridge University Press, 1983), 103. Martin Jay suggests that the critique of a Lukácsian holism also derived from the post-war identification of totality with totalitarianism. However, as Jay points out, among French Marxists, even before Sartre, there was already a stress on open rather than closed totalities, for example in the work of Lefebvre (Jay, *Marxism and Totality: The Adventures of a Concept from Lukács to Habermas* [Berkeley: University of California Press, 1984], 296–7). For further discussion of the totality/totalitarian equation, in the context of a presentation by Fredric Jameson, see *Marxism and the Interpretation of Culture*, eds Cary Nelson and Lawrence Grossberg (London: Macmillan, 1988), 358–9.

28 Levinas' ideas about justice can be compared to those of Lyotard for whom justice is also a question of respecting alterity and conflictual diversity rather than their resolution through universal laws. See in particular *The Postmodern Condition: A Report on Knowledge*, trans. Geoff Bennington and Brian Massumi (Minnesota: Minnesota University Press, 1984), and Jean-François Lyotard

and Jean-Loup Thébaud, *Just Gaming* [*Au juste*], trans. Wlad Godzich (Minneapolis: Minnesota University Press, 1985).

29 Levinas' account of the role of theory as vision, and its claim in Plato to a disinterested contemplation of being is discussed in detail by Derrida in 'Violence and Metaphysics. An Essay on the Thought of Emmanuel Levinas', in *Writing and Difference*, trans. Alan Bass (London: Routledge and Kegan Paul, 1978), 84–92.

30 Compare Lyotard again, who contests the status of theory in *Economie libidinale* (Paris: Minuit, 1974) and denounces it as terror in *Rudiments païens. genre dissertatif* (Paris: Union générale d'éditions, 1977).

31 See Paul de Man, 'Kant's Materialism', in *Aesthetic Ideology*, ed. Andrzej Warminski (Minneapolis: University of Minnesota Press, forthcoming), and Lyotard and Thébaud, *Just Gaming*. In *The Differend*, however, Lyotard returns to the Kantian problematic of the aesthetic and the sublime (161–71).

32 An example of an attempt to write such a history would be Foucault's account of the history of madness; though as Foucault found to his cost, any history as representation, even the history of the Other, must always run the risk of becoming the history of the same. See his Preface to *The Order of Things. An Archaeology of the Human Sciences* (London: Tavistock, 1970), xxiv, discussed in Chapter 5.

33 Emmanuel Levinas, *Ethics and Infinity. Conversations with Philippe Nemo*, trans. Richard A. Cohen (Pittsburgh: Duquesne University Press, 1985), 61; Levinas' sustained discussion of time comes in *Le Temps et l'Autre* (Montpellier: Fata Morgana, 1979). In *Of Grammatology*, trans. Gayatri Chakravorty Spivak (Baltimore: Johns Hopkins University Press, 1976), Derrida specifically relates his concept of '*trace* to what is at the centre of the latest work of Emmanuel Levinas and his critique of ontology: relationship to the illeity as to the alterity of a past that never was and can never be lived in the originary or modified form of presence' (70).

34 In addition to 'Violence and Metaphysics', Derrida has also written on Levinas in 'En ce moment même dans cet ouvrage me voici', in *Textes pour Emmanuel Levinas*, ed. François Laruelle (Paris: Galilée, 1980), reprinted in Jacques Derrida, *Psyché: Inventions de l'autre* (Paris: Galilée, 1987), 159–202. See also 'Of an Apocalyptic Tone Recently Adopted in Philosophy', *Oxford Literary Review* 6:2 (1984), 3–37.

35 For the difficulties inherent in the idea of an authentic speech of the other, see my discussion of Bakhtin in *The Culture of Institutions* (forthcoming).

36 Christopher Norris, *Derrida* (London: Fontana, 1987), 230. Norris' essay usefully counters the widespread assumption that the concern with ethics is a recent development; for example, in *Logics of Disintegration*, Peter Dews suggests that in the 'late 1970s onwards' it became possible to pose philosophical questions about ethics which would, he claims, have been 'unthinkable during the heady years of "anti-humanist" and "post-philosophical" experimentation' (xii). This becomes somewhat less plausible to the extent that the 'post-philosophical' itself involves the posing of ethical questions to philosophy. On Derrida and ethics, see also Robert Bernasconi, 'Deconstruction and the Possibility of Ethics', in *Deconstruction and Philosophy: The Texts of Jacques Derrida*, ed. John Sallis (Chicago: Chicago University Press, 1987), 122–39. Lacan's important Seminar on ethics, given in 1959–60, is available as *Le Séminare VIII: L'Ethique de la psychanalyse* (Paris: Seuil, 1986).

37 Richard Kearney, *Dialogues with Contemporary Continental Thinkers. The Phenomenological Heritage* (Manchester: Manchester University Press, 1984), 123.

38 Kearney, *Dialogues*, 58. Levinas here endorses the more Derridean position, in which he sees ontology and metaphysics as necessarily interdependent, first proposed in his *Otherwise than Being, or Beyond Essence*, trans. Alphonso Lingis (The Hague: Nijhoff, 1981).

39 Kearney, *Dialogues*, 69.

40 Kearney, *Dialogues*, 63.

41 Levinas, *Ethics and Infinity*, 52. On love see also *Totality and Infinity*, 254–5; Hélène Cixous, 'An Exchange with Hélène Cixous', in Verena Andermatt Conley, *Hélène Cixous: Writing the Feminine* (Lincoln: University of Nebraska Press, 1984), 143; Julia Kristeva, *Histoires d'amour* (Paris: Denoël, 1983). For Kristeva's discussions of ethics, see 'The Ethics of Linguistics', in *Desire in Language. A Semiotic Approach to Literature and Art*, trans. Thomas Gora, Alice Jardine and Leon S. Roudiez (New York: Columbia University Press, 1980), 23–35, and 'Stabat Mater', in *The Kristeva Reader*, ed. Toril Moi (Oxford: Blackwell, 1986), 160–86.

42 Levinas, 'The Trace of the Other', 348. On the gift, and the related notion of the debt, see Derrida, 'Des Tours de Babel', in *Difference in Translation*, ed. Joseph F. Graham (Ithaca: Cornell University Press, 1985), 165–205, and *Glas*, trans. John P. Leavey and Richard Rand (Lincoln: Nebraska University Press, 1986), 242a-5a.

43 Levinas, *Ethics and Infinity*, 117.

44 Gayatri Chakravorty Spivak, 'The Rani of Sirmur', in *Europe and Its Others*, I, 128.

45 Jacques Derrida and Christie V. McDonald, 'Choreographies', *Diacritics* 12:2 (1982), 69.

46 *Oxford Literary Review* seminar held with Derrida, Oxford 1979.

47 Derrida, *Writing and Difference*, 4; Michel Foucault, *The Order of Things*, xxii-iv and *passim*. In *Of Grammatology* Derrida sets up the category of the West in an explicit binary opposition with the East: '[writing] is to speech what China is to Europe' (25). The force of his argument, however, is to question the distinctness of these categories.

48 Derrida, *Writing and Difference*, 91.

49 Derrida, *Writing and Difference*, 83.

50 Derrida, *Of Grammatology*, 3.

51 Derrida, *Of Grammatology*, 120.

52 Derrida, 'Structure, Sign, and Play in the Discourse of the Human Sciences' in *Writing and Difference*, 278–93.

53 Arnold Toynbee, *A Study of History*, 12 vols. (London: Oxford University Press, 1934–61). Toynbee's early use of the term 'postmodern' is cited by Charles Jencks in *What is Post-Modernism?* (London: Academy Editions, 1986), 3. Today we can find this perspective in Eric Hobsbawm's work, particularly *The Age of Capital 1848–1875* (London: Weidenfeld and Nicolson, 1985) and *The Age of Empire 1875–1914* (London: Weidenfeld and Nicolson, 1987).

54 Toynbee, *A Study of History*, IX, 410. For an early critique of Toynbee's positivism, see R.G. Collingwood, *The Idea of History* (Oxford: Clarendon Press, 1946), 159–65.

55 cf. Paul Virilio *et al.*, *Le Pourissement des sociétés* (Paris: Union générale d'éditions, 1975). The loss of European cultural dominance gives a more significant context to Dick Hebdige's argument in *Subculture. The Meaning of Style* (London: Methuen, 1979), that all post-war subcultural phenomena in Britain have been responses to, or identifications with, British Afro-Carribean culture. For a different view, see Simon During, 'Postmodernism or Post-Colonialism Today', *Textual Practice* 1:1 (1987), 32–47. Since writing this book, I

have come across Wlad Godzich's Foreword ('The Further Possibility of Knowledge') to the English translation of a collection of Michel de Certeau's essays, *Heterologies: Discourse on the Other*, trans. Brian Massumi (Minneapolis: Minnesota University Press, 1986). Godzich's Foreword puts de Certeau's work into a context comparable to that sketched out in this introductory chapter, and is recommended to anyone interested in its general argument.

2 MARXISM AND THE QUESTION OF HISTORY

1 Pierre Macherey, *A Theory of Literary Production*, trans. Geoffrey Wall (London: Routledge and Kegan Paul, 1978); first published in French in 1966. This is not to say, of course, that there have not been works of Marxist criticism, only that there has been no new theory of Marxist criticism. For a discussion of Fredric Jameson's *The Political Unconscious. Narrative as Socially Symbolic Act* (London: Methuen, 1981) see Chapter 5; Frank Lentricchia's *Criticism and Social Change* (Chicago: University of Chicago Press, 1983), as he himself notes, is 'unrecognizably Marxist' (6); for 'Cultural Materialism', see Chapter 5.
2 The classic, and highly influential, position which rejects theory in literary criticism altogether was spelt out by F.R. Leavis in his debate with René Wellek (René Wellek, 'Literary Criticism and Philosophy', *Scrutiny* 5 [1937], 375–83, and F.R. Leavis, 'Literary Criticism and Philosophy: A Reply', *Scrutiny* 6 [1937], 59–70).
3 Frank Lentricchia, *After the New Criticism* (Chicago: University of Chicago Press, 1980), xiii.
4 Terry Eagleton, *Literary Theory: An Introduction* (Oxford: Blackwell, 1983), 150; and *The Function of Criticism: From 'The Spectator' to Post-Structuralism* (London: Verso, 1984), 96.
5 Perry Anderson, *In the Tracks of Historical Materialism* (London: Verso, 1983), 48.
6 On history as hermeneutics see in particular Martin Heidegger, *Being and Time* trans. John Macquarrie and Edward Robinson (Oxford: Blackwell, 1962), Edmund Husserl, *The Crisis of the European Sciences and Transcendental Phenomenology*, trans. David Carr (Evanston: Northwestern University Press, 1970), Paul Ricoeur, *History and Truth*, trans. Charles A. Kelbley (Evanston: Northwestern University Press, 1965), Hans-Georg Gadamer, *Truth and Method*, trans. Garrett Barden and John Cumming (New York: Crossroad, 1975), Jacques Derrida, *Edmund Husserl's 'Origin of Geometry': An Introduction*, trans. John P. Leavey (Stony Brook, N.Y.: Nicholas Hays, 1978). On history as representation see Michel Foucault, *The Order of Things. An Archaeology of the Human Sciences*, trans. anonymous (London: Tavistock Publications, 1970), and *The Archaeology of Knowledge*, trans. A.M. Sheridan Smith (London: Tavistock Publications, 1972). On history as narrative see A.J. Greimas, 'On Evenemential History', in *On Meaning: Selected Writings in Semiotic Theory*, trans. Paul J. Perron and Frank H. Collins (Minneapolis: Minnesota University Press, 1987), 204–13, Hayden White, *Metahistory: The Historical Imagination in Nineteenth-Century Europe* (Baltimore: Johns Hopkins University Press, 1973), *Tropics of Discourse: Essays in Cultural Criticism* (Baltimore: Johns Hopkins University Press, 1978), *The Content of the Form: Narrative Discourse and Historical Representation* (Baltimore: Johns Hopkins University Press, 1987), and Paul Ricoeur, *Time and Narrative*, 3 vols, trans. Kathleen McLaughlin *et al.* (Chicago: University of Chicago Press, 1984–8).

7 *Louis Althusser and Etienne Balibar, Reading Capital,* trans. Ben Brewster (London: New Left Books, 1970), 93.

8 Another concept problematized by poststructuralism and therefore, according to a common misconception, altogether excised by it, would be that of the subject. For further discussion see Chapter 4.

9 Georg Lukács, 'The Ideology of Modernism', in *The Meaning of Contemporary Realism,* trans. John and Necke Mander (London: Merlin Press, 1963), 21. Further parallels could be drawn with Lukács' other related reproaches – a preoccupation with formal elements, the attenuation of the 'real', the dissolution of subjectivity, etc.

10 Lukács, *History and Class Consciousness. Studies in Marxist Dialectics,* trans. Rodney Livingstone (London: Merlin Press, 1971), 9–10.

11 Lukács, *History and Class Consciousness,* 27.

12 Lukács, *The Theory of the Novel. A Historico-Philosophical Essay on the Forms of Great Epic Literature,* trans. Anna Bostock (London: Merlin Press, 1978), 38. The paradoxes of Lukács' argument are explored by Paul de Man in his essay 'George Lukács's *Theory of the Novel*' in *Blindness and Insight. Essays in the Rhetoric of Contemporary Criticism* (New York: Oxford University Press, 1971), 51–9. For the most comprehensive treatment of Lukács, see Jay Bernstein, *The Philosophy of the Novel: Lukács, Marxism and the Dialectics of Form* (Brighton: Harvester Press, 1984).

13 Lukács, *The Historical Novel,* trans. Hannah and Stanley Mitchell (London: Merlin Press, 1962), 41–2.

14 Jean-Paul Sartre, *Critique of Dialectical Reason. I: Theory of Practical Ensembles,* trans. Alan Sheridan Smith (London: New Left Books, 1976), 716.

15 In Britain the argument comes from the 'New Left' of the 1950s which was organized around two journals committed to 'socialist humanism', *The New Reasoner* and *Universities and Left Review*. In 1959 they amalgamated to form the *New Left Review*. Those associated with these journals included E.P. Thompson, Ralph Samuel, Raymond Williams, Stuart Hall, and Perry Anderson (see the latter's *Arguments Within English Marxism* [London: New Left Books, 1980, 131–56] for further details and for an account of the split which developed among the editors). The early books of both Terry Eagleton and Frank Lentricchia were written from a position of existentialist humanism (Terence Eagleton, *Shakespeare and Society. Critical Studies in Shakespearean Drama* [London: Chatto and Windus, 1967] and Frank Lentricchia, *The Gaiety of Language. An Essay on the Radical Poetics of W.B. Yeats and Wallace Stevens* [Berkeley: University of California Press, 1968]).

16 For such an account of Lukács, which appeared too late for consideration here in its more general claims, see John Grumley, *History and Totality: Radical Historicism from Hegel to Foucault* (London: Routledge, 1989).

17 Ronald Aronson, *Sartre's Second Critique* (Chicago: University of Chicago Press, 1987), 4–32; Maurice Merleau-Ponty, *Adventures of the Dialectic,* trans. Joseph Bien (Evanston: Northwestern University Press, 1973), 7, 97–8; Sartre, *The Communists and Peace, With an Answer to Claude Lefort,* trans. Irene Clephane (London: Hamish Hamilton, 1969). *The Communists and Peace* was also attacked from the perspective of a Marxism critical of Stalinism and the Party by Claude Lefort in 'Le Marxism et Sartre' *Les Temps Modernes* 89 (1953), 1541–70. Sartre's reply to Lefort followed immediately in the same issue of *Les Temps Modernes* 1571–1629; his response to Merleau-Ponty took rather longer – the two *Critiques* – but Simone de Beauvoir provided a more speedy riposte on his behalf in 'Merleau-Ponty et le pseudo-Sartrisme', *Les Temps Modernes* 115–5 (1955), 2072–122. See also Sartre's later essay 'Merleau-Ponty', in *Situations,* trans. Benita

Eisler (London: Hamish Hamilton, 1965), 225–326. The best analysis of the arguments between Sartre and Merleau-Ponty can be found in David Achard's *Marxism and Existentialism: The Political Philosophy of Sartre and Merleau-Ponty* (Belfast: Blackstaff Press, 1980).

18 Maurice Merleau-Ponty, *Humanism and Terror*, trans. John O'Neill (Boston: Beacon Press, 1969). For accounts of French post-war Marxism see David Caute, *Communism and the French Intellectuals, 1914–1960* (London: Deutsch, 1964), George Lichtheim, *Marxism in Modern France* (New York: Columbia University Press, 1966), Mark Poster, *Existential Marxism in Postwar France. From Sartre to Althusser* (Princeton: Princeton University Press, 1975), and Arthur Hirsh, *The French New Left: An Intellectual History from Sartre to Gorz* (Boston: South End Press, 1981); for Merleau-Ponty see Achard, *Marxism and Existentialism*, Sonia Kruks, *The Political Philosophy of Merleau-Ponty* (Brighton: Harvester, 1981), and James Schmidt, *Maurice Merleau-Ponty: Between Phenomenology and Structuralism* (London: Macmillan, 1985).

19 Merleau-Ponty, *Adventures of the Dialectic*, 91–4. Further references will be cited in the text.

20 What did this mean in political terms? A new, 'noncommunist', left with a 'new revolutionary flow' of repetition rather than teleology: for 'even if the Marxist dialectic did not take possession of our history, even if we have nowhere seen the advent of the proletariat as ruling class, the dialectic continues to gnaw at capitalist society' (228). Despite his opposition to the Algerian war and to de Gaulle, Merleau-Ponty himself, however, lapsed into political silence. Although he had anticipated and enabled much of the critical scepticism that was to be deployed in the sixties and seventies, the implications of his position for a radical politics of the left still had to be thought through.

3 SARTRE'S EXTRAVAGANCES

1 Jean-Paul Sartre, *What is Literature?*, trans. Bernard Frechtman (London: Methuen, 1950), 176.

2 Sartre, *Critique of Dialectical Reason: I: Theory of Practical Ensembles*, trans. Alan Sheridan Smith (London: New Left Books, 1976), 822. Further references will be cited in the text, preceded by the volume number. References to Volume II, *Critique de la raison dialectique: L'intelligibilité de l'histoire*, ed. Arlette Elkaïm-Sartre (Paris: Gallimard, 1985) will also be cited in the text, also preceded by the volume number. Italics are Sartre's. All students of Sartre are greatly indebted to Ronald Aronson's lucid exposition of Volume II in *Sartre's Second Critique* (Chicago: University of Chicago Press, 1987); where the same passage has been cited, the translations given here from Volume II are based (with modifications) on Aronson's. Critical accounts of Sartre tend to emphasize the earlier work; those which consider the *Critiques* include: Raymond Aron, *History and the Dialectic of Violence. An Analysis of Sartre's 'Critique de la raison dialectique'*, trans. Barry Cooper (Oxford: Blackwell, 1975), Ronald Aronson, *Jean-Paul Sartre – Philosophy in the World* (London: Verso, 1980), Joseph S. Catalano, *A Commentary on Sartre's 'Critique of Dialectical Reason. Volume 1. Theory of Practical Ensembles'* (Chicago: Chicago University Press, 1986), Pietro Chiodi, *Sartre and Marxism*, trans. Kate Soper (Brighton: Harvester Press, 1976), Thomas R. Flynn, *Sartre and Marxist Existentialism* (Chicago: Chicago University Press, 1984), André Gorz, 'Sartre and Marx', *New Left Review* 37 (1966), 33–52, Christina Howells, *Sartre: The Necessity of Freedom* (Cambridge: Cambridge University Press, 1988), Fredric Jameson, *Sartre: The Origin of a Style* (New

Haven: Yale University Press, 1961), *Marxism and Form: Twentieth Century Dialectical Theories of Literature*, (Princeton: Princeton University Press, 1971), Fredric Jameson, ed., *Sartre After Sartre*, *Yale French Studies* 68 (1985), Martin Jay, *Marxism and Totality. The Adventures of a Concept from Lukács to Habermas* (Berkeley: University of California Press, 1984), Dominick LaCapra, *A Preface to Sartre. A Critical Introduction to Sartre's Literary and Philosophical Writings* (Ithaca: Cornell University Press, 1978), Nicos Poulantzas, *La 'Critique de la raison dialectique' de J. - P. Sartre et le droit* (Paris: Archives de philosophie du droit, tome X, 1965), and Mark Poster, *Sartre's Marxism*, (London: Pluto Press, 1979).

3 *Critique of Dialectical Reason*, I, 18–21, 27–32.

4 For Sartre Kant's analytic reason was applicable to the natural but not to the human sciences. See *Critique of Dialectical Reason*, I, 18 and 823.

5 Althusser's would be the second. See Chapter 4.

6 Maurice Merleau-Ponty, 'The War Has Taken Place' (1945), in *Sense and Non-Sense*, trans. Herbert L. Dreyfus and Patricia Allen Dreyfus (Evanston: Northwestern University Press, 1964), 151.

7 Sartre, and most writers on Sartre, explain his Marxism as an attempt to add existentialism's subjectivity to Marxism's objectivity, of putting man – once more, as he argued – at the basis of Marxism. Sartre describes it as follows: 'It is precisely this expulsion of man, his exclusion from Marxist knowledge, which resulted in the renascence of existentialist thought outside the historical totalisation of knowledge.... Marxism will degenerate into a non-human anthropology if it does not reintegrate man into itself as its foundation.... From the day that Marxist thought will have taken on the human dimension (that is, the existential project) as the foundation of anthropological knowledge, existentialism will no longer have any reason for being' (Sartre, *The Problem of Method*, trans. Hazel E. Barnes, [London: Methuen, 1963], 179–81). Sartre's own explanation of the historical circumstances which gave rise to his attempt to combine existentialism with Marxism can be found at 3–34. For a critique of Sartre's account, see Jameson, *Marxism and Form*, 206–9.

8 This was obviously in itself by no means a new doctrinal crux: indeed the conflict of free-will and predetermination could be said to have always constituted the central problem for theology, just as the relation of individual to society provided the theoretical crux for the nineteenth century. The latter was effectively solved by the Marxist shift to the category of class – which Sartre could be said to have reversed back again.

9 See for example, Philip Wood, 'Sartre, Anglo-American Marxism, and the Place of the Subject in History', *Yale French Studies* 68 (1985), 15–54. For the return of individualism to Marxism see Jon Elster's argument for a theory of 'methodological individualism' in *Making Sense of Marx* (Cambridge: Cambridge University Press, 1985), and many recent works associated with the Frankfurt School.

10 Sartre, *What is Literature?*, 174; cf. *The Problem of Method*, 85.

11 Sartre, *The Problem of Method*, 87. For definition of praxis see *Critique of Dialectical Reason*, I, 734. Individual praxis constituted the fundamental principle for Sartre and he therefore sought to demonstrate that all dialectic derives from it.

12 Aronson, *Sartre's Second Critique*, 42. This was the question which Sartre was in fact unable to solve.

13 Sartre, *The Problem of Method*, 29, translation modified.

14 Sartre, *The Problem of Method*, 90.

15 *Critique of Dialectical Reason*, I, 817. Sartre continues: 'History is intelligible if the different practices which can be found and located at a given moment of the historical temporalisation finally appear as partially totalising and as connected

and merged in their very oppositions and diversities by an intelligible totalisation from which there is no appeal. It is by seeking the conditions for the intelligibility of historical vestiges and results that we shall, for the first time, reach the problem of totalisation without a totaliser and of the very foundations of this totalisation'. Sartre certainly reached the problem in Volume II.

16 See *Critique de la raison dialectique*, II, 105–28.
17 *Critique of Dialectical Reason*, I, 47; cf. 52.
18 *Critique de la raison dialectique*, II, 61.
19 Aronson discusses this problem in *Sartre's Second Critique*, 71–5, and 153n.
20 Most specifically, perhaps, with Michael Mann's *The Sources of Social Power. Vol. I: A History of Power from the Beginning to AD 1760* (Cambridge: Cambridge University Press, 1986).
21 The problem is discussed in relation to Michel Foucault, who resurrects Sartre's term 'singular universal', in Chapter 5, and to Edward Said, in Chapter 7.
22 As is evident, for example, in *Critique de la raison dialectique*, II, 72–3.
23 For a detailed discussion of these problems in Bakhtin, see my 'Back to Bakhtin', *Cultural Critique* 2 (1985–6), 71–92.
24 Louis Althusser and Etienne Balibar, *Reading Capital*, trans. Ben Brewster (London: New Left Books, 1970), 142; Michael Sprinker, *Imaginary Relations: Aesthetics and Ideology in the Theory of Historical Materialism* (London: Verso, 1987), 175.
25 Sartre, *The Problem of Method*, 78 (Sartre's emphasis).
26 *Critique de la raison dialectique*, II, 140.
27 For an analysis of Sartre's discussion of the ontology of history in the *Critique*, see Juliette Simont, 'The *Critique of Dialectical Reason*: From Need to Need, Circularly', *Yale French Studies* 68 (1985), 108–23.
28 Claude Lévi-Strauss, 'History and Dialectic', in *The Savage Mind*, (London: Weidenfeld and Nicolson, 1966). Further references will be cited in the text. Lévi-Strauss' position was supported by A.J. Greimas in his important essay 'Structure et histoire' in *Du sens: Essais sémiotiques* (Paris: Seuil, 1970), 103–115. Among the many discussions of the Sartre/Lévi-Strauss debate, see Jean Pouillon, 'Sartre et Lévi-Strauss', *L'Arc* 26 (1965), 55–60, Laurence Rosen, 'Language, History, and the Logic of Inquiry in Lévi-Strauss and Sartre', *History and Theory* 10:3 (1971), 269–94, Aron, *History and the Dialectic of Violence*, 138–58, Dominique Grisoni, 'Sartre: de la structure à l'histoire', in Dominique Grisoni, ed., *Politiques de la philosophie* (Paris: Grasset, 1976), 187–99, Simon Clarke, *The Foundations of Structuralism: A Critique of Lévi-Strauss and the Structuralist Movement* (Brighton: Harvester Press, 1981), 220–30, and Johannes Fabian, *Time and the Other: How Anthropology Makes Its Object* (New York: Columbia University Press, 1983), 52–69.
29 Sartre, *Problem of Method*, xxxiv.
30 Jacques Derrida, 'Structure, Sign, and Play in the Discourse of the Human Sciences', in *Writing and Difference*, trans. Alan Bass (London: Routledge and Kegan Paul, 1978), 278–293.
31 See Sartre, *Critique of Dialectical Reason*, I, 20.
32 For further discussion of the problems involved in Sartre's use of two types of reason see Aron, *History and the Dialectic of Violence*, 1–24, and Poster, *Sartre's Marxism*, 34–6. Howells puts the problem succinctly: 'There is an inherent contradiction in attempting to do for dialectical reason what Kant did for analytical reason: a *critique* is essentially analytic, dependent on a distance between same and other, and hence incapable of dealing with the dialectic which, Sartre maintains, transcends the analytic' (*Sartre*, 105).
33 Derrida's notion of 'stricture' is developed in *Glas*, trans. John P. Leavey and

Richard Rand (Lincoln: Nebraska University Press, 1986), (see especially 244a), in 'Restitutions', in *The Truth in Painting*, trans. Geoff Bennington and Ian McLeod (Chicago: Chicago University Press, 1987), 255–382, and in 'To Speculate – on "Freud"', in *The Post Card: From Socrates to Freud and Beyond*, trans. Alan Bass (Chicago: Chicago University Press, 1987), 257–409. See also Marian Hobson, 'History Traces', in *Poststructuralism and the Question of History*, eds Derek Attridge, Geoff Bennington and Robert Young (Cambridge: Cambridge University Press, 1987), 108–9, and Geoff Bennington, 'Deconstruction and the Philosophers (The Very Idea)', *Oxford Literary Review* 10 (1988), 80–1.

34 e.g., Lichtheim, 'Sartre, Marxism and History', *History and Theory* 3:2 (1963), 233, Poster, *Sartre's Marxism*, 54. On scarcity (*la rareté*) see *Critique of Dialectical Reason*, I, 113, 122–52 and *Critique de la raison dialectique*, II, 22–3; for the fullest treatment of the topic see Girolamo Cotroneo, *Sartre: 'Rareté' e storia* (Naples: Guida, 1976). Sartre goes out of his way to stress that scarcity is no more of an *a priori* than history: scarcity initiates just one possible history and not a universal one. However, given that he also claims that it forms the basis of all conflict this seems something of a special pleading, and appears to put Sartre closer to Malthus than to Marx.

35 It could be objected that Lévi-Strauss himself goes on to repeat this structure in his founding division of nature and culture. Although Derrida demonstrates in 'Structure, Sign, and Play in the Human Sciences' (*Writing and Difference*, 278–93), that Lévi-Strauss uses this distinction very ambivalently, in *Of Grammatology* he criticizes the ethnocentrism of the definition of culture according to the speech/writing distinction. For the structure of supplementarity through which man calls himself man see *Of Grammatology* (trans. Gayatri Chakravorty Spivak [Baltimore: Johns Hopkins University Press, 1976]), 244–5.

36 Clarke, *The Foundations of Structuralism*, 224. Sartre's distinction between 'primitive' and 'civilised' societies merely repeats his distinction between self and other ('hell is other people'); far from distinguishing Sartre's thought from that of 'primitive' societies in fact it repeats its most typical forms. To preserve this distinction Sartre even has to go to great lengths to deny that others possess the capacity of abstract thought (*Critique of Dialectical Reason*, 503) – which, logically, suggests Lévi-Strauss, would have to imply an incapacity for language itself (*Savage Mind*, 251).

37 Clarke, *The Foundations of Structuralism*, 226. The same problem is equally applicable to those who today remain close to the legacy of Sartre.

38 Lévi-Strauss is here setting up the first of the two limits of totalization detected elsewhere in his work by Derrida in 'Structure, Sign, and Play'; the second, more radical, limit is that of 'play' (*Writing and Difference*, 289).

39 For Derrida's analysis of dates, see 'Schibboleth: for Paul Celan', in G. Hartman and Sanford Budick, eds, *Midrash and Literature* (New Haven: Yale University Press, 1986), 307–47.

40 Typically in an ethnocentric manoeuvre of the sort that Gayatri Chakravorty Spivak detects in Kristeva's description of Chinese women:

> It is therefore not surprising that, even as she leaves the incredibly detailed terrain of the problem of knowing who she herself is exactly – the speaking, reading, listening 'I' at this particular *moment* – she begins to compute the reality of who 'they' are in terms of *millennia*: 'One thing is certain: a revolution in the rules of kinship took place in China, and can be traced to sometime around B.C. 1000'.

'French Feminism in an International Frame', in *In Other Worlds: Essays in*

Cultural Politics (New York: Methuen, 1986), 137, citing Julia Kristeva, *About Chinese Women* (London: Marion Boyars, 1977), 46.

41 For Lévi-Strauss, history represents only the preliminary organization of material in the first stage of understanding; he provides further analysis of the relationship between history and anthropology in the introduction to *Structural Anthropology*, I, trans. Claire Jacobson and Brooke Grundfest Schoepf (London: Allen Lane, 1968). Simon Clarke accuses Lévi-Strauss of seeing history as contingent (as, for example, in 'the contingencies of history', *The Savage Mind*, 73, and 'those irrational factors which arise from chance and from history', *The Elementary Structures of Kinship*, trans. James Harle Bell *et al.* [Boston: Beacon Press, 1969], 268); but what he says in each case is not that 'History' as such is contingent, but that history involves contingencies, which is rather different. Clarke's other objection is that Lévi-Strauss reduces 'experience, including the experience of freedom which is the basis of Sartre's philosophy, to the status of a myth' (227) – but then so would any Marxist analysis of ideology.

42 Lévi-Strauss did not, however, abjure the idea of totalization in its entirety; for Sartre's single grand diachronic totalization he wished to substitute synchronic totalizations, which would be another way of describing his set theory account of chronology, if not his theory of the human mind in general as a universal. Only a year after the publication of Lévi-Strauss' critique of Sartre, Derrida was to question this structuralist concept of synchronic totalization in the essay 'Force and Signification' (in *Writing and Difference*, 3–30).

43 'Replies to Structuralism: An Interview with Jean-Paul Sartre', *Telos* 9 (1971), 110–16.

44 Richard Kearney, *Dialogues with Contemporary Continental Thinkers. The Phenomenological Heritage* (Manchester: Manchester University Press, 1984), 58.

45 Aronson, *Sartre's Second Critique*, 234, and *Jean-Paul Sartre*, 174–7. In his *Sartre and 'Les Temps modernes'* (Cambridge: Cambridge University Press, 1987), Howard Davies gives a detailed account of this phase.

4 THE SCIENTIFIC CRITIQUE OF HISTORICISM

1 Louis Althusser, *For Marx*, trans. Ben Brewster (London: Allen Lane, 1969), and, with Etienne Balibar, *Reading Capital*, trans. Ben Brewster (London: New Left Books, 1970).

2 In other words, Hegelians such as Emile Meyerson, for whom the history of the sciences followed the same movement as the logic of consciousness in Hegel's *Phenomenology*. See, for example, Meyerson's *Identité et réalité*, 2nd ed. (Paris: Alcan, 1912).

3 Michel Foucault, 'Georges Canguilhem: Philosopher of Error', *Ideology and Consciousness* 7 (1980), 52. Foucault's account is complicated by the fact that he traces both traditions back to Husserl.

4 Gregory Elliott, *Althusser, The Detour of Theory* (London: Verso, 1987), 67; Louis Althusser, *Lenin and Philosophy, and Other Essays*, trans. Ben Brewster (London: New Left Books, 1971), 34, where Althusser cites Cavaillès and Bachelard.

5 Bachelard's argument against history as simple chronology in many ways anticipates that of Lévi-Strauss discussed in the previous chapter.

6 Gaston Bachelard, *L'Engagement rationaliste* (Paris: Presses universitaires de France, 1982), 137 (translations from Bachelard are my own). For the most substantial analysis of the relation between Bachelard and Althusser see *Theoretical Practice* 3–4 (1971–2), especially Ben Brewster, 'Althusser and Bachelard', 25–37.

7 Bachelard argues against the organization of history according to the continuity of chronology in *Le Matérialisme rationnel* (Paris: Presses universitaires de France, 1953), 209–12; Canguilhem in his essay 'L'Objet de l'histoire des sciences' in *Etudes d'histoire et de philosophie des sciences* (Paris: J. Vrin, 1968), 9–23, especially 20–1.

8 In *L'Activité rationaliste de la physique contemporaine* (Paris: Presses universitaires de France, 1951) Bachelard argues that the atom bomb, for example, means that nuclear physics is now entirely separate from the fundamental notions of traditional physics: 'Such a science has no analogue in the past. It provides a particularly clear example of the historic break in the evolution of the modern sciences' (24). For further examples see 105–18.

9 Its structure is thus, Foucault suggests with respect to Canguilhem, therefore more one of recurrence – just as discontinuity must itself be impermanent ('Georges Canguilhem', 55). The links between this Nietzschean perspective and Foucault's characterization of Canguilhem as a 'philosopher of error' (60) are fascinating to consider but would take us beyond the limits of the present chapter.

10 Bachelard, *Le Nouvel esprit scientifique* (Paris: Alcan, 1934), and *La Philosophie du non. Essai d'une philosophie du nouvel esprit scientifique* (Paris: Presses universitaires de France, 1940). For an account of Bachelard's work from this perspective, see Mary Tiles, *Bachelard: Science and Objectivity* (Cambridge: Cambridge University Press, 1984).

11 See, for example, *L'Activité rationaliste*, 25.

12 Jean Cavaillès, *Remarques sur la formation de la théorie abstraite des ensembles. Etude historique et critique* (Paris: Hermann, 1938), and *Transfini et continu* (Paris: Hermann, 1947), especially page 23.

13 See Jean Cavaillès, *Sur la logique et la théorie de la science* (Paris: Presses universitaires de France, 1947).

14 Bachelard, *Le Matérialisme rationnel*, 207–24, *L'Activité rationaliste*, 93, *La Formation de l'esprit scientifique: contribution à une psychanalyse de la connaissance objective* (Paris: Vrin, 1938), and *Le Rationalisme appliqué* (Paris: Presses universitaires de France, 1949), 102–118.

15 *Le Matérialisme rationnel*, 224.

16 'We believe, indeed, that scientific progress always reveals a break, perpetual breaks, between ordinary knowledge and scientific knowledge' (*Le Matérialisme rationnel*, 207).

17 *L'Activité rationaliste* 25, *La Formation de l'esprit scientifique*, 13–22.

18 *Le Matérialisme rationnel*, 25.

19 *Le Rationalisme appliqué*, 51; cf. also 55–7.

20 In *La Formation de l'esprit scientifique*, 55–72.

21 *Le Matérialisme rationnel*, 215.

22 *Le Matérialisme rationnel*, 18.

23 Dominique Lecourt, *Marxism and Epistemology: Bachelard, Canguilhem and Foucault*, trans. Ben Brewster (London: New Left Books, 1975), 140.

24 This argument in many ways parallels that of Lévi-Strauss with respect to Sartre, and that of Derrida with regard to Lévi-Strauss.

25 Lecourt, *Marxism and Epistemology*, 139.

26 Althusser, *Lenin and Philosophy*, 200–1. It is only to be expected, conversely, that whenever Sartre's form of history is subsequently reinvoked, its inevitable corollary takes the form of the reappearance of the autonomous human subject. As Althusser argued in his critique of Sartre, it is the subject that is the real issue (see the 'Reply to John Lewis', in *Essays in Self-Criticism*, trans. Grahame Lock [London: New Left Books, 1976], 33–99; see also 40–64, 94–9, for an extended

discussion of history as a 'process without a subject'). Direct comparisons of Sartre and Althusser are scarce, apart from Michael Sprinker's 'Politics and Theory: Althusser and Sartre', in *Imaginary Relations: Aesthetics and Ideology in the Theory of Historical Materialism* (London: Verso, 1987), 177–205.

27 Martin Jay, *Marxism and Totality: The Adventures of a Concept from Lukács to Habermas* (Berkeley: University of California Press, 1984), 422. For other recent analyses of Althusser, see Alex Callinicos, *Althusser's Marxism* (London: Pluto Press, 1976), Ted Benton, *The Rise and Fall of Structural Marxism. Althusser and His Influence* (London: Macmillan, 1984); Steven B. Smith, *Reading Althusser: An Essay on Structural Marxism* (Ithaca: Cornell University Press, 1984); Gregory Elliot, *Althusser: The Detour of Theory* (London: Verso, 1987); Sprinker, *Imaginary Relations*.

28 In particular, E.P. Thompson, *The Poverty of Theory & Other Essays* (London: Merlin, 1978). The more interesting question, on the other hand, would be what it was about Althusser that made him so attractive to certain areas of the British New Left; the classic text with which to start here would be Perry Anderson's 'Components of the National Culture', *New Left Review* 50 (1968), 3–57.

29 On the other hand, there is not such a close relation as is sometimes claimed between Althusser's thesis of 'relative autonomy' and Sartre's 'mediations', although it is true that both place greater importance on the significance of cultural and political struggles at all levels. The difference, however, would be that whereas for Sartre each element is mediated in terms of the other, i.e. according to the category of totalization, for Althusser they are characterized by radical breaks and discontinuities, distinct from each other and not totalizing; Sartre's mediations, furthermore, represent attempts to mediate between individual or group human actions and overall economic determinants. Each element therefore expresses the whole, whereas in Althusser each level remains relatively autonomous. Sprinker also distinguishes between Althusser and Sartre on this point (*Imaginary Relations*, 185–6).

30 In Ted Benton's definition, '"Historicism" consists in the attempt to impose upon 'concrete' historical processes a philosophical scheme such that, potentialities present in germ at the origins of the process, pre-figure and set in motion a process of transformation whose end result or goal is self-realization. Historical teleology ... is ... central to historicism, as is the idea of a linear series of stages through which the process must pass' (*The Rise and Fall of Structural Marxism*, 59–60).

31 In this emphasis on scientificity, Althusser is in basic sympathy with the position of Lévi-Strauss, although he lacks the latter's scepticism towards its status, with the simultaneous use of '*bricolage*'. Althusser and Lévi-Strauss are in agreement on the form of history as one of discontinuous sets.

32 For the epistemological break in Althusser, see 'Lenin and Philosophy' and 'A Letter to the Translator', in *Lenin and Philosophy*, 29–68, 323–4 and *Reading Capital*, 44–5; in Bachelard see *L'Activité rationaliste* 77, and *Le Rationalisme appliqué* 104–5; the two are discussed by Balibar in 'From Bachelard to Althusser: The Concept of "Epistemological Break"', *Economy and Society* 7:3 (1978), 207–37. For Althusser's arguments against the empiricist conception of knowledge, see *Reading Capital*, 34–40. Further references to this volume will be given in the text.

33 *Reading Capital*, 93, Althusser's italics. Althusser's basic arguments about history can be found in Chapters 4 and 5 of Part II of *Reading Capital*, 91–144; Chapter 4 is entitled 'The Errors of Classical Economics', all of which, according to Althusser, can be 'grouped around one central misunderstanding of the theoretical relationship between Marxism and history, of the so-called radical historicism of

Marxism' (92). Part III, by Etienne Balibar, represents an attempt to extend the theoretical arguments of Part II.

34 In other words, even this theory of history faces the theoretical problem of how to reconcile its stress on continuity with its simultaneous tendency to divide history into periods.

35 This is the point at which Althusser's enquiry comes particularly close to that of Derrida in *Speech and Phenomena, and Other Essays on Husserl's Theory of Signs*, trans. David B. Allison (Evanston: Northwestern University Press, 1973).

36 'The synchronic is contemporaneity itself, the co-presence of the essence with its determinations, the present being readable as a structure in an "essential section" because the present is the very existence of the essential structure' (*Reading Capital*, 96). The diachronic, as 'history', merely represents 'successive contingent presents in the time continuum'. The Hegelian concept of time is, therefore, merely borrowed from the everyday assumptions of empirical historians, in effect a form of the chronology criticized by Lévi-Strauss (for the full discussion, see 107–9).

In *Arguments Within English Marxism* (London: New Left Books, 1980), Perry Anderson objected that ordinary continuous time is not ideological but 'forms the scientific object of such institutions as the Greenwich Observatory' (75), an observation which provoked the following response from Paul Hirst: 'No, there is nothing ideological about it if one is content to look at one's watch. What *is* problematic is the identification of such time with a single historical process, in which the plenum of societal time forms part of the plenum of the one great movement in which history is made and which is identified with chronological time (*Marxism and Historical Writing* [London: Routledge and Kegan Paul, 1985], 23).

37 *For Marx*, 103–8.

38 *Reading Capital*, 136–40.

39 *For Marx*, 113.

40 *Reading Capital*, 99. It is by neglecting this part of the argument that Hindess and Hirst can claim that Althusser's totality remains essentialist (*Pre-Capitalist Modes of Production*, 275–7). As Martin Jay points out, Althusser is one of the many Western Marxists who have tried to reformulate the Hegelian assumption of a homogenous univocal temporality (*Marxism and Totality* 355) – a project by no means confined to Marxism. As Levinas argues, it was Bergson who initiated the enquiry into temporality and prepared the ground for the subsequent importation of Heideggerian phenomenology into France. Levinas comments: 'Bergson's importance to contemporary continental thought has been somewhat obfuscated; he has been suspended in a sort of limbo; but I believe it is only a temporary suspension' (in Richard Kearney, *Dialogues with Contemporary Thinkers: The Phenomenological Heritage* [Manchester: Manchester University Press, 1984], 49–50).

41 *Reading Capital*, 100. But Althusser is equally critical of the *Annales* historians who have tried to get out of such a schema by posing the possibility of 'different times in history, varieties of time, long times, medium times and short times', usually mapped against the continuum of ordinary time and with no attempt to see such 'varieties as so many *variations* to the structure of the whole although the latter directly governs the production of those variations'. In other words, as we have seen with Bachelard, while allowing the possibility of differential times, there is no attempt to 'pose them explicitly as a function of the *structure of the whole*' (96). For a defence of the *Annales* position, see Pierre Vilar, 'Marxist History, a History in the Making: Towards a Dialogue with Althusser', *New Left Review* 80 (1973), 64–106.

42 If, according to Althusser, there is no history in general (*Reading Capital*, 108), there is still the possibility of thinking a general concept of history, though this involves certain problems. The concept of history, Althusser argues, is not empirical, 'i.e. *historical* in the ordinary sense, that, as Spinoza has already put it, *the concept dog cannot bark*'. Althusser is saying that the knowledge of history as a concept is, technically speaking, ahistorical in the sense that it is a form of science, at the same time as suggesting that it is simply a question of it not being historical in the ordinary empirical sense, not subject to the ideological concept of time which cannot precede it, 'or with the ideological idea that the theory of history, *as theory*, could be subject to the "concrete" determinations of "historical time" on the pretext that this "historical time" might constitute its object' (105–6). The concept of history cannot be said to be subject to the effects of its object, a history that it has not yet conceptualized; to say that it is affected by any prior concept of history would make it pointless to try to think it through as a concept. This comes close to the analyses of history and time pursued by European phenomenologists; Derrida, it should be noted, would certainly disagree with Althusser to the extent that he would argue that any concept of history must itself already be determined by the condition of historicity which he names *différance* (for an account of this, see the final section of this Chapter).

Althusser's point, however, stands insofar as he argues that what is happening is that two incommensurate categories are being set against each other. This kind of confusion arises between theory as theory of history and history as a 'concrete' empirical history, in which the theoretical is compared to the empirical as if they were the same thing. As an example of this kind of 'short-circuit between crossed-terms which it is illegitimate to compare' (111), Althusser takes the example of the 'problem' of the action of the individual in history. The complaint is often made that a theory of history ultimately dominated by the economic seems to deny the necessity for, or existence of, individual action. But this assumes that a theory of history and a particular historical individual are comparable, as if it were possible to compare the knowledge of one thing to the existence of a person. The real problem here is 'the concept of *the historical forms of existence of individuality*' (112) for which, according to Althusser, *Capital* provides the necessary principles.

The same point would hold for all 'political', 'sociological' or 'historicizing' refutations of deconstructive arguments, as Derrida himself observes: 'One can often see in the descriptive practice of the "social sciences" the most *seductive* (in every sense of the word) confusion of empirical investigation, inductive hypothesis and intuition of essence, without any precautions as to the origin and function of the propositions advanced' (*Writing and Difference*, trans. Alan Bass [London: Routledge and Kegan Paul, 1978], 316n).

43 In arguing for the Marxist theory of history as a theory of modes of production, Althusser admitted that 'we must say that *Marx did not give us any theory of the transition from one mode of production to another, i.e. of the constitution of a mode of production*' (*Reading Capital*, 197). If this really were the case it would suggest that the objection that Althusser and Balibar did not solve the problem of the modes of transition either is a less substantial objection than is often assumed; however, for many Althusser's argument is really something of a let-out, insofar as it presumes that in every other respect up to that point his theory is identical to Marx's. For further discussion of the question of transition in relation to Foucault, see Chapter 5.

44 What went wrong was that attention to the problem of the break deflected it from the principle that necessitated it, that is the principle of totality. As in Britain, the most effective critiques of Althusserianism in France came from the

Althusserians themselves; particularly Jacques Rancière, *La Leçon d'Althusser* (Paris: Gallimard, 1974), and Althusser's *Essays in Self-Criticism*, trans. Grahame Lock (London: New Left Books, 1976). In France, Althusser's work declined rapidly in influence after May 1968, as a result of his continuing allegiance to the Communist Party which lost its prestige in those events, as well as the more general context marked by the short-lived appearance of the *nouveaux philosophes* (for critical discussions see Gayatri Chakravorty Spivak and Michael Ryan, 'Anarchism Revisited: A New Philosophy', *Diacritics* 8:2 [1978], 66–79, and Peter Dews in 'The "New Philosophers" and the End of Leftism', *Radical Philosophy* 24 [1980], 2–11).

45 For example, it made a deep impression upon journals such as *Screen, New Left Review, Economy & Society*, and upon a whole range of disciplines such as the history of science, education, anthropology, law and political theory. In the literary sphere, the ascendancy of Althusser and his collaborator and disciple, Pierre Macherey, was evident in books such as Terry Eagleton's *Criticism and Ideology*, Coward and Ellis' *Language and Materialism*, Tony Bennett's *Formalism and Marxism*, Catherine Belsey's *Critical Practice*, in the *Working Papers* of the Birmingham Centre for Contemporary Cultural Studies, and the *Essex Conference Proceedings*. For an account sympathetic to Althusserianism, see Easthope, *British Post-Structuralism since 1968* (London: Routledge, 1988), and for a more hostile estimate, Kevin McDonnell and Kevin Robins, 'Marxist Cultural Theory: The Althusserian Smokescreen', in Simon Clarke *et al.*, *One-Dimensional Marxism: Althusser and the Politics of Culture* (London: Allison and Busby, 1980), 156–231.

46 Barry Hindess and Paul Hirst, *Pre-Capitalist Modes of Production* (London: Routledge and Kegan Paul, 1975), *Mode of Production and Social Formation: An Auto-Critique of 'Pre-Capitalist Modes of Production'* (London: Macmillan, 1977); Antony Cutler, Barry Hindess, Paul Hirst, and Athar Hussain, *Marx's 'Capital' and Capitalism Today*, 2 vols. (London: Routledge and Kegan Paul, 1977–78); Paul Hirst, *On Law and Ideology* (London: Macmillan, 1979). For the arguments with the Marxist humanists see Thompson, *The Poverty of Theory*; Keith Nield and John Seed, 'Theoretical Poverty or the Poverty of Theory: British Marxist Historiography and the Althusserians', *Economy and Society* 8:4 (1979), 383–416; Paul Hirst, 'The Necessity of Theory', *Economy and Society* 8:4 (1979), 417–45; Perry Anderson, *Arguments Within English Marxism*, and *In the Tracks of Historical Materialism* (London: Verso, 1983). For other contemporary reactions in both France and Britain to Althusser from 1966 to 1975 see the Bibliography in *Essays in Self-Criticism*, 219–21.

47 For further discussion of the problems involved here, see the discussion in Chapter 5.

48 Hirst, *Pre-Capitalist Modes of Production*, 312.

49 *Reading Capital*, 97; Sartre's totalization by contrast keeps temporality as a form of presence, although such totalization is always in the process of being achieved rather than being fully realized at any moment. Michel Foucault, *Language, Counter-Memory, Practice: Selected Essays and Interviews*, ed. Donald F. Bouchard, trans. Donald F. Bouchard and Sherry Simon (Ithaca: Cornell University Press, 1977), 160.

50 *Reading Capital*, 101.

51 The classic exposition of the interpellation of the subject comes in 'Ideology and Ideological State Apparatuses (Notes towards an Investigation), in *Lenin and Philosophy*, 121–73.

52 *Reading Capital*, 106. It is for the same reason that there can be no end to ideology. Hirst (*On Law and Ideology*, 65) objects that in Althusser's account

the subject is here already constituted as a subject.

53 Louis Althusser, 'A Letter on Art', in *Lenin and Philosophy*, 204, and *Montesquieu, Rousseau, Marx: Politics and History*, trans. Ben Brewster (London: New Left Books, 1972), 186.

54 This formulation is further discussed in the following section and, with reference to Foucault, in Chapter 5.

55 Those who are not prepared to think according to this logic at all, such as Hindess and Hirst, are obliged simply to reject 'the notion of history as a coherent and worthwhile object of study' – a position which is itself an absurdity (see Hindess and Hirst, *Pre-Capitalist Modes of Production*, 321).

56 Jean-François Lyotard, *Instructions païennes* (Paris: Galilée, 1977), and *The Differend: Phrases in Dispute*, trans. Georges Van Den Abbeele (Minneapolis: Minnesota University Press, 1988). Lyotard's incommensurable histories should be distinguished from the pluralism of Braudel *et al* criticized by Althusser in which history merely reverts to a host of different stories and times.

57 Jacques Derrida, *Positions*, trans. Alan Bass (London: Athlone Press, 1981), 57–8; compare Althusser, *Reading Capital*, 100.

58 Derrida, *Positions*, 50.

59 Jacques Derrida, *Of Grammatology*, trans. Gayatri Chakravorty Spivak (Baltimore: Johns Hopkins University Press, 1976), lxxxix.

60 Derrida, *Positions*, 49–50.

61 Jacques Derrida, *Writing and Difference*, trans. Alan Bass (London: Routledge and Kegan Paul, 1978), 291.

62 Derrida, *Writing and Difference*, 279; see the discussion of 'originary delay' in Chapter 5, section IV below.

63 Derrida, *Of Grammatology*, 27.

64 Derrida, *Writing and Difference*, 4.

65 Derrida, *Speech and Phenomena, and Other Essays on Husserl's Theory of Signs*, trans. David B. Allison (Evanston: Northwestern University Press, 1973), 141.

66 Derrida, *Writing and Difference*, 147.

67 Jacques Derrida, *Edmund Husserl's 'Origin of Geometry': An Introduction*, trans. John P. Leavey (Stony Brook: Nicolas Hays, 1978), 69, 153. Strictly speaking such transcendentals are 'quasi-transcendental': see Rodolph Gasché, *The Tain of the Mirror: Derrida and the Philosophy of Reflection* (Cambridge, Mass.: Harvard University Press, 1986), and Geoffrey Bennington's discussion in 'Deconstruction and the Philosophers (The Very Idea)', *Oxford Literary Review* 10 (1988). Bennington defines quasi-transcendentals as transcendentals that are 'originarily contaminated by what they transcend' (93). In fact the quasi-transcendental 'arche-writing' ensures that this is the case for all transcendentals. For Husserl's account of history, see Paul Ricoeur's 'Husserl and the Sense of History', in *Husserl: An Analysis of his Phenomenology*, trans. Edward G. Ballard and Lester E. Embree (Evanston: Northwestern University Press, 1967), 143–74.

68 Derrida, *Writing and Difference*, 197.

69 Derrida, *Writing and Difference*, 117; cf. *Speech and Phenomena*, 102–3.

70 Derrida, *Of Grammatology*, xc, 202; on Rousseau as an untimely critic of Hegel, see Bennington, 'Deconstruction and the Philosophers', 84; for further alternatives to history as 'the linear consecution of presence', see *Positions*, 56–60.

71 Derrida, *Writing and Difference*, 90.

72 Derrida, *Writing and Difference*, 148.

73 Gasché, *The Tain of the Mirror*, 180.

74 Derrida, *Of Grammatology*, lxxxix; cf. *Positions*, 57.

75 Jean-François Lyotard, *Economie libidinale* (Paris: Minuit, 1974), 119, and 'Un Marx non marxiste', in *Dérive à partir de Marx et Freud* (Paris: Union

générale d'éditions, 1973), 36–46.
76 Jean-François Lyotard, *Driftworks*, trans. Roger McKeon *et al.* (New York: Foreign Agents Series, 1984), 109.
77 Derrida, *Writing and Difference*, 133.
78 Peter Dews, *Logics of Disintegration: Post-Structuralist Thought and the Claims of Critical Theory* (London: Verso, 1987), 233–4.
79 Perry Anderson, *In the Tracks of Historical Materialism*; G.A. Cohen, *Karl Marx's Theory of History: A Defence* (Oxford: Clarendon Press, 1978); Melvin Rader, in *Marx's Interpretation of History* (New York: Oxford University Press, 1979), also reinstates the Hegelian model of organic totality for a Marxist history. Cohen's justification of Marx's theory of history, as was almost inevitable, amounts to a Hegelianism in a new guise: see the analysis of Cohen by Paul Hirst in *Marxism and Historical Writing*:

> It makes history a single process of development *of* something, a process with a subject, and a continuously acting cause connected to the attributes of that subject which leads through successive stages of development to a final outcome in a state of affairs. An outcome perhaps not essentially necessary as our immanent becoming, but nevertheless the conclusion of a single motivated chain of events going somewhere and linked by a single subject that underlies its unity as a process. This is philosophy of history in a bad sense, a sub-Hegelian teleology without the essential immanence of the unfolding of potentiality, but unified as the purposive practice of a single subject. (25)

Hirst argues that despite his emphasis on practice rather than theoretical principles, Thompson also assumes a Hegelian concept of totality in history (57–90).

5 FOUCAULT'S PHANTASMS

1 Louis Althusser and Etienne Balibar, *Reading Capital*, trans. Ben Brewster (London: New Left Books, 1970), 16, 324. Althusser invokes Foucault again at 44–5, 103, and discusses his debt to him at 323–4.
2 Michel Foucault, *Power/Knowledge: Selected Interviews and Other Writings, 1972–1977*, ed. Colin Gordon, trans. Colin Gordon *et al.* (New York: Pantheon Books, 1980), 49–50.
3 Althusser, *Reading Capital*, 44. Foucault discusses his relation to Bachelard, Canguilhem and Althusser in the Introduction to *The Archaeology of Knowledge*, trans. A.M. Sheridan Smith (London: Tavistock Publications, 1972), 4–5.
4 Georges Canguilhem, *La Connaissance de la vie* (Paris: Hachette, 1952), and *The Normal and the Pathological*, trans. C.R. Fawcett, (Dordrecht: Kluwer, 1978). The distinction set out here between Althusser and Foucault with regard to Bachelard and Canguilhem underplays Althusser's own stress on institutional factors, particularly in his later works. He himself commented that '*my debt to Canguilhem is incalculable*' (Althusser's italics) (*Reading Capital*, 323), while Foucault observed 'take away Canguilhem and you can no longer understand much of Althusser' ('Georges Canguilhem: Philosopher of Error', *Ideology and Consciousness* 7 [1980], 51).
5 Canguilhem, *Etudes d'histoire et de philosophie des sciences* (Paris: Vrin, 1968).
6 Foucault, 'Georges Canguilhem', 55–7, citing Canguilhem, *Ideologie et rationalité dans l'histoire des sciences de la vie: Nouvelles études d'histoire et de philosophie des sciences* (Paris: Vrin, 1977), 11–20.

7 Mark Poster, *Foucault, Marxism and History. Mode of Production versus Mode of Information* (Cambridge: Polity Press, 1984), 1–3. For a more measured assessment of Foucault's relation to Marxism, see Barry Smart, *Foucault, Marxism and Critique* (London: Routledge and Kegan Paul, 1983).

8 Foucault, *Madness and Civilization: A History of Insanity in the Age of Reason*, trans. Richard Howard (New York: Random House, 1965), *The Order of Things. An Archaeology of the Human Sciences*, trans. anonymous (London: Tavistock Publications, 1970), *Discipline and Punish. The Birth of the Prison*, trans. Alan Sheridan (London: Allen Lane, 1977), *The History of Sexuality. Volume One: An Introduction*, trans. Robert Hurley (London: Allen Lane, 1979), *Volume Two: The Use of Pleasure*, trans. Robert Hurley (London: Viking, 1986), *Volume Three: The Care of the Self*, trans. Robert Hurley (New York: Pantheon, 1987). A full bibliography for Foucault up to 1982 is available in Michael Clark's *Michel Foucault, An Annotated Bibliography: Tool Kit for a New Age* (New York: Garland, 1983). Of the many critical accounts of Foucault, Mark Cousins and Athar Hussain's *Michel Foucault* (London: Macmillan, 1984) is particularly useful.

9 Foucault, 'Politics and the Study of Discourse', *Ideology and Consciousness* 3 (1978), 24.

10 Foucault, *Mental Illness and Psychology*, trans. Alan Sheridan (New York: Harper and Row, 1976), 76.

11 Jacques Derrida, *Writing and Difference*, trans. Alan Bass, (London: Routledge and Kegan Paul, 1978), 31–63. Foucault's reply, appended to the second edition (1972) of his *Histoire de la folie* (Paris: Plon, 1961), is translated as 'My Body, This Paper, This Fire' in *Oxford Literary Review* 4:1 (1979), 9–28.

12 Derrida, *Writing and Difference*, 36.

13 David Carroll, *Paraesthetics: Foucault, Lyotard, Derrida* (New York: Methuen, 1987), 77. It will be clear from this account that I do not agree with Carroll that this kind of self-reflexivity as critique extends throughout Foucault's work.

14 *The Order of Things*, xv; for the repudiation of the argument of *Madness and Civilization*, see *The Archaeology of Knowledge*, 47.

15 *Power/Knowledge*, 118–9.

16 In *Futures Past. On the Semantics of Historical Time* (Cambridge, Mass.: MIT Press, 1985), Reinhart Koselleck argues that this kind of shift came with the end of the Holy Roman Empire which had, until its dissolution, preserved all history as an eschatology. He adds: 'Bodin here played a role as historian which was as pathbreaking as his foundation of the concept of sovereignty. In separating out sacral, human, and natural history, Bodin transformed the question of the End of the World into a problem of astronomical and mathematical calculation' (10).

17 Foucault's position on the relation of Western humanism to colonialism would no doubt be similar to that outlined in his discussion of the relation of ethnography to colonialism in *The Order of Things* (376–7); for the argument that that book amounts to an ethnology of Western culture, see Axel Honneth and Hans Jonas, *Social Action and Human Nature*, trans. Raymond Meyer (Cambridge: Cambridge University Press, 1988), 131. Edward Said, on the other hand, criticizes Foucault on the ground of Eurocentrism in 'Foucault and the Imagination of Power', in *Foucault: A Critical Reader*, ed. David Couzens Hoy (Oxford: Blackwell, 1986), 149–55, as does Gayatri Chakravorty Spivak in *In Other Worlds: Essays in Cultural Politics* (New York: Methuen, 1987), 201, 209–10.

18 Foucault argues that, in any case, the distinction between science and non-science is itself primarily based on a discursive difference. See below Chapter 6.

19 *The Order of Things*, 373–86.

20 Foucault explains as follows: 'What I mean by the term is an *a priori* that is not a

condition of validity for judgements, but a condition of reality for statements'. The *a priori* are historical rather than transcendental because they are not applicable to all knowledges. More simply, they amount to a 'group of rules that characterize a discursive practice' (*Archaeology of Knowledge*, 127). The term does not survive the *Archaeology*.

21 'Foreword to the English Edition', *The Order of Things*, xi; Sartre, 'Replies to Structuralism', *Telos* 9 (1971), 110. Foucault's comments on Sartre can be found in Paolo Caruso, 'Conversazione con Michel Foucault', in *Conversazioni con Claude Lévi-Strauss, Michel Foucault, Jacques Lacan* (Milan: Mursia, 1969), 109, and in Jean-Pierre El Kabbach, 'Foucault répond à Sartre', *La Quinzaine Littéraire* 46 (1968), 20–2.

22 Foucault, *Politics, Philosophy, Culture. Interviews and Other Writings, 1977–1984*, ed. Lawrence D. Kritzman (New York: Routledge, 1988), 100.

23 Derrida, *Writing and Difference*, 94.

24 'Politics and the Study of Discourse', 11–13.

25 See, for example, Fredric Jameson, *The Political Unconscious. Narrative as Socially Symbolic Act* (London: Methuen, 1981), 26–7; for Foucault's denial that he employs the categories of cultural totalities, see *Archaeology of Knowledge*, 15.

26 'Politics and the Study of Discourse', 10; the phrase, 'cluster of transformations' is used by Foucault on page 25. Foucault's description of the *episteme* as a space of dispersion comes close to Althusser's description of the decentred structure of relative autonomy in *Reading Capital*, 99–100 (discussed in Chapter 3).

27 'My aim is to uncover the principles and consequences of an autochthonous transformation that is taking place in the field of historical knowledge' (*Archaeology of Knowledge*, 15).

28 'Politics and the Study of Discourse', 19.

29 *Archaeology of Knowledge*, 6–7.

30 A tendency discernible, for example, in Dominick LaCapra's 'Rethinking Intellectual History and Reading Texts' in Dominick LaCapra and Steven L. Kaplan eds, *Modern European Intellectual History. Reappraisals and New Perspectives* (Ithaca: Cornell University Press, 1982), 47–85, and *History and Criticism* (Ithaca: Cornell University Press, 1985), and in Clifford Geertz and James Clifford's 'interpretive anthropology' (Clifford Geertz, *The Interpretation of Cultures* [New York: Basic Books, 1973], James Clifford, 'On Ethnographic Authority', in *The Predicament of Culture. Twentieth-Century Ethnography, Literature, and Art* [Cambridge, Mass.: Harvard University Press, 1988], 21–54, 'Introduction: Partial Truths', in *Writing Culture. The Poetics and Politics of Ethnography*, eds James Clifford and George E. Marcus [Berkeley: California University Press, 1986], 1–26). *The Archaeology of Knowledge* marks a significant change from Foucault's earlier attitude to interpretation, as set out, for example in 'Nietzsche, Freud, Marx' in *Nietzsche*, Cahiers de Royaumont, Philosophie VI (Paris: Minuit, 1967), 183–92. For a discussion of this characteristic of Foucault's work, see section V of this Chapter.

31 *Archaeology of Knowledge*, 11. Any response to Foucault that takes the form of advocating a return to a historicism of whatever kind merely amounts to an identification with the earlier historical mode rather than constituting an answer to his argument for an epistemic shift. It is perhaps significant that nine years later, in 'Georges Canguilhem', Foucault ascribes the beginnings of this shift to Husserl, while he redefines the epistemic difference as a heterogeneity (52), two more examples of the kind of vacillation discussed at the end of Section V.

32 For an excellent discussion of the question of history and relativism, see Cousins and Hussain, *Michel Foucault*, 259–60.

33 *Archaeology of Knowledge*, 12.

34 Foucault describes their interdependence as follows: 'Continuous history is the indispensable correlative of the founding function of the subject: the guarantee that everything that has eluded him may be restored to him; the certainty that time will disperse nothing without restoring it in a reconstituted unity; the promise that one day the subject – in the form of historical consciousness – will once again be able to appropriate, to bring back under his sway, all those things that are kept at a distance by difference, and find in them what might be called his abode. Making historical analysis the discourse of the continuous and making human consciousness the original subject of all historical development and all action are the two sides of the same system of thought' (*Archaeology of Knowledge*, 12).

35 *Power/Knowledge*, 73–4. This does not of course mean that individuals as such did not exist before, but simply that they had not been constituted as objects for knowledge or political analysis. For further discussion of 'the individual' as artefact see *Discipline and Punish*, 189–94.

36 *Discipline and Punish*, 187–94.

37 *Discipline and Punish*, 193–4; *Power/Knowledge*, 102.

38 *Power/Knowledge*, 126–33.

39 For an analysis of this problem in the work of Edward Said, see Chapter 7.

40 Spivak, *In Other Worlds*, 208.

41 *Power/Knowledge*, 64.

42 *Power/Knowledge*, 117.

43 'Politics and the Study of Discourse', 14.

44 Foucault, *Language, Counter-Memory, Practice: Selected Essays and Interviews*, ed. Donald F. Bouchard, trans. Donald F. Bouchard and Sherry Simon (Ithaca: Cornell University Press, 1977), 178.

45 *Language, Counter-Memory, Practice*, 180, discussing Gilles Deleuze, *Différence et répétition* (Paris: Presses universitaires de France, 1969), and *Logique du sens* (Paris: Minuit, 1969). Foucault's interest in 'the event' has largely been ignored by his commentators. Two exceptions are Charles C. Lemert and Garth Gillan, *Michel Foucault. Social Theory as Transgression* (New York: Columbia University Press, 1982), and, as might be expected, Gilles Deleuze, *Foucault* (Paris: Minuit, 1986). For an excellent account of Deleuze's anti-platonism see Jean-Jacques Lecercle, *Philosophy Through the Looking-Glass: Language, Nonsense, Desire* (London: Hutchinson, 1985), 96–101, and also Ronald Bogue's recent *Deleuze and Guattari* (London: Routledge, 1989); on 'the event', with reference to Lyotard, see Geoffrey Bennington, *Lyotard: Writing the Event* (Manchester: Manchester University Press, 1988), and, with some reference to Foucault (and many others), Gillian Rose, *Dialectic of Nihilism: Post-Structuralism and Law* (Oxford: Blackwell, 1984).

46 Descombes continues: 'Consequently, the second is not that which merely arrives, like a latecomer, *after* the first, but that which permits the first to be the first. The first cannot be the first unaided, by its own properties alone: the second, with all the force of its delay, must come to the assistance of the first. It is through the second that the first is first. The "second time" thus has priority of a kind over the "first time": it is present from the first time onwards as the prerequisite of the first's priority without itself being a more primitive "first time", of course; it follows that the "first time" is in reality the "third time"' (*Modern French Philosophy*, trans. L. Scott-Fox and J.M. Harding [Cambridge: Cambridge University Press, 1980], 145).

47 Deleuze, *Logique du sens*, 122. From this account it should be clear the extent to which the basis of Foucault's genealogy differs from Popper's famous dictum that 'the historian does not recognize that it is we who select and order the facts of

history' (*The Open Society and Its Enemies*, 2 vols. [Princeton: Princeton University Press, 1966], II, 269). For similar reasons, we would also disagree with Paul Veyne's characterization of Foucault as a nominalist ('Foucault révolutionne l'histoire' in *Comment on écrit l'histoire* [Paris: Seuil, 1979], 201–42).

48 Freud's concept of deferred action, *Nachträglichkeit*, is employed most frequently in the analysis of the Wolf Man, but never elaborated formally as a concept; for a brief account see J. Laplanche and J.-B. Pontalis, *The Language of Psychoanalysis*, trans. Donald Nicholson-Smith (London: Hogarth Press, 1973), 111–14. As Laplanche and Pontalis note, the credit for drawing attention to the importance of *nachträglichkeit* must go to Lacan; for his distinction between history, memory, and remembering (*remémoration*) see *The Seminar of Jacques Lacan. Book II: The Ego in Freud's Theory and in the Technique of Psychoanalysis, 1954–1955*, ed. Jacques-Alain Miller, trans. Sylvana Tomaselli (Cambridge: Cambridge University Press, 1988), 185. Compare Fredric Jameson's discussion of repetition in 'Reification and Utopia in Mass Culture' (*Social Text* 1 [1979], 135–7).

49 Jeffrey Masson, *Freud: The Assault on Truth – Freud's Suppression of Seduction Theory* (London: Faber, 1984).

50 cf. the discussion of the ghostly persistence of essentialism in the work of Gayatri Chakravorty Spivak in Chapter 9.

51 He continues: 'A *system* is neither finite nor infinite. A structural totality escapes this alternative in its functioning. It escapes the archaeological and the eschatological, and inscribes them in itself' (Derrida, *Writing and Difference*, 123).

52 From this perspective, Althusser's symptomatic reading of Marx's account of history results from a recognition of the contradictions which it contains; but rather than seeing this as an effect of the impossibility of the concept of history itself, Althusser aims to provide Marx's texts with the full speech that he claims they are unable to articulate:

> In an epistemological and critical reading ... we cannot but hear behind the proferred word ['history'] the silence it conceals, see the blank of suspended rigour, scarcely the time of a lightning-flash in the darkness of the text; correlatively, we cannot but hear behind this discourse which seems continuous but is really interrupted and governed by the threatened irruption of a repressive discourse, the silent voice of the real discourse, we cannot but restore its text, in order to re-establish its profound continuity. It is here that the identification of the precise points of weakness in Marx's rigour is the same thing as the recognition of that rigour: it is his rigour that shows us its weaknesses; and in the brief moment of his temporary silence we are simply returning to him the speech that is his own. (*Reading Capital*, 143–4)

53 Derrida, *Writing and Difference*, 116.

54 Peter Dews, *Logics of Disintegration: Post-Structuralist Thought and the Claims of Critical Theory* (London: Verso, 1987), 234.

55 Maurice Blanchot, 'Foucault as I Imagine Him', in *Foucault/Blanchot*, trans. Jeffrey Mehlman (New York: Zone Books, 1987), 76.

56 On the limitations of resistance as a political category, see the discussion by Paul Hirst in *Marxism and Historical Writing* (London: Routledge and Kegan Paul, 1985), 143–4. The best analyses of power in Foucault include Cousins and Hussain, *Michel Foucault*, 243–47, and Jeff Minson, 'Strategies for Socialists? Foucault's Conception of Power', in Mike Gane, ed., *Towards a Critique of Foucault* (London: Routledge and Kegan Paul, 1986), 106–48. Among recent

discussions of power since Foucault, see in particular Barry Barnes' *The Nature of Power* (Cambridge: Polity Press, 1988).

57 e.g., Jameson, *The Political Unconscious*, 92.

58 On the other hand see Derrida's arguments in 'Géopsychanalyse "and the rest of the world"', in *Psyché: Inventions de l'autre* (Paris: Galilée, 1987), 327–52. For a consideration of Foucault's changing attitudes to psychoanalysis, see John Forrester, 'Michel Foucault and the History of Psychoanalysis', in *History of Science* 18 (1980), 286–301.

59 *History of Sexuality, Volume One*, 95.

60 *History of Sexuality, Volume One*, 95–6.

61 *History of Sexuality, Volume One*, 96.

62 *Politics, Philosophy, Culture*. 262.

63 Cousins and Hussain, on the other hand, point to the 'strategic limitations' of genealogy 'as a weapon of critique' (*Michel Foucault* 265), on the grounds that although it may disrupt accepted truisms and refusals to come to terms with specific histories, it cannot stand in for the 'direct assessment' of theory as such. It is interesting, however, that this argument employs the very concept of 'critique' which had been dismissed two pages earlier (262–3). Nevertheless, it is for the same reason that if Foucault's work has political significance, it does not offer a politics as such. That was not its function, a point which he argued emphatically:

> I have never tried to analyse anything whatsoever from the point of view of politics, but always to ask politics what it had to say about the problems with which it was confronted. I question it about the positions it takes and the reasons it gives for this; I don't ask it to determine the theory of what I do. I am neither an adversary nor a partisan of Marxism; I question it about what it has to say about experiences that ask questions of it ('Polemics, Politics, and Problematizations. An Interview with Michel Foucault', in *The Foucault Reader*, ed. Paul Rabinow [Harmondsworth: Penguin, 1986], 385).

In this respect we can recall his insistence that the intellectual's role does not consist in telling people what to do (*Politics, Philosophy, Culture*, 265). On intellectuals cf. the argument of Lyotard in 'La Place de l'aliénation dans le retournement marxiste', *Dérive à partir de Marx et Freud* (Paris: Union générale d'éditions, 1973), 78–166, and 'Tombeau de l'intellectuel', in *Tombeau de l'intellectuel et autres papiers* (Paris: Galilée, 1984), 9–22.

64 We shall be discussing Williams' 'Cultural Materialism' at greater length elsewhere. 'New Historicism' may be said to have begun with Stephen Greenblatt's *Renaissance Self-Fashioning: From More to Shakespeare* (Chicago: Chicago University Press, 1980); accounts of the movement include Stephen Greenblatt, Introduction to 'The Forms of Power and the Power of Forms in the Renaissance', *Genre* 15:1–2 (1982), 3–6; Jonathan Goldberg, 'The Politics of Renaissance Literature: A Review Essay', *English Literary History* 49 (1982), 514–42; Jean E. Howard, 'The New Historicism in Renaissance Studies', *English Literary Renaissance* 16 (1986), 13–43; Louis Montrose, 'Renaissance Literary Studies and the Subject of History', *English Literary Renaissance* 16 (1986), 5–12. Two recent volumes on New Historicism appeared too late for consideration here: H. Aram Veeser, ed., *The New Historicism*, (London: Routledge, 1989), and Marjorie Levinson, Marilyn Butler, Jerome McGann, and Paul Hamilton, *Rethinking Historicism: Critical Readings in Romantic History* (Oxford: Blackwell, 1989).

65 Stephen Greenblatt, 'Invisible Bullets: Renaissance Authority and Its Subversion',

Glyph 8, ed. Walter Benn Michaels (Baltimore: Johns Hopkins University Press, 1981), 48.

66 Jonathan Dollimore, 'Introduction: Shakespeare, Cultural Materialism and the New Historicism', in *Political Shakespeare*, eds Jonathan Dollimore and Alan Sinfield (Manchester: Manchester University Press, 1985), 13.

67 Greenblatt, 'Invisible Bullets', 52.

68 Foucault, 'Politics and the Study of Discourse', 21–2.

6 THE JAMESON RAID

1 Fredric Jameson, 'Cognitive Mapping', in *Marxism and the Interpretation of Culture*, eds Cary Nelson and Lawrence Grossberg (London: Macmillan, 1988), 347.

2 Fredric Jameson, *The Political Unconscious: Narrative as Socially Symbolic Act* (London: Methuen, 1981). *The Political Unconscious* was translated into German in 1988, but has yet to be translated into any other European language.

3 So Cornel West, for example, argues that Fredric Jameson effected an 'American Marxist *Aufhebung* of poststructuralism', and of contemporary criticism to ethics ('Ethics and Action in Fredric Jameson's Marxist Hermeutics', in Jonathan Arac. ed., *Postmodernism and Politics* [Minneapolis: University of Minnesota Press, 1986], 128). On feminism and male critics, see Elaine Showalter, 'Critical Cross-Dressing: Male Feminists and the Woman of the Year', *Raritan* 3 (1983), 130–49.

4 For the same reasons, the Althusserian discourse theory of Michel Pêcheux (*Language, Semantics and Ideology. Stating the Obvious*, trans. Harbans Nagpal [London: Macmillan, 1982]) achieved little impact when published in English in 1982, the year after the *Political Unconscious*.

5 Terry Eagleton, 'The Idealism of American Criticism', *New Left Review* 127 (1981), 60.

6 William Dowling, *Jameson, Althusser, Marx: An Introduction to The Political Unconscious* (London: Methuen, 1984), 14. Dowling's book is designed to give the reader unfamiliar with Jameson an account of the necessary background information on Marxism; it is all the more surprising therefore that Sartre is mentioned only once.

7 Fredric Jameson, *Marxism and Form: Twentieth-Century Dialectical Theories of Literature* (Princeton: Princeton University Press, 1971), xi, 307.

8 The contemporary political context for Marxism in the US is the major historical and situational factor that has determined the course of Jameson's work. The problem for any US Marxist criticism is that, although Marxism is perfectly acceptable in the academy, since McCarthy there has been no corresponding political culture to which it could correspond. An indication of the context as Jameson himself saw it in the early seventies comes in his chapter on Sartre in *Marxism and Form* (1971) where he remarks:

> It is worth stressing, for the American reader, the profound difference between the American and the European context in this respect: for in Europe Marxism is an omnipresent, living mode of thought, one with which every intellectual is bound to come into contact in one way or another, and to which he is obliged to react. (207)

It is clear from this citation that Jameson sees himself as writing for the 'American reader'. This accounts for his characteristic position of surveying Marxist theory from the empyrean and commodifying it for a readership presumed to be unfamiliar with such material and certainly not politically committed in relation to it, which means that Jameson can get away with theoretical arguments – and particularly theoretical syntheses – that it would be impossible to make in a European political context.

9 There is some precedent for this project: Mark Poster, for example, in *Existential Marxism in Postwar France: From Sartre to Althusser* (Princeton: Princeton University Press, 1975), instances the two rather unlikely candidates of Baudrillard (360) and Derrida (353–4) as offering the possibility of a reciprocity between the two positions. Jameson does provide some discussion of the political context of Althusser's work in the *Political Unconscious* (27n, 37, 54n). For Jameson's relation to Lukács and Sartre, and for an extended comparison between Sartre and Althusser, see Michael Sprinker, *Imaginary Relations: Aesthetics and Ideology in the Theory of Historical Materialism* (London: Verso, 1987), 153–205.

10 Dowling, *Jameson, Althusser, Marx*, 13.

11 In *Marxism and Form*, Jameson describes Sartre's move as follows::

> It is certain that, in opposition to Engels, Sartre aims at replacing the 'primacy' of the economic with that of praxis and class struggle. He wishes, he tells us at several points, 'to substitute history for economistic and sociological interpretations, or in more general terms, for all determinisms'; 'sociology and economism must both be dissolved back into *history itself*'. (293–4)

12 A device already criticized by Bachelard in his attack on 'continuists' who contrive to give history all the continuity and unity of a book by the use of narrative (*Le Matérialisme rationnel* [Paris: Presses universitaires de France, 1953], 209).

13 *Political Unconscious*, 27.

14 Fredric Jameson, 'The Re-invention of Marx', *Times Literary Supplement* 3832 (1975), 943; this project was subsequently sketched out in 'Marxism and Historicism', in *The Ideologies of Theory: Essays 1971–1986. Volume 2: The Syntax of History* (London: Routledge, 1988), 148–77, before being fully developed in *The Political Unconscious*.

15 *Political Unconscious*, 13; it should be mentioned that Jameson does qualify this phrase: '(here using the shorthand of philosophical idealism)'.

16 In this respect, Jameson differs significantly from Sartre, as well as from current initiatives to bring back the Subject.

17 Jean-Paul Sartre, *Critique of Dialectical Reason: I, Theory of Practical Ensembles*, trans. Alan Sheridan-Smith, ed. Jonathan Rée (London: Verso, 1976), 374–404, 576–83.

18 Louis Althusser and Etienne Balibar, *Reading Capital*, trans. Ben Brewster (London: New Left Books, 1970), 63.

19 *Reading Capital*, 253. Althusser continues: 'Thus the "social relations", instead of expressing the structure of these practices, of which individuals are merely the effects, would be generated from the multiplicity of these centres, i.e., they would have the structure of a practical inter-subjectivity'.

20 Cf. Anders Stephanson, in 'Regarding Postmodernism – A Conversation with Fredric Jameson': 'Your model goes from the microlevel, assorted things here and there, to the macrolevel represented by Mandel's concept of Late Capitalism. These "homologies" between the three moments of capitalism and the three moments in cultural development (realism, modernism and postmodernism) lend credence to descriptions of your position as unreconstructed Lukácsianism. It does seem a case of expressive causality, correspondences and all.... Problems arise ... with the mediating instances, the way in which you jump from the minute

to the staggeringly global' (*Social Text* 17 [1987], 35–6).

21 Barry Hindess and Paul Hirst, *Pre-Capitalist Modes of Production* (London: Routledge and Kegan Paul, 1975), cited five times in the course of Jameson's opening theoretical chapter. Further references will be given in the text.

22 *Pre-Capitalist Modes of Production*, 275–7.

23 *Political Unconscious*, 97.

24 *Critique of Dialectical Reason*, I, 579.

25 Here Jameson counters the argument that links totalizing thought to totalitarianism, that as he puts it there is a straight line from Hegel's Absolute Spirit to Stalin's Gulag, on rather different grounds. In a cunning riposte to post-structuralists, he argues that if this were true it would constitute an example of an expressive causality between different levels which would be in contradiction with the anti-Hegelian position of those who make it (see Jameson, 'Cognitive Mapping', 354).

26 Similarly, although he allows Althusser's refutation of the master narratives of historicism in which history is rewritten in terms of an underlying self-realizing meaning, Jameson himself nevertheless goes on to propose a new ' "fundamental" ... hidden master narrative' (*Political Unconscious*, 28).

27 *Pre-Capitalist Modes of Production*, 318.

28 *Pre-Capitalist Modes of Production*, 311.

29 In fact that particular truism had been pointed out long before by Sartre and Lévi-Strauss among others, who had observed that 'history is a method with no distinct object corresponding to it' without feeling the need to draw Hindess and Hirst's absurdly literal conclusion and to condemn history as such (Sartre, 'Replies to Structuralism', *Telos* 9 [1971], 114, cited in the *Political Unconscious*, 47, and Lévi-Strauss, *The Savage Mind* [London: Weidenfeld and Nicolson, 1966], 262). Hindess and Hirst's rejection of history here assumes that other objects, apart from history, can be known outside representation. The realization that they cannot leads Hindess and Hirst, in *Mode of Production and Social Formation: An Auto-Critique of Pre-Capitalist Modes of Production* (London: Macmillan, 1977), to reject epistemology (that is, epistemological guarantees) altogether (9–33) – which only means that knowledge is back where non-Marxist science in the twentieth-century has always thought it was, uncertain. For criticisms of Hindess and Hirst's position, see Tony Skillen, 'Discourse Fever: Post-Marxist Modes of Production', *Radical Philosophy* 20 (1978), 3–8, and Andrew Collier, 'In Defence of Epistemology', *Radical Philosophy* 20 (1978), 8–21.

30 Paul Q. Hirst, *Marxism and Historical Writing* (London: Routledge and Kegan Paul, 1985), vii. Deleuze's account of the 'crisis of representation' comes in Deleuze and Guattari, *Anti-Oedipus: Capitalism and Schizophrenia* (trans. Robert Hurley *et al.* (New York: The Viking Press, 1977).

31 For example, Perry Anderson, *In the Tracks of Historical Materialism* (London: Verso, 1983), Frank Lentricchia, *After the New Criticism* (Chicago: University of Chicago Press, 1980).

32 Jacques Derrida, 'Le Facteur de la vérité', in *The Post Card: From Socrates to Freud and Beyond*, trans. Alan Bass (Chicago: Chicago University Press, 1987), 413–96.

33 Jameson, 'Marxism and Historicism', 164.

34 Samuel Weber, *Institution and Interpretation* (Minneapolis: Minnesota University Press, 1987), 50.

35 Particularly, as Weber argues, that of Stanley Fish in *Is There a Text in This Class? The Authority of Interpretive Communities* (Cambridge, Mass.: Harvard University Press, 1980).

36 cf. Geoff Bennington, 'Not Yet', *Diacritics* 12:3 (1982), 23–32.

37 *Political Unconscious*, 10.

38 Jameson introduces his book on Sartre with a discussion of the importance of style (*Sartre: The Origin of a Style* [New Haven: Yale University Press, 1961], vii); since the end of his Althusserian period Eagleton has placed an increasing value on style and rhetoric, advocating a rhetoric of persuasion rather than the traditional Marxist appeal to absolute verities (see for example his discussion of Jameson, 'Fredric Jameson: The Politics of Style' in *Diacritics* 12:3 (1982), 14–22, and the last chapter of Eagleton, *Literary Theory: An Introduction* [Oxford: Blackwell, 1983]). Jameson and Eagleton have also been followed by Frank Lentricchia who rejects Marxism as a 'true' scientific theory, substantiated by appeals to the laws of history, and sees Marxism instead as a persuasive rhetoric, its goal 'the formation of genuine community' (*Criticism and Social Change* [Chicago: University of Chicago Press, 1983], 12).

39 Jameson, Foreword to Jean-François Lyotard, *The Postmodern Condition: A Report on Knowledge*, trans. Geoff Bennington and Brian Massumi (Minneapolis: Minnesota University Press, 1984), viii–ix.

40 Erich Auerbach, *Mimesis: The Representation of Reality in Western Literature*, trans. Willard Trask (New York: Anchor Book, 1957), 19. All further references will be given in the text.

41 See Tzvetan Todorov's illuminating essay on patristic exegesis in *Symbolism and Interpretation*, trans. Catherine Porter (Ithaca: Cornell University Press, 1982), 97–130.

42 See Mark Cousins and Athar Hussain, *Michel Foucault* (London: Macmillan, 1984), 260–2. Foucault's position here would distinguish him from contemporary historians such as de Certeau, who see the historian's task as a matter of joining together the two incommensurable realms of the real and writing (Michel de Certeau, *L'Ecriture de l'histoire* (Paris: Gallimard, 1975), 5; cf. Jean-François Lyotard, *Des dispositifs pulsionnels* (Paris: Union générale d'éditions, 1973), 180–2, and *The Differend*, trans. Georges Van Den Abbeele (Manchester: Manchester University Press, 1988), 32–58.

43 *Political Unconscious*, 40, 91–102.

44 Jameson, 'Postmodernism, or the Cultural Logic of Late Capitalism', *New Left Review* 146 (1984), 53–92. Further references will be given in the text.

45 See Andreas Huyssen, 'Mapping the Postmodern', in *After the Great Divide: Modernism, Mass Culture, Postmodernism* (Bloomington: Indiana University Press, 1986), 179–221.

46 This was one of the aspects of Jameson's 'Postmodernism' article most disputed in the responses to it; see in particular Terry Eagleton, 'Capitalism, Modernism and Postmodernism', *New Left Review* 152 (1985), 60–73.

47 'The Politics of Theory: Ideological Positions in the Postmodernism Debate', in Jameson, *The Ideologies of Theory*, II, 111; cf. Jameson's comment in 'Regarding Postmodernism': 'The languages that have been useful in talking about culture and politics in the past don't really seem adequate to this historical moment' (37).

48 This simultaneous experience of fragmentation and totalization has become a constant preoccupation for Jameson, as it was for Sartre. For example: 'rather than clinging to this particular mirage of the "centered subject" and the unified personal identity, we would do better to confront honestly the fact of frag-mentation on a global scale', or, 'we Americans, we masters of the world, are in something of the same position. The view from the top is epistemologically crippling, and reduces its subjects to the illusions of a host of fragmented subjectivities' (Jameson, 'Third-World Literature in the Era of Multinational Capitalism', *Social Text* 15 [1986], 67, 85).

49 The problem might be said to start with Jameson's postmodern 'hyperspace': a way of thinking against its seamless homogeneity, might be to read it against Foucault's 'Of Other Spaces' (*Diacritics* 16:1 [1986], 22–27). On paranoia and the missing body of the father in Jameson, see Weber, *Institution and Interpretation*, 54–8.

50 'Writing and Gender' Conference, London, July 1986. On utopia see Jameson's 'Of Islands and Trenches: Neutralization and the Production of Utopian Discourse', *The Ideologies of Theory*, II, 75–101, and Barbara Goodwin and Keith Taylor, *The Politics of Utopia: A Study in Theory and Practice* (London: Hutchinson, 1982).

51 Jameson, 'Reification and Utopia in Mass Culture', *Social Text* 1 (1979), 135–8.

52 Jameson, 'Third World Literature', 85.

53 cf. Frantz Fanon's argument that Third World countries ought not to have to choose between the capitalist and socialist systems, which would only define them according to the Western systems (*The Wretched of the Earth*, trans. Constance Farrington [Harmondsworth: Penguin Books, 1967], 77–8).

54 *Marxism and Form*, 231; cf. 165.

55 It is significant that in *Marxism and Form* Jameson follows the Sartrean position whereby pre-capitalist societies are not considered to be part of History:

> It is only on this condition that history as a whole can have a meaning, or a single direction, in the sense that projects are acquiring increasingly vaster fields of influence in all senses. We may anticipate the thesis of the projected second volume of the *Critique [of Dialectical Reason]* hinted at here and there in the [first] volume, by saying that the 'meaning' of history is just such a totalization. It is a becoming rather than a being; and in genuine dialectical fashion, we may assume that in prehistoric times, when men lived in unrelated groups and tribes, history, in effect, had no single meaning. Only now, when the world is becoming one, and when events in any given area are involved in and affect the very being of people in wholly distinct countries and societies, can we begin to have even a vague realization of what human life would be like if it were a single project, had a single meaning, constituted a single 'totalization in course'. (231–2)

By the time of *The Political Unconscious*, however, as we have seen, everyone is included. The shift discernible here, whereby all history, prehistoric or otherwise, is assimilated into one grand narrative, is exactly paralleled by the complaint that late capitalism, or its cultural form of postmodernism, has assimilated everything to the extent that Marxism has lost any 'exterior' perspective.

56 'Third-World Literature', 68–9; cf. *Political Unconscious*, 92.

57 'Third-World Literature', 68–9. For a comparable gesture, on a less politically sensitive topic, see 'Reification and Utopia', 147: 'All contemporary works of art ...'.

58 'Third-World Literature', 65.

59 Aijaz Ahmad, 'Jameson's Rhetoric of Otherness and the "National Allegory"', *Social Text*, 17 (1987), 3–25.

60 Similarly Jameson slips from 'nation' to 'culture', 'society', 'collectivity', as if these were interchangeable terms.

61 See 'Third-World Literature', 79–80: 'Such allegorical structures ... are not so much absent from first-world cultural texts as they are *unconscious*, and therefore they must be deciphered by interpretative mechanisms that necessarily entail a whole social and historical critique of our current first-world situation. The point here is that, in distinction to the unconscious allegories of our own cultural texts, third-world national allegories are conscious and overt'. In 'Magic Realism in

Film' (*Critical Inquiry* 12:2 [1986], 301–25), Jameson suggests that, in a similar way, magic realism in Latin American film offers 'as a possible alternative to the narrative logic of contemporary post-modernism', its more direct presentation of 'narrative raw material'; Third-World films present 'historical raw material in which disjunction is structurally present', a reflection of conflicting pre-capitalist and capitalist modes of production. The implicit assumptions at work here are all too obvious.

62 *Political Unconscious*, 92.
63 Jameson, 'Postmodernism', 87; cf. also 78–80.
64 'Postmodernism', 92.
65 'Postmodernism', 89, 92. On mapping, totalizing, and colonialism see José Rabasa, 'Allegories of the *Atlas*', in *Europe and Its Others*, ed. Francis Barker *et al.* (Colchester: University of Essex, 1985), II, 1–16.
66 The postmodern condition, Lyotard tells us, is only a symptom of 'the most highly developed societies' (*The Postmodern Condition*, xxiii), and Jameson concurs by using it almost as a synonymous term for American culture as such ('global American postmodernist culture', 'Third-World Literature', 65).
67 'Regarding Postmodernism', 33. Jameson describes cognitive mapping as 'the invention of ways of using one object and one reality to get a mental grasp of something else which one cannot represent or imagine' (45); cf. Robert John Ackermann, *Wittgenstein's City* (Amherst: University of Massachusetts Press, 1988). In 'Cognitive Mapping' (350–1), Jameson advances a theory of three types of space which correspond to the three stages of capitalism (postmodern space therefore corresponds to late capitalism).
68 'If we want to go on believing in categories like social class, then we are going to have to dig for them in the insubstantial bottomless realm of cultural and collective fantasy' ('Reification and Utopia', 139).
69 'Cognitive Mapping', 353, citing Kevin Lynch, *The Image of the City* (Cambridge, Mass.: MIT Press, 1960).
70 Reyner Banham, *Los Angeles: The Architecture of Four Ecologies* (London: Allen Lane, 1971).
71 'Third-World Literature', 87.
72 Jameson, *Nationalism, Colonialism and Literature: Modernism and Imperialism* (Derry: Field Day Pamphlets 14, 1988), 11.
73 *Political Unconscious*, 102. Jameson admits that 'the project of cognitive mapping obviously stands or falls with the concept of some (unrepresentable, imaginary) global social totality that was to have been mapped'('Cognitive Mapping', 348; cf. 356, 358–60).
74 Fanon, *The Wretched of the Earth*, 251–4.

7 DISORIENTING ORIENTALISM

1 Aimé Césaire, *Discourse on Colonialism*, trans. Joan Pinkham (New York: Monthly Review Press, 1972), 54.
2 Frantz Fanon, *The Wretched of the Earth*, trans. Constance Farrington (Harmondsworth: Penguin, 1967), 81. Further references will be cited in the text.
3 As is evident from Marcel Merle's extremely useful anthology, *L'Anticolonialisme européen, de Las Casas à Marx* (Paris: Colin, 1969); see also Peter Hulme, *Colonial Encounters. Europe and the Native Caribbean, 1492–1797* (London: Methuen, 1986), and Tzvetan Todorov, *Nous et les autres: La Réflexion française sur la diversité humaine* (Paris: Seuil, 1989).
4 Georg Lukács, *The Historical Novel*, trans. Hannah and Stanley Mitchell

(London: Merlin Press, 1962), 28–9. For contemporary discussions of humanism, see also Sartre's Conclusion to *Being and Nothingness*, trans. Hazel E. Barnes (New York: Philosophical Library, 1958), and *Existentialism and Humanism*, trans. Philip Mairet (London: Methuen, 1948); Maurice Merleau-Ponty, *Humanism and Terror*, trans. J. O'Neill (Evanston: Northwestern University Press, 1964), Heidegger, 'Letter on Humanism', in *Basic Writings*, ed. David Farrell Krell (London: Routledge and Kegan Paul, 1978), 193–242, and Louis Althusser, 'Marxism and Humanism', in *For Marx*, trans. Ben Brewster (London: New Left Books, 1969), 219–47, and 'Reply to John Lewis', in *Essays in Self-Criticism*, trans. Grahame Lock (London: New Left Books, 1976), 33–99. A detailed account of some of the recent arguments about the complexities of the problems involved in humanism can be found in Kate Soper's *Humanism and Anti-Humanism* (London: Hutchinson, 1986).

5 Abdul R. JanMohammed, 'The Economy of Manichean Allegory: The Function of Racial Difference in Colonialist Literature', *Critical Inquiry* 12:1 (1985), 61–2.

6 Roland Barthes, 'The Great Family of Man', in *Mythologies*, trans. Annette Lavers (London: Jonathan Cape, 1972), 100–2. Further references will be cited in the text.

7 Chandra Talpade Mohanty, 'Under Western Eyes: Feminist Scholarship and Colonial Discourses', *Boundary 2* 12:3/13:1 (1984), 340.

8 Compare Paul Gilroy's analysis of the 1983 Conservative Election poster, 'Labour Says He's Black, Tories say He's British' in *There Ain't No Black in the Union Jack: The Cultural Politics of Race and Nation* (London: Hutchinson, 1987), 57–9.

9 Jean-Paul Sartre, *Critique of Dialectical Reason: I. Theory of Practical Ensembles*, trans. Alan Sheridan-Smith (London: New Left Books, 1976), 752.

10 Mill, *On Liberty* in the *Collected Works of John Stuart Mill*, ed. J.M. Robson (London: Routledge and Kegan Paul, 1963–), Vol. 18, 224, *Considerations on Representative Government*, Vol. 19, 562–77 ('Of the Government of Dependencies by a Free State'), and 'Thoughts on Parliamentary Reform', Vol. 19, 324 (for detailed analysis of Mill's views in relation to India see Eric Stokes, *The English Utilitarians and India* [Oxford: Clarendon Press, 1959]); Kant, *The Critique of Judgement*, trans. James Creed Meredith (Oxford: Clarendon Press, 1952).

11 Spivak, *In Other Worlds*, 202. It should be obvious from the present discussion that I disagree with Spivak's argument that imperialism constitutes a 'symptomatic blank in contemporary Western anti-humanism' (209). For further discussion of Spivak's analysis of the production of the European sovereign subject, see Chapter 9.

12 Aimé Césaire, *Discourse on Colonialism*, 14–15; Fanon, *The Wretched of the Earth*, 71, 80; cf. also Paul Virilio, *Speed and Politics*, trans. Mark Polizzotti (New York: Semiotext(e), 1986), 106ff.

13 Louis Althusser and Etienne Balibar, *Reading Capital*, trans. Ben Brewster (London: New Left Books, 1970), 141.

14 Homi Bhabha, 'Sly Civility', *October* 34 (1985), 74. With respect to this Western time, contrast the essays in the special issue of *Diogenes* (42 [1963]), 'Man and the Concept of History in the Orient'.

15 Edward W. Said, *Orientalism* (London: Routledge and Kegan Paul, 1978). Further references will be cited in the text.

16 *Diacritics* 6:3 (1976), 38.

17 Edward W. Said, 'Orientalism Reconsidered', in *Europe and Its Others*, 2 vols, ed. Francis Barker *et al.* (Colchester: University of Essex, 1985), I, 17. Further references will be cited in the text as OR.

18 Such critiques of *Orientalism* are discussed by Said in 'Orientalism Reconsidered'. For further analysis of the reviews of *Orientalism*, see Lata Mani and Ruth Frankenberg, 'The Challenge of *Orientalism*', *Economy and Society* 14:2 (1985), 174–92; Emmanuel Sivan's 'Edward Said and His Arab Reviewers' (*Interpretations of Islam Past and Present* [Princeton: Darwin Press, 1985], 133–54) discusses Arab reviews of, and reactions to, Said's book, which criticize Said for his 'totalising' (139), 'ahistorical, essentialist mode' (135), and argue that Said inadvertently serves the cause of contemporary Arab 'Orientalism in reverse' (141–2). On the question of the representation of Islam, see Said, *Covering Islam* (London: Routledge and Kegan Paul, 1981), *After the Last Sky* (London: Faber and Faber, 1986), 'In the Shadow of the West', *Wedge* 7/8 (1985), 4–11, and, for an attempt at it, Michael Gilsenan, *Recognizing Islam: An Anthropologist's Introduction* (London: Croom Helm, 1982); Cf. also Anouar Abdel-Malek, 'Orientalism in Crisis', *Diogenes* 44 (1963), 102–40.

19 *Orientalism*, 259, 263.

20 Samuel Weber, 'The Intersection: Marxism and the Philosophy of Language', *Diacritics* 15:4 (1985), 111.

21 *Orientalism*, 246, 211, 238.

22 Said finds such 'profound humanism' endorsed in the modern scholars whom he admires most, Auerbach (259–61) and Massignon (264–70). Said reinvokes Auerbach as his model for the critic in 'Secular Criticism', in *The World, the Text, the Critic*, (Cambridge, Mass.: Harvard University Press, 1983), 5–9.

23 *Orientalism*, 110, 44, Similar points are made at 87, 93, 96, 108, 116, 120, 141, 146–8, 261, 291, 326.

24 *Orientalism*, 45.

25 *Orientalism*, 46, 266, 246, 328, 267. It is characteristic of Said's identification with the values of humanism that he always opposes 'human', never materialist, history to idealist history (246).

26 James Clifford, 'On Orientalism', in *The Predicament of Culture: Twentieth-Century Ethnography, Literature, Art* (Cambridge, Mass.: Harvard University Press, 1988), 263.

27 *The World, the Text, the Critic*, 175.

28 In effect, Said tries to assimilate 'experience' to the function of the 'event' in Foucault or Lyotard; but as a category of consciousness, it clearly cannot work as the antithesis of appropriating knowledge and theory in the same way. A similar problem with the category of consciousness arises in Hayden White's *Metahistory: The Historical Imagination in Nineteenth-Century Europe* (Baltimore: The Johns Hopkins University Press, 1973).

29 Said, *The World, the Text, the Critic*, 177. Said further affirms the identity of the cultural and imperialist projects in *Nationalism, Colonialism and Literature: Yeats and Decolonization* (Derry: Field Day Pamphlets 15, 1988), 7.

30 Said, *The World, the Text, the Critic*, 176.

31 See Chapter 1, section II.

32 Foucault's idea of the 'specific' intellectual is elaborated in *Power/Knowledge, Selected Interviews and Other Writings, 1972–1977*, ed. Colin Gordon (New York: Pantheon Books, 1980), 126–33.

33 Spivak, in 'Criticism, Feminism and the Institution. An Interview with Gayatri Chakravorty Spivak', *Thesis Eleven* 10/11 (1984/85), 176–8. The same criticism could be made of Frank Lentricchia's discussion of the role of 'the intellectual' in *Criticism and Social Change* (Chicago: University of Chicago Press, 1983), 2–11 (Lentricchia, it is worth noting, broadly speaking takes up a position similar to Said's, describing himself as a 'university humanist' [7] and advocating a form of 'oppositional criticism' [15]). In *Tombeau de l'intellectuel et autres papiers* (Paris:

Galilée, 1984), Jean-François Lyotard argues that Foucault's notion of the 'specific intellectual' is incoherent, and indeed that the idea of 'the intellectual' can no longer be sustained (11–22).

34 'Right now in American cultural history, "Marxism" is principally an academic, not a political, commitment' (Said, 'Secular Criticism', in *The World, the Text, the Critic*, 28; cf. 'Reflections on American "Left" Literary Criticism', 160–6).

35 Said, 'Secular Criticism', in *The World, the Text, the Critic*, 16–24.

36 Said, 'The Problem of Textuality: Two Exemplary Positions', in *Critical Inquiry* 4:4 (1978), 673–714; revised version published as 'Criticism Between Culture and System' in *The World, the Text, the Critic*, 178–225.

37 *Orientalism*, 40, 143–5, 149–53, 161, 194, 209.

38 *Orientalism*, 272. The significance of this question, and the extent to which it remains unanswered, is suggested by the fact that Said closes the book by raising it again (325).

39 As his narrative proceeds to the period between the two world wars, Said himself identifies a more overt form of confrontation : 'The Orient now appeared to constitute a challenge, not just to the West in general, but to the West's spirit, knowledge, and imperium' (248). Much as this might support our own thesis that postmodernism constitutes a recognition of a certain loss of US and European political and cultural dominance, Said's suggestion that it is only at this point that the Orient began to appear as a threat is contradicted by his own book, which shows the extent to which it has always done so.

40 *Orientalism*, 206–7, 233.

41 *Orientalism*, 27, 286.

8 THE AMBIVALENCE OF BHABHA

1 Homi K. Bhabha, 'Difference, Discrimination, and the Discourse of Colonialism', in *The Politics of Theory*, ed. Francis Barker *et al.* (Colchester: University of Essex, 1983), 199 (hereafter cited as DDDC). Bhabha's other articles will be cited in the text as follows: 'The Other Question', *Screen* 24:6 (1983), 18–35: OQ; 'Of Mimicry and Man: The Ambivalence of Colonial Discourse', *October* 28 (1984), 125–33: OMM; 'Sly Civility', *October* 34 (1985), 71–80: SC; 'Signs Taken for Wonders: Questions of Ambivalence and Authority under a Tree Outside Delhi, May 1817', in *Europe and Its Others*, 2 vols, ed. Francis Barker *et al.* (Colchester: University of Essex, 1985), I, 89–106 (reprinted in *Critical Inquiry* 12:1, 1985, 144–65): STW; 'Foreword: Remembering Fanon: Self, Psyche and the Colonial Condition', in Franz Fanon, *Black Skin, White Masks*, trans. Charles Lam Markmann (London: Pluto Press, 1986): BSWM.

2 Edward W. Said, *Orientalism* (London: Routledge and Kegan Paul, 1978), 95.

3 Jean Baudrillard, *In the Shadow of the Silent Majorities ... Or the End of the Social, and Other Essays*, trans. Paul Foss, Paul Patton and John Johnston (New York: Foreign Agents Series, 1983), 20–2.

4 *C.O.D.* 1982 (Seventh edition). The first account of religious fetishism was Charles du Brosses' *Du culte des dieux fétiches, ou Parallèle de l'ancienne religion de l'Egypte avec la religion actuelle de Nigritie* (Paris, 1760); its first use in the realm of psychology occurs in Alfred Binet's 'Le Fétichisme dans l'amour' in *Etudes de psychologie expérimentale* (Paris: Doin, 1888), 1–85, cited by Freud in the *Three Essays on the Theory of Sexuality* (1905).

5 Gilles Deleuze and Félix Guattari, *Anti-Oedipus: Capitalism and Schizophrenia*, trans. Robert Hurley, Mark Seem, and Helen R. Lane (New York: Viking Press, 1977), 170. Deleuze and Guattari are arguing in particular against Marie-Cécile and Edmond Ortigues, *Oedipe africain* (Paris: Plon, 1966)

6 Bhabha continues: 'Its predominant strategic function is the creation of a space for a "subject peoples" through the production of knowledges in terms of which surveillance is exercised and a complex form of pleasure/unpleasure is incited. It seeks authorization for its strategies by the production of knowledges of colonizer and colonized which are stereotypical but antithetically evaluated. The objective of colonial discourse is to construe the colonized as a population of degenerate types on the basis of racial origin, in order to justify conquest and to establish systems of administration and instruction' (DDDC 198). This emphatically Foucauldian account is, however, soon intermeshed with the discourses of psychoanalysis and deconstruction.

7 Lacan's discussion of mimicry comes in Chapter 8 of *The Four Fundamental Concepts of Psycho-Analysis*, trans. Alan Sheridan (London: Hogarth Press, 1977), 97–100.

8 OMM 129. In Bhabha's psychoanalytic analogy, the process is compared to Lacan's account of anamorphosis in *The Four Fundamental Concepts of Psycho-Analysis* (85–90) where he illustrates the structure of desire through the unrecognizable skull in the foreground of Holbein's *The Ambassadors*.

9 Lacan, *The Four Fundamental Concepts of Psycho-Analysis*, 99.

10 For Derrida, a deconstructive strategy, whether written by 'man' or by 'woman', can avoid a simple reversal by inscribing heterogeneity within an opposition so as to displace it and disorient its antagonistic defining terms. But how do you displace an opposition without simply replacing it? The answer is not to replace it at all, but to subvert it by repeating it, dislocating it fractionally through parody, dissimulation, simulacrum, mime, a mimicry that mocks the binary structure, travestying it (see *Spurs: Nietzsche's Styles*, trans. Barbara Harlow [Chicago: Chicago University Press, 1979], 95, 99, 101 119, 139; *Dissemination*, trans. Barbara Johnson [Chicago: Chicago University Press, 1981], 206–8). This repetition, however, is also not identical to itself:

> What announces itself here is an internal division within *mimesis*, a self-duplication of repetition itself.... Everything would then be played out in the paradoxes of the supplementary double: the paradoxes of something that, added to the simple and the single, replaces and mimes them, both like and unlike, unlike because it is – in that it is – like, the same as and different from what it duplicates. (*Dissemination*, 191)

This parodic doubling *reinscribes* the relation of alterity between the same and the other, woman as truth and as falsehood: it is the same as that which it simulates but necessarily also different from it, a doubling that can easily be mistaken for the real thing, leading to the accusations of essentialism. In other words, it repeats the relations that it finds, so that 'woman' mimes herself without being herself, providing the customary specular reflection but in a relation of dissymmetry. It is this, rather than the Lacanian form of mimicry, that is invoked by Irigaray in *This Sex Which Is Not One*, trans. Catherine Porter (Ithaca: Cornell University Press, 1985). cf. also Bhabha's discussion of the mask and the veil, BSWM xxii-iii.

11 Bhabha substantiates this by citing a report from the Missionary Register in which a group of Indians gathered together to study a Bible translated into a native language are sceptical when told that this is the European religion of the Sahibs. Bhabha suggests that they resist the idea of the Christian sacrament because they are vegetarian, although it has to be said that the logic of not taking the sacrament because it symbolizes the eating of human flesh would apply equally to all non-cannibal Europeans; moreover, in the context of India, it seems at least as likely that it is the alcohol of the communion wine that is being refused. Bhabha does not discuss the possibility that the story may be showing how the

natives prefer their own Christian study group to the promise of institutionalized religion with a priest, church, baptism, and the taking of the sacrament which they resist in particular. The question becomes whether it is the 'colonial text [that] emerges uncertainly' (149), or whether the natives have in fact accepted the text but resist the much more obvious aspects of institutionalized imperial power. In addition, the complication that the entire reported discussion takes place between two native Indians suggests that the 'subject' of colonial discourse cannot be generalized any more than its effects. Bhabha's instance of 'intervention', therefore, is equally readable as a questioning of a colonial institution in which 'hybridization' has produced a recognition of cultural difference. To what extent has such recognition become 'subversion'? And to what extent has hybridization occurred at all – as opposed to an ambivalence of the Christian text when placed in a new context?

12 Christopher Hibbert, *Africa Explored. Europeans in the Dark Continent, 1769–1889* (London: Allen Lane, 1982), 258.

13 As Fanon puts it, 'the native replies to the living lie of the colonial situation by an equal falsehood.... In this colonialist context there is no truthful behaviour: and the good is quite simply what is evil for "them"' *The Wretched of the Earth* (Harmondsworth: Penguin, 1967), 39. In this context, see also Ashis Nandy, *The Intimate Enemy: Loss and Recovery of Self under Colonialism* (Delhi: Oxford University Press, 1983).

14 Albert Memmi, *The Colonizer and the Colonized* (London: Souvenir Press, 1974).

15 Stephen Greenblatt, 'Invisible Bullets: Renaissance Authority and Its Subversion', *Glyph* 8, ed. Walter Benn Michaels (Baltimore: Johns Hopkins University Press, 1981), 52.

16 Fanon, *The Wretched of the Earth*, 29–35.

17 An example of the use of psychoanalysis as a truth-statement would be the following: 'what is denied the colonial subject, both as colonizer and colonized, is that form of negation which gives access to the Symbolic' (DDDC 203).

18 Chapter Two of *Black Skin, White Masks* is concerned with 'The Woman of Colour and the White Man', Chapter Three with 'The Man of Colour and the White Woman'.

19 In a footnote to 'Difference, Discrimination and the Discourse of Colonialism' Bhabha himself offers the criticism that he has not addressed the questions of class and sexual difference. In the revised version later printed in *Screen*, this admission is repeated, but not extended.

20 *The Wretched of the Earth*, 31 (further revision of Marx comes at pages 86–98, where Fanon defines the peasantry not the working class as the revolutionary force). This leads to certain questions: if Fanon replaces economics with psychology as the motor of revolution, then what is the politics of the psychologist who treats the native, or even the colonizer who, Fanon implies, is equally psychotic? This raises the question of the normative role of psychiatry and psychoanalysis in society generally, and anticipates Laing's and Foucault's stress on madness as a subversive force in a repressive society. This in turn leads to Foucault' rejection of psychoanalysis, and the theoretical questions raised by Bhabha's use of it. Bhabha's politics have been criticized by Abdul R. JanMohammed in 'The Economy of Manichean Allegory: The Function of Racial Difference in Colonialist Literature', *Critical Inquiry* 12:1 (1985), 59–61; however, JanMohammed's criticisms seem to be based on a serious misunderstanding of Bhabha's work.

21 *The Wretched of the Earth*, 9.

22 Jean-Paul Sartre, *What is Literature?*, trans. Bernard Frechtman (London: Methuen, 1950), 59.
23 In his account of Fanon, however, Bhabha does not allow for such deconstructive tactics, and mildly reproves Fanon for utilizing Sartre's existential humanism, commenting on 'the intricate irony of turning the European existentialist and psychoanalytic traditions to face the history of the Negro which they had never contemplated' (BSWM xxiv). This underestimates the degree to which psychoanalysis was employed in the colonial context, as well as the place of colonialism in Sartre's work – for example, the *Critique of Dialectical Reason*, his Preface to *The Wretched of the Earth*, or, particularly, the 1948 text translated as *Black Orpheus*, trans. S.W. Allen (Paris: Présence africaine, 1976); cf. also *Anti-Semite and Jew*, trans. George J. Becker (New York: Schocken Books, 1948). The relation of psychoanalysis to colonialism is a question to which we shall return.

9 SPIVAK: DECOLONIZATION, DECONSTRUCTION

1 Spivak, in Angela McRobbie, 'Strategies of Vigilance. An Interview with Gayatri Chakravorti [*sic*] Spivak', *Block* 10 (1985), 8.
2 Colin MacCabe, Foreword to Gayatri Chakravorty Spivak, *In Other Worlds: Essays in Cultural Politics* (New York: Methuen, 1987), ix.
3 Spivak, in 'Criticism, Feminism and the Institution. An Interview with Gayatri Chakravorty Spivak', *Thesis Eleven* 10/11 (1984/85), 187.
4 On 'imperialism' as a term see Richard Koebner and Helmut Dan Schmidt, *Imperialism: The Story and Significance of a Political Word, 1840–1960* (Cambridge: Cambridge University Press, 1964), as a theory see Anthony Brewer, *Marxist Theories of Imperialism: A Critical Survey* (London: Routledge and Kegan Paul, 1980).
5 Spivak's 'French Feminism in an International Frame' has recently been collected in *In Other Worlds*, 134–53. Further references to this volume will be given in the text as IOW. Other essays by Spivak will be referred to as follows: 'The Rani of Sirmur', in *Europe and Its Others*, 2 vols, ed. Francis Barker *et al.* (Colchester: University of Essex, 1985), I, 128–51: RS; 'Can the Subaltern Speak? Speculations on Widow Sacrifice', *Wedge* 7/8 (1985), 120–30 (revised version reprinted in *Marxism and the Interpretation of Culture*, ed. Cary Nelson and Lawrence Grossberg [London: Macmillan, 1988], 271–313): CSS; 'Three Women's Texts and a Critique of Imperialism', *Critical Inquiry* 12:1 (1985), 243–61: TWT; 'Imperialism and Sexual Difference', in *Sexual Difference*, ed. Robert Young, *Oxford Literary Review* 8 (1986), 225–40: ISD.
6 RS 141.
7 'Ai margini della storia (Storia dei gruppi sociali subalterni)', Notebook 25 (1934): Gramsci, *Quaderni del carcere*, ed. Valentino Gerratana, 4 vols (Turin: Einaudi, 1975), III, 2277–94, especially 2283–4, 2287–9, partially excerpted in *Selections from Prison Notebooks*, trans. Quentin Hoare and Geoffrey Nowell Smith (London: Lawrence & Wishart, 1971).
8 *Prison Notebooks*, 26n.
9 Jacques Derrida, *Of Grammatology*, trans. Gayatri Chakravorty Spivak (Baltimore: Johns Hopkins University Press, 1976), 145.
10 Ranajit Guha, 'On Some Aspects of the Historiography of Colonial India', *Subaltern Studies*, Vol. I, ed. Ranajit Guha (Delhi: Oxford University Press, 1982), 3.
11 IOW 208.
12 Spivak, in McRobbie, 'Strategies of Vigilance', 10.

13 Chandra Talpade Mohanty, 'Under Western Eyes: Feminist Scholarship and Colonial Discourses', *Boundary* 2 12:3/13:1 (1984), 333; Cf. Felicity Eldhom, Olivia Harris and Kate Young, 'Conceptualising Women', *Critique of Anthropology* 3 (1977), 101–03.

14 Mohanty, 'Under Western Eyes', 352.

15 CSS 120, 130; TWT 254.

16 Spivak, 'Criticism, Feminism and the Institution', 182–3.

17 IOW, 241

18 For example, Benita Parry, 'Problems in Current Theories of Colonial Discourse', *Oxford Literary Review* 9 (1987), 27–58.

19 cf. CSS 120, TWT 243–6 (Spivak here cites Elizabeth Fox-Genovese's 'Placing Women's History in History', *New Left Review* 133 (1982), 5–29 as showing us 'how to define the historical moment of feminism in the West in terms of female access to individualism') and ISD, passim. Related writings on feminism by Spivak include 'Displacement and the Discourse of Woman', in Mark Krupnick ed., *Displacement: Derrida and After* (Bloomington: Indiana University Press, 1983), 169–95 and 'Love Me, Love My Ombre, Elle' in *Diacritics* 14:4 (1984), 19–36.

20 IOW 267; in a footnote Spivak speculates that ' "Stanadayini" as *énonciation* might thus be an example of an ever-compromised affirmative deconstruction'.

21 IOW 240, 253–4.

22 IOW 246. As Spivak's comment implies, the problem of the term 'Third World' arises from the assumption that it only signifies an identity with no difference.

23 For the difficulties of a reverse ethnocentrism, see in particular Fanon's essay 'On National Culture' in *The Wretched of the Earth* (Harmondsworth: Penguin, 1967), 166–99; Spivak's essay also 'operates on the notion that all such clear-cut nostalgia for lost origins are suspect, especially as grounds for counter-hegemonic ideological production' (CSS 129).

24 In other words, the colonial subject forms a metonymic mirror image of Europe as sovereign subject; cf. RS 128, and Rana Kabbani's, *Europe's Myths of Orient* (London: Macmillan, 1986), a work which, though avoiding the theoretical difficulties raised by Said, complements his *Orientalism* by chronicling the sexual fantasies implicit in European literary and artistic representations of the Orient. Kabbani concludes that such artistic representation followed the same structure as Spivak describes: 'the gaze into the Orient had turned, as in a convex mirror, to reflect the Occident that had produced it' (85).

25 TWT 254. For a discussion of the problems of such nostalgia in a different context, see Richard Kearney, *Transitions: Narratives in Modern Irish Culture* (Dublin: Wolfhound Press, 1988).

26 Lata Mani, 'The Production of an Official Discourse on Sati in Early Nineteenth-Century Bengal', in *Europe and Its Others*, I, 107–29. Among the many other discussions of *sati*, see also Ashis Nandy, 'Sati: A Nineteenth Century Tale of Women, Violence and Protest', in *At the Edge of Psychology: Essays in Politics and Culture* (Delhi: Oxford University Press, 1980), 1–31.

27 Guha, 'On Some Aspects of the Historiography of Colonial India', 3–8; cf. IOW 245, where Spivak criticizes Benedict Anderson's *Imaginary Communities: Reflections on the Origins and Spread of Nationalism* (London: Verso, 1983). For other recent discussions of the problem of nationalism see in particular Partha Chatterjee, *Nationalist Thought and the Colonial World: A Derivative Discourse* (London: Zed Books, 1986), and Homi K. Bhabha, ed., *Nation and Narration* (London: Routledge, 1990).

28 Edward Said, 'Orientalism Reconsidered', in *Europe and Its Others*, I, 25; IOW 253.

29 CSS 120, and Spivak, 'Criticism, Feminism and the Institution', 182.
30 IOW 104.
31 Spivak, 'Criticism, Feminism and the Institution', 180.
32 For example, RS 131–2, IOW 15–17, 26, 103, 134–5.
33 IOW 263; cf. CSS 123.
34 CSS 120–1; see also the section of 'The Rani of Sirmur' entitled 'Freud as the Monitory Model for the Critic's Desire' (RS 136–7).
35 Spivak, 'Criticism, Feminism and the Institution', 178.
36 RS 140.
37 RS 147; cf. IOW 150, where Spivak points out that institutional changes against sexism may mean further harm for women in the Third World.
38 IOW 109. A more detailed analysis of Spivak's relation to Marxism would perhaps start with her remark in CSS where, commenting on the essentialism/anti-essentialism debate, she notes that for Marx 'the curious persistence of essentialism within the dialectic was a profound and productive problem' (120); Spivak's writings on Marx include 'Scattered Speculations on the Question of Value' (IOW 154–75), and 'Speculations on Reading Marx: after reading Derrida', in Post-Structuralism and the Question of History, eds Derek Attridge, Geoff Bennington and Robert Young (Cambridge University Press, 1987), 30–62.
39 See Spivak, in McRobbie, 'Strategies of Vigilance', 7–9, 'Criticism, Feminism and the Institution', 183–4, and IOW 205.
40 Hazel V. Carby, 'White Woman Listen! Black Feminism and the Boundaries of Sisterhood', in The Empire Strikes Back: Race and Racism in 70s Britain, Centre for Contemporary Cultural Studies (London: Hutchinson, 1982), 213. Fanon, The Wretched of the Earth, 78.
41 Salman Rushdie, 'The New Empire Within Britain', New Society, 9 December 1982.
42 See Errol Lawrence, 'Just Plain Common Sense: The "Roots" of Racism', in The Empire Strikes Back, 80–85.
43 Homi K. Bhabha, 'The Commitment to Theory', New Formations 5 (1988), 5–23.

Index